# Exorcising Translation

Literatures, Cultures, Translation

*Literatures, Cultures, Translation* presents a new line of books that engage central issues in translation studies such as history, politics, and gender in and of literary translation, as well as opening new avenues for study. Volumes in the series follow two main strands of inquiry: one strand brings a wider context to translation through an interdisciplinary interrogation, while the other homes in on the history and politics of the translation of seminal works in literary and intellectual history.

Series Editors
Brian James Baer, Kent State University, USA
Michelle Woods, The State University of New York, New Paltz, USA

Editorial Board
Rosemary Arrojo, The State University of New York, Binghamton, USA
Paul Bandia, Concordia University, Canada, and Harvard University, USA
Susan Bassnett, Professor of Comparative Literature, Warwick University, UK
Leo Tak-hung Chan, Lingnan University, Hong Kong, China
Michael Cronin, Dublin City University, Republic of Ireland
Edwin Gentzler, University of Massachusetts Amherst, USA
Carol Maier, Kent State University, USA
Denise Merkle, Moncton University, Canada
Michaela Wolf, University of Graz, Austria

# Exorcising Translation

## Towards an Intercivilizational Turn

Douglas Robinson

Bloomsbury Academic
An imprint of Bloomsbury Publishing Inc

B L O O M S B U R Y
NEW YORK · LONDON · OXFORD · NEW DELHI · SYDNEY

**Bloomsbury Academic**
An imprint of Bloomsbury Publishing Inc

| | |
|---|---|
| 1385 Broadway | 50 Bedford Square |
| New York | London |
| NY 10018 | WC1B 3DP |
| USA | UK |

www.bloomsbury.com

**BLOOMSBURY and the Diana logo are trademarks of Bloomsbury Publishing Plc**

First published 2017

© Douglas Robinson, 2017

All rights reserved. No part of this publication may be reproduced or transmitted in any form or by any means, electronic or mechanical, including photocopying, recording, or any information storage or retrieval system, without prior permission in writing from the publishers.

Douglas Robinson has asserted his right under the Copyright, Designs and Patents Act, 1988, to be identified as Author of this work.

No responsibility for loss caused to any individual or organization acting on or refraining from action as a result of the material in this publication can be accepted by Bloomsbury or the author.

**Library of Congress Cataloging-in-Publication Data**
Names: Robinson, Douglas, 1954- author.
Title: Exorcising translation : towards an intercivilizational turn / Douglas Robinson.
Description: New York : Bloomsbury Academic, 2016. | Series: Literatures, cultures, translation | Includes bibliographical references and index.
Identifiers: LCCN 2016022353 (print) | LCCN 2016038021 (ebook) | ISBN 9781501326059 (hardback) | ISBN 9781501326066 (ePub) | ISBN 9781501326073 (ePDF)
Subjects: LCSH: Translating and interpreting--Cross-cultural studies. | Literature--Translations--History and criticism. | Literature and transnationalism. | East and West. | BISAC: LITERARY CRITICISM / General. | LITERARY CRITICISM / Semiotics & Theory.
Classification: LCC P306.2 .R59 2016 (print) | LCC P306.2 (ebook) | DDC 418/.04--dc23
LC record available at https://lccn.loc.gov/2016022353

ISBN: HB:   978-1-5013-2605-9
PB:   978-1-5013-2604-2
ePub: 978-1-5013-2606-6
ePDF: 978-1-5013-2607-3

Series: Literatures, Cultures, Translation

Cover design: Daniel Benneworth-Gray
Cover image © iStock

Typeset by Fakenham Prepress Solutions, Fakenham, Norfolk NR21 8NN

# Contents

Preface     vii
   0.1 Panicked Eurocentrism     xiii
   0.2 The Structure of the Book     xxiii
   0.3 Acknowledgments     xxv

1   Sakai Naoki on Translation     1
   1.1 Sakai's Model     3
   1.2 Implications for Civilizational Spells     25

2   The Casting of Civilizational Spells: Nietzsche as Precursor, Bloom as Ephebe     37
   2.1 Nietzsche 1: Slave Morality as a Civilizational Spell     38
   2.2 Nietzsche 2: The Mnemotechnics of Pain     42
   2.3 Bloom 1: The Western Canon as a Tug-of-War Between Civilizational Spells     56
   2.4 Bloom 2: The Canon as Memory as Pain     68
   2.5 Nietzsche 3: Guilt and Debt     76
   2.6 Nietzsche 4: The Desomatization of Somatic Codes     82
   2.7 Bloom 3: The Western Canon, Universalized     92
   2.8 Cofiguration?     103

3   East and West: Toward an Intercivilizational Turn     107
   3.1 An East-to-West Countertradition as a Cofigurative Regime of Translation     107
   3.2 The Occidentalist Attack on "Immature, Self-Centered Western Minds"     110
     3.2.1 Kirkland on Distortions of Daoism     111
     3.2.2 Problems in Kirkland's Attack     114
   3.3 Three Historical Stages of *Laozi* Translation     119
     3.3.1 Christianity     120
     3.3.2 Esotericism     125
     3.3.3 Romanticism     129

3.4 First Conclusion: Civilizational Spells, Again   135
3.5 Second Conclusion: Eurocentrism, Decentered   140
3.6 Third Conclusion: An Intercivilizational Turn?   142

Notes   147
References   155
Index   169

# Preface

The transition from this book's main title, *Exorcising Translation*, to its subtitle, *Towards an Intercivilizational Turn*, is apparently disjunctive—what does exorcism have to do with civilizations?—but that is because the subtitle is an abridgement of a longer and more explicit (but also more cumbersome) phrasing, which made the transition clear: "Exorcising Translation: From Civilizational Spells to an Intercivilizational Turn." The move towards an Intercivilizational Turn would, obviously, be the intervention that would ideally "exorcise" the "civilizational spells" from the global body of translation.

The inspiration for that elided transitional trope—the idea of civilizational spells—comes from a 2010 piece about the apparent oddity of the collocation "Asian theorist," where the Japanese theorist Sakai Naoki (2010: 441) tropes our sense of that oddity supernaturally:

> If not completely oxymoronic, the pairing of theory and Asia may strike many readers as a sort of quirk or defamiliarizing trick. At best, it can have the effect of exposing the presumption often taken for granted in fields dealing with certain aspects of what we understand as Asia: namely, that theory is something we do not normally expect of Asia. Precisely because this sense of oddity invoked when theory is associated with Asia is no more than a certain presumptive or conditional reflex, neither theory nor Asia receives rigorous scrutiny, and both are by and large left rather vague in conceptual articulations. Rarely have we asked ourselves why we do not feel unsettled about this feeling of incongruity, where this discomfort comes from, or how we might possibly explicate the reasons why we take this underlying presumption for granted. As long as this reflex remains presumptive and refuses to be further objectified conceptually, I suspect that it will become something which one might well call a *"civilizational spell"*, and it will continue to cast a curse on us. In other words, we will remain haunted by this presumption about theory and Asia. (Emphasis added)

A spell? A curse? A haunt? The "it" that casts the spell, that curses and haunts us, is what he calls a "reflex": there is, in other words, a mysterious force of some sort that makes us feel this way. We don't know what that force is; we don't know where it comes from, or how it acts on us. We can't explain it. So we "explain" it figuratively—which is to say, we throw metaphors at it, knowing that those metaphors don't really explain it, don't really say much about it at all, but not knowing any better way of getting a handle on the situation.

Such mysterious forces are something of a recurring interest of mine. My somatic theory and, more recently, my icotic theory are my attempts to trace those forces back to psychosocial processes that are "mysterious" only because they are mostly unconscious. They work below the level of our awareness—or, to use another metaphor, they fly under our radar. I've written one whole book about the supernatural trope of "spirit-channeled" translation—*Who Translates? Translator Subjectivities Beyond Reason* (2001)—but religious and magical tropes for such forces recur repeatedly throughout my work, from Augustine's eschatological perfectionism in *The Translator's Turn* (1991), to the fear of divine retribution for improperly translating sacred texts and Schleiermacher's invocation of witches "going doubled" in *Translation and Taboo* (1996), to the mysterious "sway" wielded by norms (which those operating under a competing set of norms may thematize as bias) in *Translation and the Problem of Sway* (2011), to Laozi's 道 dao in *The Dao of Translation* (2015a), to Mengzi's 天 tian ("heaven") in *The Deep Ecology of Rhetoric in Mencius and Aristotle* (2016a).

What strikes me as especially interesting in Sakai's trope, however, is this notion that the spell is *civilizational*—that we are conditioned to fear and respect and obey certain forces not just vaguely by "religion" or "superstition," and not just by secularized versions of those forces like "ideology" or "norms," either, but by whole civilizations. Implicit in Sakai's trope, obviously, is something like "Orientalism" or "Eurocentrism," the quite reasonable notion that "Europe" or "the West" as a massive and perhaps even in some sense monolithic civilization is under a spell, is cursed or haunted by some kind of mysterious cultural/ideological "witch" or force that associates theory with thought and modernity, and excludes Asia from that association. Westerners theorize; Asians are (occasionally) the target of Western theory. An "Asian theorist" like Sakai himself, therefore, is a kind of category error—or else, since he lives in the United States and holds an endowed chair at Cornell, he can be grandfathered in as a kind of honorary Westerner.

That kind of civilizational "grandfathering" is insulting, of course. There is no "intrinsic" or "empirical" reason (whatever that might mean) why a Japanese scholar like Sakai should not be celebrated as an *Asian* theorist. But think of it in reverse. I have lived in Hong Kong for several years now. Upon my arrival in greater China I became interested in ancient Chinese thought, began reading Mengzi intensively, comparing the various translations against the Chinese original—which I couldn't exactly read, but had just enough Chinese to study—and then began doing the same with Laozi. What I found in those ancient thinkers was a deep intellectual kinship. Mengzi in particular turned out to be a brilliant somatic theorist. He was theorizing what I had been calling somatics more than two millennia before I was born. I felt immediately at home in his writing. Laozi was more alien, harder to "feel" as my intellectual kin; but the more I studied him, the more at home I felt in his writing as well. Why? What did that mean? Was this just more Orientalism, just more of the Western colonizer's appropriation of "Eastern wisdom"?

The line I want to pursue in this book runs through a challenge to the kind of either-or thinking that binarizes East and West, draws a big fat line between them, and derogates all apparent crossovers between them to "ethnocentric" "appropriation." West is West; East is East. What the West has is the West's and the West's alone; the East should keep its civilizational hands off it. What the East has is the East's alone; the West should not try to appropriate it either. There is no intellectual or cultural traffic between the two "macrospatial" or "super-national" regions, no history of cultural cross-pollination. Sakai reading Jean-Luc Nancy (1986/2004, Conner 1991) and developing his contrast between homolingual and heterolingual address, in this civilizational binarization, is not exploring and expanding upon a crossover intellectual tradition between East and West—say, the German Romantic tradition from Herder to Heidegger drawing on ancient Indian and Chinese thought, and the Kyoto School. It's just an Asian scholar learning to think by reading Western thinkers. In reading Mengzi and Laozi and feeling at home in them, I was not prepared for that at-homeness by my long saturation in the Western dissident—say, radical esoteric, Romantic, pragmatic, and phenomenological—intellectual traditions that have long been steeped in Asian thought; I'm just appropriating them. It has to be that way, because crossovers are impossible. Westerners are Eurocentric; Asians are Asiacentric. There is a deep ditch between the two. Any attempt to cross that ditch is to be dismissed aggressively as an ethnocentric appropriation.

Obviously I think there's more to it than that. Crossovers are not only possible; they have been a reality for several centuries. Yes, the potential for misunderstanding is very real. Yes, power differentials skew our attempts to assimilate intellectual trends across civilizational boundaries. But then power differentials skew everything. Power differentials and other forms of cultural sway skew our attempts to understand our nearest and dearest—our parents and siblings, our close friends, our significant others. Why should intercivilizational dialogues be any different? It's clear why radical binarization of cultural and civilizational difference should be so attractive: boundaries have explanatory power. A man can't understand women and a woman can't understand men, because they come from radically different cultures. Gender lines, racial lines, class lines, age lines, civilizational lines bring welcome definition to the confusions of our encounters with other people. Difference is everywhere, and everywhere frustrating; how much simpler things seem if we can draw clear lines between Self and Other, and attribute the difficulties that we have making sense of the Other to some imagined impossibility of crossing those lines. To understand men you have to be a man. But of course also to understand a working-class man you have to be a working-class man, and to understand a working-class black man you have to be a working-class black man, and to understand a working-class gay black man you have to be a working-class gay black man, and so on. The problem, of course, is that even after you've eliminated all possible differences, the working-class gay black man finds it frustrating trying to understand his working-class black husband. Categories are attractive labels in the sorting out of difference; but they don't eliminate difference. In the end they only mystify it.

Drawing on Nancy, Sakai theorizes this "categorical" thinking about difference as the regime of homolingual address: the notion that communication, and thus understanding, is perfect and automatic and instantaneous among members of any given group, and all but impossible across group lines. To this regime Sakai opposes what he calls the attitude of heterolingual address: the notion that difference is endemic to the human condition, and so cannot be eliminated categorically, but that we also find ways to address each other across those differences, and to make ourselves partially understood, and to understand others in limited, pragmatic ways.

In the regime of homolingual address, Westerners instantaneously understand other Westerners and Asians instantaneously understand other Asians, because each "civilization" is perfectly unified, and so not only promotes internal understanding and external misunderstanding but is based upon the normative presumption of such (mis-)understanding. In that regime, it is to be expected, normatively, that Westerners will be under a civilizational spell that denies to Asians the ability to theorize, to think theoretically. Of course that's how things work! How else could they?

Rethinking and retheorizing this spell through Sakai's attitude of heterolingual address does not banish it, of course. Misunderstanding is not only always possible; it is always inevitable. What the attitude of heterolingual address banishes is the dogma of *absolute* misunderstanding—the idea that Westerners will never understand anything about Asians, and Asians will never understand anything about Westerners, and that any apparent understanding between the two civilizations is a deplorable (probably exploitative) illusion, because each civilization is perfectly and normatively trapped in its own prison of homolinguality.

Sakai's most brilliant theory of intercivilizational relations entails the creation and operation of what he calls "cofigurative regimes of translation"—the notion that we are always not only translating across cultural lines, and so struggling to diminish the inevitable misunderstandings of heterolinguality, but working *cofiguratively* to diminish those misunderstandings. In fact the chief form taken by the cofigurative regime of translation is the homolingual binary according to which translation is a crossing from one unified cultural entity to another unified cultural entity—because in this ideological formation cultural entities *are normatively* unified, and so require translation between them (but not within them). Sakai's great insight is that it is practical *enunciations* of translation across ubiquitous cultural difference that generate the need to retheorize/normativize intercultural communication in terms of ideological *representations* of translation across perfectly binarized cultural difference.

In other words, the "civilizational spells" that curse and haunt us with ethnocentric misunderstandings of other cultures and other civilizations, while they may be inevitable, are not inexorable. We only resign ourselves to them if we accept the binaries implicit in the regime of homolingual address. Translation as enunciation, which is to say as a practical act, is for Sakai always an effort to achieve cross-cultural understanding; and even when that effort partially fails (and it always does), the cross-cultural relationship that is thereby engaged works cofiguratively to organize the potential for understanding, even if only in the representational form of the binary regime of translation. The normative homolingual assumption that we will always "perfectly" misunderstand people from a different culture or civilization is itself a kind of understanding: we understand why we misunderstand. What that kind of homolingual "understanding" obscures, of course, is the undercurrent of repressed partial/pragmatic understanding that tends to accompany heterolingual address. By becoming normatively convinced that we understand why we misunderstand people from a different culture, we also normatively misunderstand the actual extent of our partial/pragmatic understanding.

"Cofigurative regimes of translation" tend to be negatively valenced in Sakai's thought, but only, I suggest, because Sakai is railing against the Translation Studies (TS) tendency to naturalize them as "reality." I understand them as icoses, group-plausibilized *constructions* of reality that are extraordinarily useful as counterevidence to the East-is-East-and-West-is-West dogma. "Regimes of translation" tend to be homolingual constructions for Sakai, for binary reasons—translation is only necessary in the *regime* of homolingual address across the rigid lines of national language difference—but it seems to me that they can also be usefully theorized in the attitude of heterolingual address, as organized attempts to manage or "cofigure" difference whenever it occurs, whether between close friends or distant civilizations.

## 0.1 Panicked Eurocentrism

Another manifestation of Sakai's "civilizational spells" is what I want to call, with a nod to Judith Butler (1991), panicked Eurocentrism. A Chinese translation scholar I know in Hong Kong came to me a few years ago, incensed at a reader's report he had gotten that accused him of being "Eurocentric" for stating his belief that European translation theories are more interesting than the homegrown ones developed by Chinese scholars. He asked me indignantly whether I thought that was a fair accusation. How could he be Eurocentric, he railed, if he's not even European? I waffled, said I didn't know, suggested that I might need to read the piece in question; but I was thinking that I'm not European either, and have felt pretty Eurocentric myself at various points in my life. Obviously there is often a strong inclination in what postcolonial scholars call the formerly colonized "periphery" to favor the intellectual traditions of what they call the colonial "center"—and, rich and powerful as the United States and Hong Kong both are these days, both are postcolonies still on the formerly colonized periphery of Europe, and leave their citizens feeling a little inferior to those from the center.

This "strong inclination" to value the colonial center over one's own native land is an example of what Sakai calls "civilizational spells"—but then, so too is the inclination to feel uneasy about that preference, to suspect that one may be secretly guilty of some unnamed crime against the motherland, and so to worry about being caught red-handed, so to speak, and publicly shamed. So is the inclination, when caught, to deny all charges, indignantly protest one's innocence.

Nor was this encounter with my Chinese colleague an isolated incident. Talk of Eurocentrism in TS, which seems like a fairly obvious and even expected phenomenon to point out and discuss, has increasingly become, or come to be perceived as, a *problem* in the field. Andrew Chesterman (2014), for example—an English linguist-become-translation-scholar who has been living in Finland since 1968—wrote a long position-piece denying and defending against the accusation for *Translation Studies*, which used it as a springboard for a forum on "Universalism in translation studies" that was carried over across two issues (7.1 and 7.3), with four responses in each issue, by Ronit Ricci, Rita Kothari, Judy Wakabayashi, and Maria Tymoczko in issue 1, and by Şebnem Susam-Saraeva, Kathryn Batchelor, Siobhán McElduff, and Douglas Robinson in issue 3.

It's not for me to pronounce, as if I could possibly know, on Chesterman's emotional state prompting his writing of this position piece; but just by the logic of denial his proclamations strike me as an even better example of Butlerian "panic" than my colleague's indignation in Hong Kong. Like the straight people who take heterosexuality to be a "natural" and therefore stable and safe category, but belie that naturalization and the sense of security it ostensibly brings by micro-guarding against the ever-present danger of *becoming gay*, Chesterman naturalizes and universalizes what he takes to be the core values of Western thought—namely, mainstream Enlightenment (for him Popperian) scientism—as a stable and safe category, but belies the sense of security it should theoretically bring him by writing a rather nervously exaggerated defense of his position. There is, after all, no good historical reason to reduce all Western thought to that Enlightenment master-narrative; and as anyone—except perhaps Chesterman himself—might have expected, that reductivist move had the effect of irritating his respondents: *we're now supposed to universalize not only Western thought but an extremely cold and cramped and alien **strain** of Western thought?* The powerful influence of "critical theory" and "Continental philosophy" on TS, the powerful influence of German Idealism/Romanticism on Continental philosophy/critical theory, and the powerful influence of "Oriental" (especially ancient Chinese and Indian) thought on German Idealism/Romanticism—all of which has led this counterhegemonic strain of Western thought in TS to reject and scorn the Enlightenment with great incredulous passion—makes it rather problematic for Chesterman to "forget" that the West is not the Enlightenment. A more tolerantly Olympian, more calmly inclusive, pluralistic, even relativistic understanding of the Western thought that he wanted to universalize might better have concealed the defensive agitation that now so clearly signals his *panicked* Eurocentrism. (But of course the impulse not only to universalize but to *naturalize* one's universalizations—treat them as *intrinsically* universal—militates quite effectively against that kind of pluralistic tolerance.)

To provide only the briefest sampling of Chesterman's (82–3) arguments and the various responders' counterarguments:

1. Chesterman's summary of what he takes to be cultural relativists' critique of Eurocentrism in TS:
   [a] "It is ... argued that current Eurocentric views cannot account adequately for some translation practices in non-Western cultures."
   - That might be a concern, yes, but the pressing issue is that European theories tend to be shaped—and therefore limited—by European intellectual history. Every lens,

by focusing one's sight on one set of objects, necessarily blinds one to numerous other sets. Chesterman's own assumption that Popper's scientific philosophy has "universal" applicability is a prime example of this kind of limitation. Even in Europe there is a world of social practices that cannot be accounted for through the narrow lens of scientism (see e.g. Denzin and Lincoln 2011 for a world of alternatives within qualitative research methodologies alone).

[b] TS "is particularly affected by cultural relativity, and has been dominated for too long by European culture; it needs shaking up."

- No, it's not that TS "is *particularly* affected by cultural relativity"; it's that *everything* is affected by cultural relativity, and only an extremely narrow dogmatism insists on ignoring the resulting complexity through an appeal to universalized (local) canons of proof and persuasion.

[c] There is "a 'Western', socioculturally determined conceptualization of translation, let us say, which (so the argument goes) Western scholars have assumed is universal but is not, because non-Western conceptualizations are different."

- No one has ever claimed that there is a *single* "'Western', socioculturally determined conceptualization of translation"; the critical theorists among Chesterman's respondents tend to disagree with him rather comprehensively on the best way to study translation. There may be certain family resemblances among the many Western conceptualizations of translation, among them the notion that empirical verification is the only acceptable arbiter of truth; but the cultural-relativist attack on TS Eurocentrism does not rest on any methodological or theoretical unity in what they attack.

[d] "This paradigm has arisen (partly) as a result of the colonial dominance of the West and the hegemony of some of its major languages, notably English."
- No argument.

[e] "The paradigm persists (partly) because of the entrenched and institutionalized nature of this hegemony, and ultimately reflects a continuing cultural imperialism."
- No argument.

[f] "On this view, TS will advance by overthrowing its Western paradigm, or by expanding it to incorporate non-Western concepts and theories."
- Among the Western assumptions in that sentence that need to be challenged: [i] a discipline must "advance" (the master narrative of "progress"); [ii] there is (1c) only one "Western paradigm" (the master narrative of "unity"); [iii] that one "Western paradigm" is a state or a fortress that is in danger of being "overthrown" from the inside (the master narrative of "revolution") or the outside (the master narrative of "barbarian invasion"); and [iv] the only conceivable peaceful result of this assault on the hegemony of the one single "Western paradigm" is that, though it continues to rule supreme, it might be expanded so as to make room for foreigners (the master narrative of the "melting pot").

[g] "We in the West therefore need to know more about Chinese or Indian theories, for instance, in order to make TS more universally applicable."
- Why would cultural relativists, who believe that all culture is characterized by relativity, conceive the goal of achieving "universal applicability"? This is a universalist's panicky phantasmatic projection.

[h] "Note that this relativist view seeks universality, but argues that this cannot be achieved with our current Western-centric theories."

- The universalist phantasm continues here. Several responders commented on the odd assumption that relativists "seek universality." If the one single "Western paradigm" is reduced far enough, of course, so that the only conceivable Western conceptualization of translation is by default universalist, then Chesterman's assumption is not so strange; but it's still astonishingly blind to the very issues he proposes to address.

2. Chesterman's Popperian/universalist counterargument to (1):
   [a] "All scientific endeavour is intrinsically universalist."
   - Not only is the universalism of "all scientific endeavor" not a particularly weighty selling point for humanists, but "scientific endeavour" is far too narrow a methodology to account for the complexity of translation activities in the world.
   [b] "Hypotheses and theories can emerge anywhere, in a given context of discovery, but they are assessed anywhere they can be assessed, in a universalist context of justification."
   - The adverbial tag there, "in a universalist context of justification," modifying as it does the declarative passive "are assessed," seems to suggest that this is simply what always happens. In fact while "are assessed" is indeed a simple fact, "in a universalist context of justification" is a crypto-optative: in an ideal world, as Chesterman imagines it, all hypotheses and theories *would be* "assessed in a universalist context of justification."
   [c] "There is no added value in assessing them specifically in country or culture X, any more than there is added value in the fact that they were first formulated in country or culture Y."
   - The issue is not whether there is "added value" in the location of formulation or assessment; the issue is whether a field organized around Eurocentric norms of

formulation and assessment is even capable of noticing, let alone assessing, scholarship organized around competing (non-Western) cultural norms.

[d] "For universalists, the above-mentioned relativist position commits the genetic fallacy, according to which an idea, hypothesis or theory is valued (or not) according to its origin."

- While there may empirically exist some relativists who value theories or methodologies based on their geopolitical origins, as an account of "the above-mentioned relativist *position*" this is a straw man. What the *position* values is a certain fractal kind of negativity, or subtractivity: whatever approach is touted as the "only" one, or the "correct" one, or even the "best" one, isn't. Indeed, cultural relativists would probably argue that Chesterman has it backwards: Western "universalists" like Chesterman who only value "an idea, hypothesis or theory" if it meets their universalist/scientific criteria are the ones who are valuing that idea etc. according to its origin. Chesterman is projecting his own mystified ethnocentrism onto his opponents.

[e] "In other words, to claim that TS would be enriched by ideas, etc. that originate in non-Western cultures *because* they arise there, is a bad argument."

- And since no one actually argues that ideas etc. are better simply because they originate outside the West, the proper response to this is that a straw-man argument is a bad argument.

I do not propose to dwell on that debate here; I will take passing snippets of Chesterman's position paper as illustrations of this or that perception in the field, but mostly I want to present the debate as a sign or symptom of a certain inflammation in the field surrounding Eurocentrism, a disorder that I propose to take as an opportunity to talk about large and weighty matters that are global and historical in scope and understandably divisive in impact. Drawing on the theoretical innovations of Sakai Naoki, I propose to segue from talk about universalism/objectivism and relativism/perspectivism to a rethinking of Eurocentrism in terms of the grand multicentury intercivilizational projects of Orientalism and Occidentalism, specifically as "cofigurative regimes of translation." The interesting thing about those *cofigurative* projects, as we'll see, is that they aren't centered anywhere: they're relationships, *co*figurations. The fact that they are intercivilizational relationships with an unequal distribution of power does not make the more powerful (or thematically more favored) civilization the "center."

In Chesterman's rhetorically neutralized—"objectified" but cryptoironic—double-voiced report[1], "relativist" TS scholars (1g in my tabulation) apparently argue that "We in the West therefore need to know more about Chinese or Indian theories, for instance, in order to make TS more universally applicable." The respondents to Chesterman's provocation wondered why the cultural relativists he was attacking would want to "make TS more universally applicable"—it seems not even to occur to Chesterman that some TS scholars might prefer complexity over conformity—but I suggest that Sakai (2010: 441) would pick out a very different sour note in Chesterman's claim, namely, "the presumption often taken for granted in fields dealing with certain aspects of what we understand as Asia: namely, that theory is something we do not normally expect of Asia." Would Sakai be wrong to hear that note of careful image-management in Chesterman's double-voiced report, that sense that Chesterman is working very hard *not* to express a dubiety about the very existence of "Chinese or Indian theories"?

Of course, the very fact that as a renowned Japanese theorist Sakai himself gives the lie to the "sense of oddity" he documents, but without quite banishing it, supports his suggestion that we might be under a "civilizational spell"—that we are *haunted* by the reflex, cursed by it. Sakai is an Asian theorist; he theorizes translation in ways that bear a certain family resemblance to postcolonial translation theories offered by other Asian scholars, from Talal Asad (1986) through Vicente Rafael (1988/1993) and Tejaswini Niranjana (1992) to Harish Trivedi (Bassnett and Trivedi 1999) and Gayatri Chakravorty Spivak (1993); in Hong Kong alone the list of Chinese translation theorists would include at least Martha Cheung, Zhu Chunshen, Sun Yifeng, Leo Chan, Rachel Lung, Chang Namfung, Isaac Hui, and Eugene Eoyang; surely that is scientific evidence enough to confirm that our skepticism about "the pairing of theory and Asia" is wrong and should be discarded? And yet the sense of oddity remains difficult to shake: a phenomenological (experiential, bodily, situated) resistance to the kind of steely propositional logic championed by "universalists" and scientific objectivists.

Nor does the Western assumption that "Asia" and "theory" don't colligate remain (only) Western: through (post/neo)colonial domination, through the geopolitical dispersal of "the West" throughout the world, Western Orientalist notions of the inferiority of the "Orient" to the "Occident" have become "universal." This would be propositions 1d and 1e in my tabulation. Or, to put it in Chesterman's terms: (2b) "Hypotheses and theories can emerge anywhere, in a given context of discovery, but they are assessed anywhere they can be assessed, in a universalist context of justification." It doesn't matter that the "sense of oddity" we feel when he writes of familiarizing ourselves with (1g) "Chinese or Indian theories" was originally a Western Orientalist orientation, because it can be assessed in a universalist (globalized) context of justification today. Or, as he adds, (2c) "There is no added value in assessing them specifically in country or culture X, any more than there is added value in the fact that they were first formulated in country or culture Y." And again (2d): "For universalists, the above mentioned [1] relativist position commits the genetic fallacy, according to which an idea, hypothesis or theory is valued (or not) according to its origin." It is fallacious to dismiss the "sense of oddity" we feel about "Chinese and Indian theories" as wrong on the mere grounds that its origins were in Europe. The only universalist justification for a dismissal of that sense must be objective evidence, adduced according to "universal" canons of logic and proof. (And don't try to demean the universalism of those canons by tracing them back to Plato and Aristotle. They are accepted *everywhere*. And if you can show me a culture or a cultural pocket where they are not accepted, we can dismiss those thinkers as not scientifically credible. QED.)

And yet ... what happens when we accept that evidence as valid, when we have personally read Chinese and Indian theories, personally listened to presentations by Chinese and Indian theorists, and *still* feel haunted by the reflex that rejects "Chinese and Indian theories" as unlikely in the extreme? What if we are ourselves Chinese or Indian theorists, and still find ourselves unable to undo the "civilizational spell" that tells us that there are no Chinese or Indian theorists? (We must <sigh> be doing something other than theory.)

Another extension of this panic: the reviewers of my 2015 article for *Translation Studies* (revised as bits and pieces of this book, including this section and sections 3.1 and 3.4–6) worried that I had not sufficiently defined my terms. What do I mean by "the West," or "the East"? What do I mean by Europe and Asia? Which Orientalism am I talking about? Can I really use China as a representative example of Asia? Are Talal Asad and Gayatri Spivak really Asian theorists, after all these years in the West? Can I really use Andrew Chesterman as a representative example of scientizing universalism, and thus of Eurocentrism? Aren't the boundaries around my various categories porous, and therefore in danger of allowing leakage? The fact that they explicitly stated their (quite correct) understanding of my project as being about *relationality*, and thus about border-crossings, and professed themselves in full agreement and sympathy with that project, did not prevent them from experiencing what I take to be panicked scientism about the leaky boundaries around my categories. *What if something escapes our net!?*

In an important sense, in fact, this book is about boundaries, and leakage across them. In the broadest purview, the civilizational spell that Sakai identifies "curses" or "haunts" us with the notion that there have to be boundaries, borderlines, and that they must necessarily (normatively) be hermetically sealed; any leakage across them is to be ignored as far as possible, and, to the extent that a specific instance of such leakage forces itself upon our consciousness, condemned as wrong, appropriative, even exploitative, and in any case a very bad thing. Following Sakai into the attitude of heterolingual address and the intercivilizational cofigurations of translation that result, I want to suggest that the current furor over Eurocentrism might well be marking the taking of a new turn in TS: an Intercivilizational Turn. According to the anti-Eurocentric critique of TS, the field is organized around assumptions that derive entirely from European intellectual traditions, and are therefore blind to the cultures and the intellectual traditions from the rest of the world. But while that critique is perfectly on target in regard to, say, Andrew Chesterman's Popperian scientizing universalism—as indeed his indignant protests against that critique attest—it doesn't tell the whole story. There are already, and arguably have been for at least two centuries, influential East-West crossovers at work in the field that keep insistently expanding "leakage across boundaries" into transformative theoretical and methodological innovations.

## 0.2 The Structure of the Book

I begin in Chapter 1, "Sakai on Translation," by outlining Sakai's 1997 theory of translation, in particular the key distinction between homolingual and heterolingual address and the super-categories of cofiguration and regimes of translation. After a general overview, I zero in on Sakai's telling 2010 phrase that is the focus of this book, "civilizational spells," building a rough working model out of the parallels between the supernaturalism of Sakai's "spells" trope and Friedrich Schleiermacher's condemnation of writers who write well in a foreign language as witches who "go doubled" like ghosts.

In Chapter 2, "The Casting of Civilizational Spells: Nietzsche as Precursor, Bloom as Ephebe," I read Friedrich Nietzsche in *On the Genealogy of Morals* (1887) interleavingly with Harold Bloom in *The*

*Western Canon* (1994): first (2.1) Nietzsche on masters and slaves and (2.2) the use of pain to train Western civilization to "remember" (to become docile through memory); then (2.3) Bloom on masters and slaves and (2.4) the literary canon as built on and out of pain-based memory; then (2.5) Nietzsche on the early somatic economics of justice and (2.6) the later desomatization of justice; and finally (2.7) Bloom on the desomatization and universalization (what Sakai Naoki would call the homolingualization) of the canon through the "forgetting" of translation, and (2.8) a conclusion raising the issue of cofiguration.

If Chapter 2 tracks parallel interdictions of cofigurativity in a blinkered focus on the West, the target of Chapter 3's critique also seeks to interdict cofigurativity by assigning truth and purity exclusively to "the East"—not only to China but to a very specific Chinese Daoist tradition—and error and arrogance to the West, specifically American translations and adaptations of the *Laozi*. The chapter's focal condemnation of cofiguration is offered in a 1997 lecture given by Russell Kirkland, an American Sinologist who has specialized in Daoism; his argument is that what makes Americans misread the *Laozi* is pure unadulterated Americanism (no cofigurative influence from China), and that the only way to read the *Laozi* correctly is to embargo all cofigurative influences from the West. What makes his lecture a useful case study of this anti-cofigurative project is that his own examples relentlessly prove him wrong: cofiguration is everywhere at work in them.

Nietzsche and Kirkland attack the West; Bloom uses an approach very like theirs, and certainly heavily indebted to Nietzsche, to defend it, or to defend one canonization of its literature, but also to attack the (multi)cultural relativists whom he accuses of perversely seeking to destroy the Western Canon. One might argue that all three (one German, two Americans) are Western Occidentalists, seething with rage at the West, the Occident, for its predations, its narrow bigotries, its blithe self-satisfied ignorance. Kirkland upbraids Americans in particular for not understanding Daoism as Chinese Daoists do, for not magically transforming themselves into Chinese Daoists and understanding the religion from the inside; and Nietzsche and Bloom, while seeming to conform to Kirkland's angry stereotype—they aren't Chinese, they don't think like the Chinese, they don't know the Chinese language, they never think about the Chinese, they are totally focused on the West—at some level seem to join him in his campaign. As they accuse the West of a petty, pusillanimous kind of ire that they variously call *ressentiment* and resentment, their accusations uncannily anticipate and echo Kirkland's, and begin to limn in that larger global conversation that Sakai calls *cofiguration*. In all three there is a nostalgic origin myth at work—the original aristocratic master as Strong Man in Nietzsche and Strong Poet in Bloom, the original Daoist believer (from the Liu-Song Dynasty, mid-fifth century CE) in Kirkland, the present as a falling away from that early pristine greatness—that in important ways prejudices them against the historical dissemination of their positive values. Dissemination is decay. The farther the world drifts out of sight of that lost Golden Age, both temporally and spatially—in both historical and global circulations—the worse things get.

My task here is to reverse and oppose that (image of) decay, not temporally but theoretically: to explore the ways in which the global flows and exchanges of knowledge create not only the ideological turbulences that these thinkers deplore but their inclination to deplore them, and the tropes they marshal to express their disapproval.

## 0.3 Acknowledgments

This book began to take shape for me at the "China in Translation: Theory, History, Practice" conference at the Fairbank Center at Harvard University, November 21–22, 2014, where I presented portions of what eventually became Chapter 3 here (especially sections 3.2–4); thanks to Uganda Kwan, Mark Elliott, and Alan Chan for organizing that conference and inviting me, and to Maria Tymoczko for her comments and suggestions as discussant. I also served as a discussant for Michael Hill's working paper titled "Sino-Arabic Enlightenments: At the Limits of Translation and Comparison," in which he drew in passing on Sakai

Naoki's work; reading Sakai's work in preparing my response to that began to open Sakai's theory to me.

My colleague at Hong Kong Baptist University, Robert Neather, head of the Centre for Translation, invited me to give the Centre's Thursday evening lecture March 5, 2015, and the talk I gave there (Robinson 2015b) became in revised form most of the rest of Chapter 3 (sections 3.1 and 3.4–6). Thanks not only to Robert for inviting me but to the audience members at that talk for a rousing and challenging Q&A session—especially Dennitza Gabrakova, who knows Sakai's work quite well, and Sarah Aubry, who kept asking the kinds of bolshy questions that can really liven up a Q&A session and refocus a speaker's thinking.

The Bloom sections (2.3–4 and 2.5.7) of Chapter 2 were presented at St. Petersburg State University, on December 9, 2010, at the invitation of Ivan Delazari. The Q&A that followed the talk was especially helpful—in particular the searching questions asked by Valeriy Timofeev. Ivan and I have recurred to those discussion many times in the years since, and his insights have guided my thought on these matters at a level of which I have not always been aware.

The approach to the study of translation that I borrow from Sakai Naoki—and have elsewhere called Critical Translation Studies (Robinson 2017)—is fundamentally a cultural-studies approach, and the most transformative conversations I have had with a cultural-studies scholar on these and related matters have been conducted at home, with Svetlana Ilinskaya. To her I dedicate this book.

# 1

# Sakai Naoki on Translation

There is a group of scholars that have been publishing studies of translation for twenty years—without calling themselves translation scholars, indeed disavowing any connection with Translation Studies (TS)—who take as their task the tracing of the socio-ideological *prehistory* of TS, namely, the preparatory steps by which the unified and idealized conception of translation that TS takes as its field of study was created. For these scholars the TS "primal scene" of translation, in which a text in a unified national language cannot be understood by speakers of another unified national language until it is translated, was not primal at all; rather, it was a fairly recent historical development, closely linked to the birth of the nation-state in the early modern period, and was conditioned by the sociopolitical and socioeconomic practices that are the focus of their research.

That constitutes quite a trenchant challenge to the very foundations of TS, obviously. What struck me about this work as I began reading it was how little TS scholars know about it—to the point of almost total ignorance. The group has been loosely confederated around the leadership of Lydia Liu and Sakai Naoki (who publishes in English under the Western-resequenced name Naoki Sakai), in the monographs Liu (1995) and Sakai (1997), then the essay collections Liu (1999c) and Sakai and Solomon (2006), then converging in the special issue of *translation* coedited by Sakai and Sando Mezzadra in 2014 (containing articles by Liu and Solomon). Chinese TS scholars tend to know Liu, because she's Chinese; but my impression is that they don't seem to know quite what to do with her work. Sakai has been moving recently into the peripheries of TS scholars' awareness, and was asked by Siri Nergaard to coedit the special issue of *translation*; but again, TS scholars who do know his work seem to be mostly at a loss with it, perhaps because there doesn't seem to be any obvious TS work that can be done with it. The work he does with it, beginning in 1997 with his study of the eighteenth-century creation of the Japanese national language, doesn't seem to be TS work; the contribution of Jon Solomon in Sakai and Solomon (2006) seems to push his thinking about translation into the world of political economics, and Solomon's contribution to Sakai and Mezzadra (2014) is even more overwhelmingly a high-level retheorization of political economics, with only passing references to translation.

Not only that: these scholars don't seem to have a name for their approach to the study of translation. I have elsewhere (Robinson 2017) named them Critical Translation Studies, or CTS for short, based on Lydia Liu's self-description as a critical translation theorist on her Columbia faculty web page; but I have never seen anyone else use that term.

For twenty years, then, "CTS scholars" have been theorizing translation, without a name, and translation scholars have not known (much) about them; nor, for the most part, have the "CTS scholars" been reading us. Sakai (1997) mentions Benjamin (1923/72), Jakobson (1959), and Quine (1960: 27–79)—all major TS texts, of course, especially the first two, but not exactly indicative of an intimate familiarity with the field over the last half century. In *Translingual Practice* Liu (1995) mentions a double handful of TS scholars, including me, but very much in passing, as if by way of due diligence[1]; by *Tokens of Exchange* (Liu 1999c) she has pretty much written us off, hinting in rather terse break-up lines ("we can no longer talk about translation as if it were a purely linguistic or literary matter" [1999a: 1]) that TS has nothing to offer the approach she is developing—without giving any indication that she has actually read anything in the field, except (again) Benjamin and Jakobson.

To be fair, though, the logocentric assumptions that she dismissively associates with TS as a whole are not only still very much present in the field, but remain in some sense definitive for the field as a whole. The fact that some of us associate those assumptions with the linguistic approaches that dominated TS before the Cultural Turn began to take hold from the late seventies to the early nineties—and shudder to see the field caricatured along those lines—does not mean that TS is not still in (large?) part about that "process of verbal transfer or communication, linguistic reciprocity or equivalences" (Liu 2014: 149) that she pins on TS as a whole.

And to be even fairer, where are the intelligent, complex, nuanced assessments of CTS by TS scholars? Where is the evidence that TS scholars are even reading Liu and Sakai and the others?

My *Critical Translation Studies* (Robinson 2017) was an attempt to redress that neglect; it offered three series of Critical Theses on Translation, summarizing (1) Sakai (1997), (2) Sakai and Solomon (2006), and (3) Solomon (2014) and offering four chapters on Liu (1999c). Rather than simply referring you to that introduction, I propose here to offer a very brief summary of Sakai (1997), but with a very specific focus on the civilizational spells that he mentions in passing in Sakai (2010).

## 1.1 Sakai's Model

Sakai begins his 1997 book *Translation and Subjectivity*, on the historical mobilization of practical acts (or "enunciations") of translation to create a unified Japanese nation and national language, by challenging the standard account of translation as "a somewhat tritely heroic and exceptional act of some arbitrator bridging two separate communities" (3). The "separate communities" are, we assume, nations, national cultures, each speaking a single unified national language that is utterly incomprehensible to the other. The "somewhat tritely heroic and exceptional act" is specifically a *secondary* act that follows the (ideo)logically primary act of homolingual address: the normative act of communication is to address speakers/readers of one's own national language, homolingually; translation, then, is a deviant act of rewriting that homolingual text in another unified homolingual sign system. Translation is of course a *necessary* act of rewriting, due to language difference, but nonetheless deviant, because it deviates from the normative regime of homolingual address.

Sakai identifies this set of assumptions as an ideological byproduct of the modern European nation-state, beginning in the early modern period and most influentially theorized by the German Romantics, according to whom there is a "natural" or "organic" relation between a nation and the *single* language spoken in it by the *single* ethnic group that comprises its entire population. This is not, in other words, a "natural" scene for translation. It is a cultural achievement—and a fairly recent one, articulated by a handful of German-speaking patriots two centuries ago, distressed at the occupation of the German-speaking principalities by Napoleon, convinced that the only thing that could protect "the German Nation" from future such incursions was a German Empire, the unification of German-speaking peoples into a true pan-Germanic Nation. German Romantic nationalists in the early decades of the nineteenth century, more than a half century away from actual political unification—it did not happen until 1871—tended to speak and write of the German Nation as if it were already a reality, populated with everyone who spoke "German"—some Germanic dialect, at any rate.

This nationalist conception of the integration of nation, people, and language—*Ein Land, Ein Volk, Eine Sprache* "One Land, One People, One Language"—meant that reality had to be brought into alignment with this ideological principle as much as was humanly (socially, politically) possible. The most extreme form this kind of reality-rectification has taken, of course, is ethnic cleansing, the deportation or even genocide of "foreigners"—people of a non-majority ethnicity, speaking a language that is not the One Language of the One Land and the One People—even if "they" have been living in the One Land for centuries. But there are many subtler forms of this reality-rectification as well. In his 1813 Academy address on the different methods of translating, for example, Friedrich Schleiermacher argues that:

Denn so wahr das auch bleibt in mancher Hinsicht, daß erst durch das Verständniß mehrerer Sprachen der Mensch in gewissem Sinne gebildet wird, und ein Weltbürger: so müssen wir doch gestehen, so wie wir die Weltbürgerschaft nicht für die ächte halten, die in wichtigen Momenten die Vaterlandsliebe unterdrückt, so ist auch in Bezug auf die Sprachen eine solche allgemeine Liebe nicht die rechte und wahrhaft bildende, welche für den lebendigen und höheren Gebrauch irgend eine Sprache, gleichviel ob alte oder neue, der vaterländischen gleich stellen will. Wie Einem Lande, so auch Einer Sprache oder der andern, muß der Mensch sich entschließen anzugehören, oder er schwebt haltungslos in unerfreulicher Mitte. (Schleiermacher 1813/2002: 87: 25–35)

For true as it remains in many ways that one cannot be considered educated and cosmopolitan without a knowledge of several languages, we must also admit that cosmopolitanism does not seem authentic to us if at critical moments it suppresses patriotism; and the same thing is true of languages. That highly generalized love of language that cares little what language (the native one or some other, old or new) is used for a variety is not the best kind of love for improving the mind or the culture. One Country, One Language—or else another: a person has to make up his mind to belong somewhere, or else hang disoriented in the unpleasant middle. (Robinson 1997/2002b: 235)

While Schleiermacher is clearly placing a patriotic limitation on cosmopolitanism here—the German Romantic dictum *Ein Land, Eine Sprache* "One Country, One Language" is pretty far from cosmopolitanism as we would normally define it—he is just as clearly *not* arguing for patriotism in place of cosmopolitanism. He wants both, in a mixture with unspecified proportions. It's good to be cosmopolitan, good to learn foreign languages, good to read foreign literatures, but only up to a point—namely, the point at which cosmopolitanism begins to trump patriotism. As long as cosmopolitanism is clearly subordinate to patriotism, it's okay. The form of cosmopolitanism whereby the native speaker of any given language no longer even notices what language s/he is speaking, and doesn't care, is not a *patriotic* kind of cosmopolitanism, and is therefore to be avoided. The *rechte und wahrhaft bildende* "right and truly educational" love of language is at least implicitly the kind that loves the mother tongue first and most, and relegates foreign languages to second place.

Note that the idea is not just that people brought up monolingually will *tend* not to learn foreign languages well enough not to notice or care what language they are speaking. Nor is it just that more patriotic people, or people who feel so thoroughly at home in the culture(s) in which they have spent their childhoods (the cultures of family, friends, neighborhood, language, values, country, and so on) that they don't mind being described as patriotic, may tend not to learn foreign languages well—perhaps because unconsciously they are afraid that learning a foreign language well would send a signal to their friends and family that they aren't happy with them, that they want out, that foreign cultures look more attractive and enticing than their local one. This would be a social-dispositional *tendency* that might convincingly be attached to patriotism in some form. No, Schleiermacher is saying more specifically that patriotic people who aspire to being thought "educated and cosmopolitan" should *consciously and systematically resist* taking that extra step from rough amateurish proficiency in one or more foreign languages to feeling at home in them. This is the operative *rectification of reality* so as to make it align more perfectly with the ideological (nationalistic) norm. Apart from those freaks of nature who learn several languages well enough that they forget what language they're speaking, Schleiermacher says, "alle andere Menschen, wie geläufig sie eine fremde Sprache auch lesen, behalten doch immer dabei das Gefühl des Fremden" (80: 37–9)/"all other people, no matter how fluently they read foreign languages, always have the Feeling of the Foreign while reading them" (232; translation modified).

Speaking foreign languages with a "native" accent is unpatriotic. Getting so caught up in a conversation in a foreign language (or several foreign languages) that one speaks fluently that one doesn't notice what language one is speaking with whom is a slur to one's native land. Ironically, "das Gefühl des Fremden"/"the Feeling of the Foreign" is the feeling of belonging to one's native land and its culture. Anthony Pym

(1995: 9) argues persuasively that "Schleiermacher's prime concern is not translation as such but something as vague and as vast as a sense of living in a community, at home, at ease with oneself and with others, in the present and in the future, but most importantly within certain limits, particularly the spatial limits of community as place. Let me summarize this complex concern as a problematic of social 'belonging.'" Learning an L2 well enough to feel entirely at home in it, even to prefer speaking it over the L1, and to prefer living among native speakers of it as one of them, is an implicit rejection of, and even insult to, one's L1 community. In order to declare one's loyalty to that "local" or "home" culture, in order to signal (and thus to sustain and protect) one's belonging, one must hold back from learning foreign languages *well*, which is to say, from assimilating to foreign language-use communities. Speaking the L2 rarely and reluctantly, and retaining a strong L1 accent and halting rhythms and displaying frequent syntactic interference from the L1 when one does speak it, are useful signs of loyalty to one's first language—and one should *only* have one first language—and its community of speakers.

So important is this ideological hierarchy that Schleiermacher tends to offer apparently "empirical" descriptions of the way things will typically go—*der wird sich doch wohl bewußt seyn ...*/"will be perfectly aware that ..."—when he is surreptitiously pursuing his nationalistic agenda:

> Dasselbe ist der Fall mit dem romanischen. Wer gezwungen und von Amtswegen eine solche Sprache schreibt, der wird sich doch wohl bewußt seyn, daß seine Gedanken im ersten Entstehen deutsch sind, und daß er nur sehr früh während der Embryo sich noch gestaltet schon anfängt sie zu übersetzen, und wer sich einer Wissenschaft wegen dazu aufopfert, der wird sich auch nur da leicht ungezwungen und ohne geheimes Uebersetzen finden, wo er sich ganz in der Gewalt des Gegenstandes fühlt. (87: 39–88: 5)

> The same is true of the Romance languages. Anyone required to write one of them in an official capacity will be perfectly aware that his thoughts in their first embryonic state are German, and that he

merely begins to translate them early on, while the embryo is still being formed; and anyone who dedicates himself to scholarly writing in one of them will only find his task easy, unforced, and unaccompanied by covert translation when he feels utterly under the sway of the object. (235)

What makes this ostensibly empirical description problematic is that he has just finished lamenting that

> unserm großen König waren alle feineren und höheren Gedanken durch eine fremde Sprache gekommen, und diese hatte er sich für dieses Gebiet auf das innigste angeeignet. Was er französisch philosophirte und dichtete, war er unfähig deutsch zu philosophiren und zu dichten. (86: 18–22)

> every fine and noble thought came to our great king, for example, through a thoroughly internalized foreign language; he could not have written in German the philosophical and poetic works he wrote in French. (235)

What he says literally is that Frederick the Great had "appropriated" (*angeeignet*) French as a foreign language "for this realm/domain to the innermost" (*für dieses Gebiet auf das innigste*)—though French was in fact Frederick's *first* language, which he learned from the French governess who mostly raised him. French was the language not only of his governess, of course, but of European culture and intellect, and thus to his mind of modernism and cosmopolitanism; German was the language of his father's narrow parochial militarism. In rebellion against his father, the young Frederick refused to speak German, dressed in French clothes, and affected a foppish French manner. Some speculate that his reputed homosexuality—there was no direct evidence of this, and he may have been asexual, but he encouraged rumors of his romantic preference for men throughout his life—was part of this "French" rebellion against his father. And while he grew into one of the greatest military geniuses of all time—his rebellion against his father's militarism was far from total—he wrote poetry and speculative philosophy in French, changed the language of the Royal

Academy of the Sciences to French, inducted French thinkers into the Academy, and worked hard throughout his forty-six-year reign to modernize Prussia on the French model. But for Schleiermacher the king of Prussia had to be a native speaker of German; his French had to be a foreign language. The primacy of German for "Germans," citizens of the imaginary "German Nation," is not an empirical fact; it is an ideological norm, in accordance with which empirical reality must be revised until it fits.

Increasingly, however, this German Romantic nationalist ideology is now being undermined by global capitalism, global communication, and global mobility. We like to complain that globalization has meant the universal dominance of Global English, and at a highly abstract level of Occidentalist ideologization that is arguably the case: if everyone speaks English, then all communication becomes effortless because monolingual, and therefore guaranteed to succeed. But the more closely one examines actual social relations on the ground, the less convincing that complaint becomes; and Sakai's project challenges every assumption in that if-then proposition. Not only does everyone *not* speak English; those who do speak English (as a Lingua Franca) refract "English" as One Global Language into regional Englishes that are "dialects" in the sense that Platt, Ripuarian, Franconian, Hessian, Thuringian, Silesian, Wymysorys, Sathmarisch, Siebenbürgisch, and the dialects of Bavaria, Austria, Switzerland, Alsace, and Liechtenstein are dialects of German (not to mention Dutch and Yiddish). And of course while something called (and even perhaps here and there approaching) Standard English is increasingly adopted as the medium of instruction in schools and universities around the world, the classroom reality is quite different. In Hong Kong, where I write this, all eight universities are officially MOIE—English-medium-of-instruction—but in the Arts Faculty at HKBU, English is officially the medium of instruction only in 53 percent of the classrooms, and according to student reports the ratio of English to Cantonese used in MOIE classrooms is on average 8 or 9 to 1. And there are inevitably cases where a course supposedly taught entirely in English is in fact taught entirely in Cantonese, because the instructor's English isn't good enough, or because the instructor gets frustrated with the students not understanding his or her English, or because the instructor is lazy. And even when the instructor doggedly uses English throughout, typically the English is Hong Kong English. And in most other cultural contexts Cantonese with some Hong Kong English mixed in dominates speech, and standard Chinese (Putonghua) dominates writing, with signage also in Hong Kong English ("COULD NOT ACCESS TO THIRD FLOOR BY THIS ENTRANCE"), both necessitating and exemplifying not only translation but what Sakai calls "the heterolingual address."

What makes this distinction between homolingual and heterolingual address so interesting for the study of translation is that it explains why translation should have come to be perceived as at once essential and invisible. It is *essential* because, in Sakai's (1997: 3–4) words,

> [Ø]  Homolingual address is "a regime of someone relating herself or himself to others in enunciation whereby the addresser adopts the position representative of a putatively homogeneous language society and relates to the general addressees, who are also representative of an equally homogeneous language community"—

—and obviously that doesn't cover all communication situations. That image of communication idealizes most (perhaps even all) of the complexities of real-world communication out of the picture. Translation is necessary to handle some of those airbrushed complexities—and must remain *invisible* in order to preserve the airbrushing. At the very least:

> [Ø′]  When a homolingual address has potential readers/hearers that are rendered incapable of reading it by their cultural-linguistic exclusion from that "equally homogeneous language community"—they are "foreigners" who can't read the source language—"interlingual" translation becomes necessary. These recipients may remain normatively invisible and unknown to

the writer/speaker; the possibility that the source text might need to be translated may also remain normatively invisible and unknown to the source author; hence also the translator, and the (f)act of translation, will typically need to remain invisible as well, to protect the (Ø) normative homolinguality of the address.

That's a reassuringly familiar binary, I trust: (Ø) homolingual address understood easily, automatically, by source readers who are native speakers of the source language, and (Ø′) homolingual address misunderstood totally, "perfectly," by non-native speakers of the source language who depend upon a translation for understanding. But Sakai next asks us to consider a problematically dual middle ground between those two poles:

[1] "Foreign" readers of the source text whose command of the source language is near-native read the source text with a facility that is so great as to be virtually indistinguishable from a native speaker's. They do not stop to look words up in the dictionary. They do not do painstaking syntactic analyses to figure out what complex sentences mean. They do not translate mentally into their first language as they go along.

[1′] "Foreign" readers of the source text whose command of the source language is weaker than that in (1) do frequently look words up in the dictionary, and do analyze sentences syntactically, and do translate mentally as they read along.

The (1) near-native "foreign" readers there might be thought of as near-perfect simulacra of (Ø) the intended native addresses of the homolingual source text (ideal source readers); the (1′) weaker "foreign" source readers, since they translate mentally, might correspondingly be thought of as rough simulacra of (Ø′) the translators who make the source text available to those target readers with no knowledge at all of the source language.

Tellingly, these two reader-types are the main focus of Schleiermacher's address—his positive and negative exemplars for translators. The (1′) readers who read with a "Feeling of the Foreign" are his ideal, the model that all (Ø') translators should emulate; the (1) readers who should by rights be foreigners to the text and its author and its ideal readers (and its homolingual community), and should therefore be reading with a Feeling of the Foreign, but instead perversely emulate native speakers of the source language, are unpatriotic cosmopolitans whose ability to "go doubled like a ghost" he condemns as a *frevelhafte und magische Kunst* "wicked and magical art":

> Es giebt freilich auch außerdem eine freie Liebhaberei am lateinisch oder romanisch schreiben, und wenn es mit dieser wirklich darauf abgesehen wäre in einer fremden Sprache gleich gut wie in der eigenen und gleich ursprünglich zu produciren: so würde ich sie unbedenklich für eine frevelhafte und magische Kunst erklären, wie das Doppeltgehen, womit der Mensch nicht nur der Geseze der Natur zu spotten, sondern auch andere zu verwirren gedächte. So ist es aber wol nicht, sondern diese Liebhaberei ist nur ein feines mimisches Spiel, womit man sich höchstens in den Vorhöfen der Wissenschaft und Kunst die Zeit anmuthig vertreibt. Die Production in der fremden Sprache ist keine ursprüngliche; sondern Erinnerungen an einen bestimmten Schriftsteller oder auch an die Weise eines gewissen Zeitalters, das gleichsam eine allgemeine Person vorstellt, schweben der Seele fast wie ein lebendiges äußeres Bild vor, und die Nachahmung desselben leitet und bestimmt die Production. Daher auch selten auf diesem Weg etwas entsteht, was außer der mimischen Genauigkeit einen wahren Werth hätte; und man kann sich des beliebten Kunststükkes um so harmloser erfreuen, als man die gespielte Person überall deutlich genug durchblikkt. Ist aber jemand gegen Natur und Sitte förmlich ein Ueberläufer geworden von der Muttersprache, und hat sich einer andern ergeben: so ist es nicht etwa gezierter und angedichteter Hohn, wenn er versichert, er könne sich in jener nun gar nicht mehr bewegen: sondern es ist nur eine Rechtfertigung, die er sich selbst schuldig ist, daß seine Natur wirklich ein Naturwunder ist gegen alle Ordnung und Regel, und eine Beruhigung für die andern, daß er wenigstens nicht doppelt geht wie ein Gespenst. (Schleiermacher 1813/2002: 88: 5–29)

To be sure, some write in Latin or one of the Romance languages for their own pleasure; and if their intentions in this were to write as well and as originally in the foreign language as in their own, I would unhesitatingly pronounce it a wicked and magical art akin to going doubled, an attempt at once to flout the laws of nature and to perplex others. But that is truly not their aim; their hobby is but an exquisite mimetic game with which to beguile away the hours out on the margins of philosophy and art. Writing in a foreign language is never original; rather remembrances of specific authors or of the manner of a certain era, which flesh forth as it were a collective persona, float before the soul almost like living simulacra that, when imitated on paper, give the writing direction and definition. This is also why this approach rarely produces anything of true value, except perhaps the mimetic accuracy it undeniably fosters. It also affords the reader much harmless enjoyment of a beloved work of art, since the person imitated so clearly shines through everywhere. If on the other hand, in defiance of nature and morality, a writer becomes a traitor to his native language by surrendering his verbal life to another, it is no false or affected self-mockery when he protests that he can no longer move about in that language; it is rather his attempt to vindicate himself by portraying himself as a wonder, a miracle surpassing all natural rule and order, and a relief to others that he at least does not go doubled like a ghost. (Robinson 1997/2002b: 235–6)

I have elsewhere analyzed the moral horror at black magic in this passage (Robinson 1996: 176–82) and the bad logic according to which, because it is impossible to write well in a foreign language, it is wicked to imitate such writing while translating, or even to use the image of such writing as a heuristic while translating (Robinson 2013b: 125–30); my point here is mainly that 1/1' is a middle ground inside Ø/Ø' that, through Schleiermacher, already has considerable traction in TS. The fact that, also through Schleiermacher, that middle ground also resonates with Sakai's "civilizational spells" is significant, but is for now a secondary concern: the cosmopolitan German who speaks French or English so well that s/he forgets what language s/he is speaking is for Schleiermacher something like the Asian monster or freak who "thinks" well enough to be a (by definition Western) theorist, and so "goes doubled" as a Westerner. I want to come back to this attribution of supernatural evil to crossover language proficiency; for now, note only that the fear-mongering (ideo)logic that resorts to metaphorical witch-hunting when faced with a crossover like this is by definition zealously binary. The supernatural accusations are directed at phenomena that flout rigid binaries—that occupy *infelicitous middles*: "Wie Einem Lande, so auch Einer Sprache oder der andern, muß der Mensch sich entschließen anzugehören, oder er schwebt haltungslos in unerfreulicher Mitte" (Schleiermacher 1813/2002: 87: 25–35)/"One Country, One Language—or else another: a person has to make up his mind to belong somewhere, or else hang disoriented in the unpleasant middle" (Robinson 1997/2002b: 235).

What I would like to suggest, in fact, is that Sakai's homolingual/heterolingual binary is beset by some of that same anxious rigidity—and that, *pace* Sakai and his nervous binarism, heterolinguality can be logically inserted right into that disorienting middle that we've been expanding:

[2] Even within the "putatively homogeneous language society" there are subcultures whose language usages vary from the putative norm: male and female cultures, straight and gay cultures, social class cultures, ethnic cultures, age cultures, professional cultures, and so on. Putative homogeneity or homolinguality is only an ideological imputation—an ideal toward which language communities may strive, but which always inevitably reflect the heterogeneity or heterolinguality *against* which they strive. Speakers of the same ostensibly "homolingual" language who are members of different subcultures will have to "translate" to understand each other.

[2'] Even in the same family, siblings of the same sex will often misunderstand each other. Even when all subcultural differences are removed, in other words, "translation" is still necessary.

If Ø/Ø' there is the regime of homolingual address, 2' is the extreme statement of the attitude of heterolingual address—but the sequence

∅/∅′>1/1′>2>2′ suggests that the cardinal numbers in it mark not progressive stages of a trajectory from falsehood to truth, or from illusion to reality, as it mostly seems to be for Sakai, but expansions of the slashes that mark the middles:

$$\emptyset\backslash 1\backslash 2\backslash/2'/1'/\emptyset'$$

For Sakai, homolingual address is an ideological construct that distorts the reality of communication, and must be cleared away before proper (heterolingual) rehistoricization can begin; for me, *both* the regime of homolingual address and the attitude of heterolingual address are ideological constructs. Or, better, they are both social ecologies, which is to say *icoses*, sociosomatically constructed "realities" that cannot and should not be derogated as illusions. While agreeing with Sakai that the attitude of the heterolingual address is in almost every way more attractive than the regime of homolingual address, and even that it seems to fit my intuitions about the way human communication *really works* far better than the regime of homolingual address, I submit that that attractiveness and that intuitive sense of rightness do not make (2/2′) the attitude of the heterolingual address "truer" or "more real" than (∅/∅′) the regime of homolingual address. It just makes it more icotic for critical theorists.

The corollaries that Sakai posits for (2/2′) the attitude of heterolingual address are counterintuitive, in a way, but in a way that surreptitiously flatters us critical theorists who have long been steeped in poststructuralist thought (Freudian displacement, the Lacanian mirror-stage, Derridean *différance*) as Romanticism's dark side. We long for precisely this kind of counterintuitivity; we expect it from theorics that we respect as smart; when we find it, we nod knowingly, and congratulate ourselves on our receptivity to such transvaluations of traditional values. In that sense these corollaries are ultimately the least problematic part of Sakai's theoretical project.

The first corollary is that *everyone* we want to address is a foreigner to us: "In this respect, you are always confronted, so to speak, with foreigners in your enunciation when your attitude is that of the heterolingual address. Precisely because you wish to communicate with her, him, or them, so the first, and perhaps most fundamental, determination of your addressee, is that of the one who might not comprehend your language, that is, the foreigner" (Sakai 9).

The second corollary is that we are foreigners to ourselves: "what is addressed to the addressee is not automatically delivered precisely because of the disparity between addressing and communicating, of a disparity that also expresses the essential *distance* not only of the addressee from the addresser but also of the addressee or addresser from himself or herself" (8–9). We don't know ourselves. We don't know what we want to say, because we don't know what we want in general—until we begin addressing others, begin translating our emerging wants for the foreigners in our environment and the foreigners in ourselves. Only as we venture across those boundaries do we begin to collect the ingredients that might eventually, emergingly, be baked into something resembling a self—which is thus always collective first, individualized second (if at all; see Sakai 51).

The third corollary is that all address is translation: "Every translation calls for a countertranslation, and in this sort of address it is clearly evident that within the framework of communication, translation must be endless" (Sakai 8). Because we are all foreigners to each other and to ourselves, we are also all translators. Not only do we have to translate everything other people say to us, before we can begin to try and make sense of it; we have to translate everything we say to ourselves. More: not only is every heterolingual address to an other a translation across the gap of exteriority—from one perspective on the world to another—but every *reception of* or *response to* every heterolingual address is a (counter)translation of that address as well. "Thus, in the heterolingual address, the addressee must translate any delivery, whether in speech or writing, in order for that delivery to actually be received" (8). "Reception" is not passive but active, an active responding as a *translational speech act*.

I should add that Sakai takes this conception of community loosely from Jean-Luc Nancy's *La communauté désœuvrée/The Inoperative Community*, who builds it out of his close engagements with Heidegger:

C'est-à-dire qu'il [Bataille] renonça à penser le *partage* de la communauté, et la souveraineté dans le partage ou *la souveraineté partagée*, et partagée *entre* des *Dasein*, entre des existences singulières qui ne sont pas des sujets, et dont le rapport—le partage lui-même—n'est pas une communion, ni une appropriation d'objet, ni une reconnaissance de soi, ni même une communication comme on l'entend entre des sujets. Mais ces êtres singuliers sont eux-mêmes constitués par le partage, ils sont distribués et placés ou plutôt *espacés* par le partage qui les fait *autres* : autres l'un pour l'autre, et autres, infiniment autres pour le Sujet de leur fusion, qui s'abîme dans le partage, dans l'extase du partage : "communiquant" de ne pas "communier". Ces "lieux de communication" ne sont plus des lieux de fusion, bien qu'on y *passe* de l'un à l'autre ; ils sont définis et exposés par leur dis-location. Ainsi, la communication du partage serait cette dis-location elle-même. (1986/2004: 64–5)

That is to say he [Bataille] gave up thinking the *sharing* [*partage*] of community and the sovereignty in the sharing or *shared sovereignty*, shared *between Daseins*, between singular existences that are not subjects and whose relation—the sharing itself—is not a communion, nor the appropriation of an object, nor a self-recognition, nor even a communication as this is understood to exist between subjects. But these singular beings are themselves constituted by sharing, they are distributed and placed, or rather *spaced*, by the sharing that makes them *others*: other for one another, and other, infinitely other for the Subject of their fusion, which is engulfed in the sharing, in the ecstasy of the sharing: "communicating" by not "communing." These "places of communication" are no longer places of fusion, even though in them one *passes* from one to the other; they are defined and exposed by their dislocation. Thus, the communication of sharing would be this very dis-location. (Connor 1991: 25)

"Le Sujet de leur fusion"/"The Subject of their fusion" would be something like Sakai's regime of homolingual address; "le partage qui les fait *autres*"/"the sharing that makes them *others*" would be the heterolingual address.

Where Sakai's binary model really becomes interesting—which is to say, problematic—is when he uses it to explain why in the regime of homolingual address the translator must be "erased" from communication. This erasure of the translator is an "enemy" move in TS, something against which the TS community rails—"stop assigning us merely 'instrumental' value, as if we weren't even human! stop treating us as invisible!"—but Sakai insists that it follows inexorably from the regime of homolingual address within which TS traditionally works. One could represent this necessity syllogistically:

    P1.    The regime of homolingual address entails the repression of heterolingual address.
    P2.    The translator must operate within the heterolingual address.
    C.    Therefore, the regime of homolingual address entails the repression of the translator's work.

In (Ø) the regime of homolingual address, there is (Ø′) no translation. It has to be that simple. (Ø′) No one translates.

The regime of homolingual address as Sakai describes it is a regime in which each language is ideally isolated from every other, with the speakers of each able to communicate easily and freely, and indeed automatically, with each other, and utterly unable to communicate with the "foreigners" that have been relegated in advance to other isolated languages. There is, obviously, no room in this idealized model for the translator—and yet it depends not just for its proper functioning but for its very theorization on the mediatory work done by the translator:

> Precisely because of her positionality, the translator has to enunciate for an essentially mixed and linguistically heterogeneous audience. In order to function as a translator, she must listen, read, speak, or write in the multiplicity of languages, so that the representation of translation as a transfer from one language to another is possible only as long as the translator acts as a heterolingual agent and addresses herself from a position of linguistic multiplicity: she necessarily occupies a position in which multiple languages are implicated within one another. (9)

But for that very same reason, in order for communication to be represented within the regime of homolingual address, the translator must be "erased": "The translator who is present to both the writer and the readers regulates communicative transactions, but her mediation must be erased in the representation of translation according to which the message issued by the writer in one language is translated into an equivalent message in another language, which is then received by the readers" (9–10). The idea remains in the "homolingual" representation of translation that the written or spoken text can be understood by its audience because it is *essentially* homolingual—because the "foreign" author somehow magically wrote or spoke it in the "local" language of its (monolingual) audience. I suggest, in fact, that this is the theoretical critique of "bringing the author to the reader" toward which Schleiermacher was so haplessly groping in his 1813 address to the Academy, and that his followers among the foreignizers have so far been unable to formulate more effectively for him: "The assumption that one can make oneself understood without perceptible hindrance, as long as one belongs in the same linguistic community, survives intact here" (Sakai 10). As Sakai would see it, the difference between domestication and foreignization for Schleiermacher and his many followers should have been, not that the former takes the author to the reader and the latter takes the reader to the author, nor that the former is immoral and unpatriotic and the latter is the only "true" form of translation (as Schleiermacher insists), nor that the former makes the target culture complicit with capitalism and the latter makes the target culture dissident (as Venuti insists), but that the former is conditioned by the regime of the homolingual address and the latter is an embrace of the attitude of the heterolingual address.

By far Sakai's most intriguing theoretical solution to the slippages he tracks in the movement from Ø to Ø' is his suggestion that in the practical act of translating, the "erasure" of the translator's work makes the translator a "subject in transit" (13). Noting the familiar conundrum that the translator in translating cannot "speak" in his or her own person, and therefore "must be responsible for her translation, for every word of it, but she cannot be held responsible for what is pledged in what she says" (11), Sakai underscores "the extremely ambiguous and unstable positionality the translator has to occupy with regard to the original addresser and the addressee" (11). The translator is the addresser of the translation, but is required to vacate that subject-position in favor of the source author; and is the addressee of the source text, but is required to vacate that subject-position in favor of the target reader. The translator must act as if the source author both is and is not writing to him or her and as if the target reader both is and is not reading her or him. "The addressee for the enunciation of the addresser must not be located at the site where the translator is, so that the addressee is always located elsewhere in translation" (11).

Sakai frames this dislocation in Benvenistean terms:

> In the enunciation of translation, the subject of the enunciation and the subject of the enunciated are not expected to coincide with one another. The translator's desire must be at least displaced, if not entirely dissipated, in translational enunciation. Thus, the translator cannot be designated either as "I" or as "you" straightforwardly: she disrupts the attempt to appropriate the relation of the addresser and the addressee into the *personal* relation of first person vis-à-vis second person. To follow the determination of a "person" as espoused by Émile Benveniste—that is, that only those directly addressing and addressed in what he calls "discourse" as distinct from "story" or "history" can be called persons, and that those who are referred to or talked about in the capacity of "he," "she," or "they" in "story" or "history" cannot be "persons"—the addresser, the translator, and the addressee cannot be persons simultaneously; the translator cannot be either the first or second or even third "person" undisruptively. (12–13)

Sakai pauses for a moment to contrast Benveniste's depersonalization of the third person with Foucault's "explicitly antipersonalist" (12) conception of discourse, but returns to note that, to the extent that we want to personalize address, translation destabilizes that project, destabilizes "the putatively *personal* relations among the agents of speech, writing, listening, and reading" (12). The translator cannot be the full (monolingual) "person" or "individual" that is Romanticized in the regime of homolingual address, empowered by membership in a single unified language community to "confirm" her unique individual personality by expressing it:

> At best, she can be a *subject in transit*, first because the translator cannot be an "individual" in the sense of *individuum* in order to perform translation, and second because she is a *singular* that marks an elusive point of discontinuity in the social, whereas translation is the practice of creating continuity at that singular point of discontinuity. Translation is an instance of *continuity in discontinuity* and a poietic social practice that institutes a relation at the site of incommensurability. This is why the aspect of discontinuity inherent in translation would be completely repressed if we were to determine translation to be a form of communication. And this is what I have referred to as the *oscillation or indeterminacy of personality in translation*. (13)

In the regime of homolingual address, there are no discontinuities. It is by definition the realm of perfected (because imagined) continuity. It is precisely in order to protect that imagined continuity that the translator's work is repressed or "erased." Because the translator is precisely the "disimagined" laborer whose job it is to smooth out the real discontinuities, and create continuities in their place, s/he is effectively positioned "in transit" between stable communities and stable subjectivities, simultaneously destabilizing the homolingual ideal and restabilizing the resulting discontinuities for reassimilation into the homolingual ideal. Nor should the subjective "transit" be imaged as a continuous becoming; it is, rather, a stop-frame shift, very much like the rabbit-duck illusion, in which the translator's subjectivity is perceived first as this, then as that, alternatingly, and, since the two subjectivities are mutually incompatible, and thus as ultimately impossible, the whole process dissolves into illusion, and stands revealed as something to which no attention needs to be paid.

And it is precisely this "poietic social practice that institutes a relation at the site of incommensurability" that makes practical ("enunciative") translation constitutive of the ideological *regime* of translation that for Sakai organizes heterolinguality into an incommensurability between *national* subjectivities and *national* languages: "Through the labor of the translator, the incommensurability as difference that calls for the service of the translator in the first place is negotiated and worked on. In other words, the work of translation is a practice by which the initial discontinuity between the addresser and the addressee is made continuous and recognizable" (Sakai 14)—recognizable, that is, as involving a transfer of meaning from one national language to another. The translator's transitory subjectivity, by working on disconcerting discontinuities in the heterolingual address, plying "the initial discontinuity between the addresser and the addressee," makes it "continuous and recognizable," as a gap not between any two human beings who are irrevocably foreigners to each other but between languages, language unities, unified language communities: "Only retrospectively and after translation, therefore, can we recognize the initial incommensurability as a gap, crevice, or border between fully constituted entities, spheres, or domains. But, when represented as a gap, crevice or border, it is no longer incommensurate" (14). It is a gap or a crevice that can be jumped, a border that can be crossed.

According to Sakai, the specific representation of translation as this kind of border-crossing between two stable language unities has had the historical effect of giving rise to the idea of consolidating a geographically based collection of dialects and styles and genres into a single stable national language, but "cofiguratively," in what Sakai calls the "schema of cofiguration." In this notion "the comparative framework of Japan and the West" is *imaginary*, but in the complex sense that it is an *image* that organizes the *imagination*, and so is "practical in its ability to evoke one to act toward the future" (52)—and specifically as a *relational* practicality, a practicality that is embedded in a mutually constitutive relationship between a collectivized self and a collectivized other:

> The relation to the self cannot be determined unless the relation to the other has already been determined. Not to mention Hegel on self-consciousness, it is a rudimentary premise, when dealing with the problem of identity in cultural and social contexts, that the relation to the other logically precedes that to the self. What is at issue here,

indeed, is not a dialectic of the self and the other for individual consciousnesses, but a process in which the comparative framework of Japan (the self) and the West (the other) is installed. This framework is not merely epistemological in that it offers a means of comparative mapping. As I have repeatedly stressed, its function is also practical, since it fashions the shape of desire for the students of Japanese thought. (51)

More aphoristically: "desire for 'Japanese thought' is invoked through the schema of cofiguration in the regime of translation" (51). This "desire for 'Japanese thought'"—the desire to create it or imagine it as a unique and original contribution to "thought in general" or "world thought," the desire to identify with a unique and original "Japanese thought" that already exists and, in so doing, to help bring it into being—is "mimetic," or perhaps better "co-mimetic," as it emerges out of an intertwined global network of imitations. The desire to identify with a strikingly original Japan is "mediated by the mimetic desire for the West" (52), and "within the discipline of the history of Japanese thought—and, by extension, Japanese studies—the insistence on the West's uniqueness would, in turn, be a testimony to the students' disavowed desire to imitate what is expected of the West by the Japanese" (52).

Sakai notes that this representation of translation is not an inevitable one: "As the practice of translation remains radically heterogeneous to the representation of translation, translation need not be represented as a communication between two clearly delineated linguistic communities" (15). All the interesting work done on "cultural translation" in various borderlands, one complexly mixed code being translated into another, often with slightly different mixtures of the same codes, should remind us that the "standard" form of translation, with a single coherent source language and a single coherent target language, is an *ideal* that has been imposed upon translation in the modern era, with the rise of the nation-state. As Sakai goes on, "there should be many different ways to apprehend translation in which the subjectivity of a community does not necessarily constitute itself in terms of language unity or the homogeneous sphere of ethnic or national culture. The particular representation of translation in which translation is understood to be communication between two particular languages is, no doubt, a historical construct" (15).

But what we now take to be the "standard" representation of translation did emerge and take hold, several hundred years ago, "and it is this particular representation of translation that gave rise to the possibility of figuring out the unity of ethnic or national language together with another language unity" (15). In other words, the representation of translation as "a communication between two clearly delineated linguistic communities" gave rise to the "schema of cofiguration," which he defines as "a means by which a national community represents itself to itself, thereby constituting itself as a subject," but specifically as a *relational* self-representation: "it seemed to me that this autoconstitution of the national subject would not proceed unitarily; on the contrary, it would constitute itself only by making visible the figure of an other with which it engages in a translational relationship" (15–16).

His prime example of this "autoconstitution of the national subject" is Japan, the country in which he was born and raised: "Indeed, this is one or the reasons for which I have claimed that the Japanese language was born, or stillborn, in the eighteenth century among a very small portion of literary people, when the schema of cofiguration came into being" (15). And indeed this is his model for the study of the creation of "Japan," and the reason he writes his long and densely brilliant Introduction on translation. He also insists that this origin story is not unique to Japan:

> By now it should be evident that, given my analysis of the regime of translation and the homolingual address, culturalism in which Japanese culture and nation are obstinately reified and essentialized is, as a matter of fact, not particular to Japanese journalism and academia at all. Culturalism that endorses nationalism in terms of national language and ethnic culture is as persistently endemic in Japanese Studies in the United States, Europe, and elsewhere as in Japan today.

For, as I will show in some of the following chapters, behind Westerners' as well as Japanese insistence on Japanese cultural uniqueness looms an equally obstinate essentialization of the West. (17)

It is this historical generalizability of Sakai's concepts of "the representation of translation" and "the schema of cofiguration" that makes them useful tools in the study of translation in terms of Eurocentrism and Orientalism/Occidentalism (see Chapter 3).

## 1.2 Implications for Civilizational Spells

Now let us return to Sakai's 2010 notion of the "civilizational spell" that makes it seem odd to speak of an Asian theorist, in the context now of Sakai's own earlier model of the aporias in the regime of homolingual address. In section 1.1 I suggested an isomorphism between the nationalistic ethos that generates a horror of trans-binary crossovers, which Schleiermacher associated with witchcraft ("going doubled"), and the civilizational—specifically, Orientalist—value hierarchy that as Sakai notes associates "theory" or "thought" with modernism and thus with the West. Is this just an isomorphism, or might there be a causal relationship between the two?

There are of course several divergences between the two "supernatural" "accusations": Schleiermacher (jokingly? figuratively?) "accuses" the writer who writes well in a foreign language of "going doubled like a ghost," which is to say, of being a witch whose black magic is wielded on *travel between worlds*; Sakai (jokingly? figuratively?) "accuses" the West of being under a civilizational spell that blinds us to the existence of Asian theorists, which is to say, of being "cursed" by a witch or "haunted" by a ghost whose black magic is wielded on *obscuring the true nature of reality*. It is pretty clear that Sakai does not lodge his "accusation" seriously, literally: it is a trope. Things are less clear in Schleiermacher. He seems to be supernaturalizing the ability to write well in a foreign language figuratively, and obviously the extremism of the moral horror that a literal reading would impute to it would seem to suggest that he is speaking figuratively, and perhaps even jokingly; but there is an irrational zealotry to his atrocious logic here that arguably suggests the opposite as well, or perhaps some fractal return-of-the-repressed position between opposites, such as that he *thinks* he's joking but deep down cannot help but mean it seriously.

Setting aside the knotty problem of Schleiermacher's possibly conflicted intentions, then, let us narrow the divergences down to just two: on the issues of [1] *who the witch is* and [2] *what kind of black magic the witch practices*.

1. For both thinkers, the witch is clearly an Other, but a rather different Other: the writer like Beckett or Nabokov who writes well in a foreign language for Schleiermacher, some sort of deep ideological agent in Orientalist thinking for Sakai. Schleiermacher's Other is *wrong*, and possibly even *frevelhaft* "wicked," because s/he deviates from what I have called Schleiermacher's henolingual norm (Robinson 2013b: 146–65): just as in what Schelling dubbed henotheism there are many gods but each culture has its own, which it reveres above all others, so too for Schleiermacher are there many languages, each of them valuable in its own right, but each culture has its own, which it loves and speaks better than all others. A xenophobic norm would require that every individual speak his or her own language well and no others at all; Schleiermacher's henolingualism is a nationalistic brand of cosmopolitanism that encourages openness to xenolanguages and xenocultures, but only if those others remain radically secondary to the henolanguage. The henolingual norm is for every human being to speak one language well and one or more others *badly*, with an ever-present Feeling of the Foreign. This norm becomes important to Schleiermacher as a model for the translator to emulate: the translator should translate so as to give the target reader that Feeling of the Foreign, as if that reader could actually read the source language, but badly. The "witch," for Schleiermacher, in other words, is not the domesticating translator, who translates so as to give the target reader the feeling that s/he is a native speaker of the source language, or

indeed as if the source author had originally written the text in the target language. That translator for Schleiermacher is only *imitating* the witch.

Sakai's focus, by contrast, is not on the caster of the spell, the witch, but on the spell's target, the victim, namely, the West—or perhaps, rather, the whole world as a realized simulacrum of the West's Orientalist orientations. His passing supernaturalization of ideology does not specify what force he would identify as the witch.

2. The divergence that I want to place center stage in this book, however, is the other one: that Schleiermacher is interested in *travel between worlds*, Sakai in the *obscuring of the true nature of reality*. The rectification I want to bring to that divergence is a simple grab-and-go: I want to adjust both models so as to enable us to have it both ways. Schleiermacher's geocultural focus on *travel between worlds* is essential for discussions of translation; Sakai's epistemological focus on *obscurantism* is essential for discussions of the relations between theory and practice. In order to incorporate both, I propose to assimilate each to the other: to rethink [a] Sakai's trope of civilizational spells in terms of the witch that not only travels between worlds but travels in disguise, stays in World X while sending his or her double out into World Y, where it is mistaken for a local (a homolingual Y-ian); and to rethink [b] Schleiermacher's trope of the "wicked and magical art" of "going doubled like a ghost" in terms of those disguises, the mistaken identity that focuses our attention on the epistemological problems of theorizing experience.

a. *Sakai's trope in terms of travel between worlds*: The Asian thinker—say, Sakai himself—travels to the West as a theorist. That travel is either physical, by plane, to deliver conference papers or guest lectures, or to take up a job as a professor in a Western university—say, Cornell—or virtual, by publication, reputation, and so on. Once he gets there, something feels not quite right about his reception. There is an odd disconnect that is difficult to explain. This Asian theorist, this Sakai, gradually comes to thematize that disconnect in terms of a "civilizational spell": his Western hosts are "cursed," or "haunted," by an

Orientalist ideology according to which Asians don't really think philosophically, aren't critical theorists in anything like the Western (normative-becoming-universal[ized]) sense. And yet here is this real person, this Asian thinker, who presents himself as a theorist, who manifestly is engaged in theorizing things of considerable importance to his Western counterparts. They can't exactly deny that he's an Asian *and* a theorist; and yet the colligation seems indisputably odd. Superimposing Schleiermacher's image of the witch going doubled allows us to explain that feeling of oddity as an existential angst at an apparent imposture, someone pretending to be what he's not, in this case an Asian coming "here" (where we are all exactly the same, members of this homolingual super-nation that we lovingly Romanticize as "the West") and pretending to be one of us, when obviously he can't possibly be, because he's a foreigner, and not a Western foreigner at all, but a Japanese, someone from outside the homolingual Western super-nation. Two hundred years ago, if we had been German National Romantics in Berlin, we would have directed this kind of epistemological suspicion at any French "thinker" trying to pass himself off as a philosopher (and thus as fundamentally German); indeed in his study of ghostly hauntings and doubles in Heidegger, Jacques Derrida has an amused moment when he finds the great post-Romantic German philosopher still indulging this kind of nationalistic hubris a century and a half later, in the 1966 *Spiegel* interview, when he says that when the French begin to think, "ils parlent allemand" (quoted in Derrida 1987: 111)/"they speak German" (quoted in Bennington and Bowlby 1989: 69). In the twenty-first century, by contrast, we are global citizens, cosmopolitans in a far more open and receptive frame than Schleiermacher or Heidegger was willing to countenance: we not only accept thinkers from other European countries as theorists; we are even willing to accept Asian thinkers as theorists, even to give them endowed chairs at Ivy League universities. And yet … that nagging feeling of oddity persists. We can't shake the suspicion that they aren't *really* theorists. They are somehow *disguised* as theorists. There must be some trick, some impersonation, some kind of epistemological flimflam.

b. *Schleiermacher's trope in terms of epistemological suspicion*: It is of course extraordinarily easy to prove Schleiermacher wrong when he claims that no one can write brilliantly original literature in a foreign language. I've mentioned Beckett and Nabokov; in *Schleiermacher's Icoses* (2013b: 159) I list two dozen other well-known counterexamples as well, writers who have published great works in "foreign" languages learned after childhood. I also list exceptions to his rule that no writer ever successfully translated his or her own works into a foreign language (160), and challenge his claim that diplomats and writers like Grotius and Leibniz, who wrote and published in both Latin and their national vernaculars, are exceptions to the rule (161-5). All these famous and highly esteemed writers and translators, including many in Schleiermacher's own day and before—people of whose work he should have been aware—did what he claimed was flat-out impossible, and, even if it were possible, would be a "wicked and magical art akin to going doubled." And yet ... if we imagine Schleiermacher alive today, and reading my empirical refutations, shouldn't we also imagine him still resisting my counterexamples? Shouldn't we assume that Schleiermacher too, even had he admitted the empirical force of my argument, would have gone on feeling that nagging feeling of oddity?

In icotic terms, as Aristotle remarks in the *Rhetoric*, given a choice between a true story that is implausible and a false story that is plausible, we will almost always choose the latter, because that feeling of plausibility is our indication that the story has been vetted by the community. Whatever is plausible—*eikos*, and so "icotic"—must be true, and must therefore be believed even in the face of apparently incontrovertible evidence that undermines it. Even if we meet, listen to, read, or are an Asian theorist, somehow we must go on believing that "Asian" and "theory" don't colligate. Even if dozens of well-known writers have written brilliantly in and translated brilliantly into foreign languages, somehow we must go on believing that "one" (the normative self) can only write well in "one's" "own" (homo/henolingual) language.

This communal "plausibilization" or vetting of normativized opinions as truths and realities—icosis—is my explanation of the civilizational "spell" or the "curse" or the "haunt" that makes Schleiermacher think that no one can write well in a foreign language and Orientalists think that Asians can't be theorists; I will be exploring that icotic explanation more fully in Chapter 2. For now, though, let us ask what the "plausibility" in question actually consists in. If we collapse Schleiermacher's nationalist/henolingual plausibility together with the Orientalist plausibility that Sakai calls a "civilizational spell," what is at stake in "our" inclination to believe the plausible story over what is arguably the true one? What in the end is "the story" that we believe?

It would appear to be non-controversial that "the story" in question involves rigidly exclusive binaries and value hierarchies, and is enforced not only as "true" but as *necessarily* true, as binding not only on our thought but on reality. In each case, perhaps unsurprisingly, the reigning binary would seem to be the Me and the Not-Me, the Self and the Other. For Schleiermacher the Me is the (putative) German Nation, and the Not-Me is first the French, then the rest of the world; for Sakai's imagined Orientalist, the Me is the West, the Not-Me is Asia, "the Orient." One would assume further—again, unsurprisingly—that the Me should be assigned the higher rung in the value hierarchy: smarter, better educated, more cultivated, more civilized.

But now things get complicated. For Schleiermacher and the other German Romantics, Germans were superior to the French precisely because they were *less* civilized, *less* cultured, and therefore more open and receptive to the world on its own terms. It is important to remember that Schleiermacher gave his 1813 Academy address on the different methods of translating in a Berlin that was occupied by Napoleon's troops: the French were militarily superior, and their military strength was at least in part attributed to their civilizational superiority. But for that very reason the Germans—so argued the Romantics—had the moral/cultural high ground. Their lack of French cosmopolitan sophistication lowered their threshold to accepting the foreign.

Even more interestingly, that German Romantic moral/cultural high ground was transformed over the centuries into an Occidentalist opposition to Western superiority, on very much the same Orientalist grounds by which the West's superiority had earlier been established. Yes, the West's military superiority gave it not only geopolitical hegemony over the world it colonized but (the impression of) cultural superiority as well, especially in the areas of science, technology, and generally practical reasoning; but the East was *spiritually* superior, in a primitive, mystical, even magical sense, better connected with a projected primordial spirituality that was ranked lower on the Orientalist value hierarchy than Western science and Christianity. As Western dissident thought was channeled down from the Renaissance and Enlightenment esoterics to the Romantics, and on to the pragmatists and phenomenologists, however, that Orientalist sense of the East's spiritual superiority was gradually reframed as a true and authentic superiority; and the classical texts from ancient India and China, which had been translated into Latin and the European vernaculars by Orientalists to prove the superiority of Christianity and Western thought, were increasingly read by Western Occidentalists against the grain, in support of the West's spiritual bankruptcy and the East's spiritual ascendancy. And as this Western Occidentalism was increasingly picked up by non-Western thinkers and activists, so that it gradually came to channel "the Rest's" anti-Westernism, it took on ideological and political complexity and nuance as a radical transvaluation of Orientalist values:

1. it emerged out of the Orientalist cofiguration aimed at establishing the superiority of the West and the inferiority of Asia;
2. it reversed (1) in order to establish the inferiority of the *dominant* West and the superiority of a *peripheralized* West in league with an older and more "authentic" Asian thought;
3. it accomplished (2) through the agency of intellectual *readers* of translations that were originally produced in the service of (1)—it was a regime of translation (re)directed not by Orientalist translators but by dissident target readers; and
4. it was pursued for several centuries by (3) peripheralized Western intellectuals without cofigurative collaboration with

their Asian counterparts, through that (1>2) series of cofigurative East-to-West borrowings, but gradually grew into cofigurative reciprocity, and ultimately came to seem like a non-Western movement against the West.

Buruma and Margalit (2005) define this (2-3-4) Occidentalist reversal of (1) Orientalism not just as anti-Westernism—not just an anti-Orientalist or anti-colonialist resistance movement and ideology among non-Westerners—but rather more broadly a movement and ideology that in its values and origins is decisively

(a) *rural*: oriented to the family, the clan, the farm, and the village, and so anti-urban, anti-decadence, and generally anti-modernist;
(b) *religious*: oriented to ancient rituals and obedience to "higher powers," and so anti-secular, anti-rationalist, and generally anti-intellectual;
(c) *ascetic*: oriented to spirit and spirituality, and so to abstinence from sex, strong drink, rich food, and the raucous high spirits that tend to accompany those things (generally, from the pleasures of the body, the easy indulgence of which is condemned as immature);
(d) *collectivistic*: oriented to group norms and conformity, and so anti-individualist and generally inclined to associate individualism with selfishness, isolation, soulless anonymity, and alienation;
(e) *heroic*: oriented to honor and death, and so anti-bureaucratic and generally anti-capitalistic;
(f) *organic*: oriented to nature and the natural, and so anti-mechanical and generally anti-artifice; and
(g) *nativist*: oriented to home-grown communal authenticity, and so anti-stranger and generally xenophobic.

Not every Occidentalist group embraces all of these tendencies. The esoteric movements coming out of the Renaissance, for example, embraced (b) anti-intellectual (mystical) religious tendencies against what they perceived as the over-intellectualization of religion in the state churches, but this orientation diminished markedly in Romanticism, and then even more in phenomenology and pragmatism, which became progressively more secular and more intellectual. The German Romantics through Heidegger were strongly (a) anti-modernist, (e) anti-bureaucratic, (f) anti-mechanical, and (g) inclined to heroize the German Nation; but they also argued, from Herder and the Schlegel brothers through Schleiermacher and Goethe up to Heidegger, that the German nation was perfectly suited and positioned to translate and so to repackage the foreign cultures of the whole world as an expanded and expansive German culture "damit nun durch Hülfe unserer Sprache, was die verschiedensten Zeiten schönes gebracht haben, jeder so rein und vollkommen genießen könne, als es dem Fremdling nur möglich ist" (Schleiermacher 1813/2002: 92: 22–39)/"so that with the help of our language everyone can enjoy, as purely and as perfectly as a foreigner can, all the beauty that the ages have wrought" (Robinson 1997/2002b: 238). This still heroizes the German nation, of course, and condescendingly denigrates the foreigners who will be reading "world literature" in German, and will be able to enjoy it only "as purely and as perfectly as a foreigner can"; but at least they aren't so xenophobic as to despise foreign cultures and bar them entry into the German nation.

Buruma and Margalit make a strong case for the origins of Occidentalism in German Romanticism, and its continued perpetuation in German post-Romantic thinkers like Schopenhauer, Nietzsche, and Heidegger, noting that it has since "spread" to the rest of the world—those parts of the world that are engaged in anti-colonial and anti-Western struggles (Russia, Mainland China, Iran, Al Qaeda, Islamic State, North Korea, and so on). This etiology would suggest another cofigurative regime of translation, one that began as far back as the Renaissance, perhaps even earlier, and by the early seventeenth century was importing key mystical/experiential notions from Daoism, Confucianism, Buddhism, and other "Oriental" philosophies/religions. It was, in other words, an ancient-to-modern and East-to-West translation regime that eventually became East<>West cofigurative.

Sakai's discussion of civilizational spells is all about "colonial modernism"; the launching-pad for my argument here is the manifest geopolitical fact that colonial modernism is everywhere engaged in conflict with *anti-colonial anti-modernism*, and the attendant ideological fact that the two intertwined historical trajectories that generated that conflict are *both* East<>West cofigurative regimes of translation, operating on different social, political, and cultural strata in the various regions, and organized and driven by groups with different (indeed opposed) social, political, and cultural agendas. Implicit in that suggestion is also the intimation that an exclusive focus on Orientalism and its ideological subjugation of Asia to the West's military, economic, scientific, technological, and epistemic power is too narrow: the cofigurative engagement between the West and the Rest (however we want to define those geopolitical "areas" or "civilizations") gave rise to opposed regimes of translation, opposed translation-driven ideological agendas, here called Orientalism and Occidentalism.

The three Western thinkers whose explorations of these relationships that I explore in this book, one German (Friedrich Nietzsche) and two Americans (Harold Bloom and Russell Kirkland), are all Occidentalists. All three despise the mainstream West. Of the three, only Nietzsche is purely negative: the *Streitschrift* "polemic" of his *Genealogy of Morals* is specifically an attack on Western power, diagnosed as dominated by the slave morality of the Jews and the Christians; he has no admirable culture to hold up as a positive counterpoint to the negativity he attacks. Bloom is a Jewish mystic who in his anxiety-of-influence work in the mid-seventies combined Kabbalism with Nietzschean critiques of slave morality and Freudian father-son dynamics, but by *The Western Canon* in 1994 was peddling a hybrid message consisting of part anxiety-of-influence negativity, part standards-and-genius positivity—though one could also characterize both sides of that hybrid as Nietzschean, the negativity coming out of Nietzsche's critiques of slave morality (what Bloom calls the School of Resentment), the positivity effectively constituting a conservative transmogrification of Nietzsche's celebration of the Strong Man, the aristocrat warrior, who in Bloom becomes the

Strong Poet. And Kirkland, an American Sinologist, despises everything American except his own Sinology, celebrating a purified and Romanticized version of Chinese Daoism that one must be born Chinese (and somehow ideally protected against Western corruption) to appreciate. Of the three, in other words, if only Nietzsche is entirely negative, only Bloom strives to achieve some accommodation with the Orientalist celebration of the West's superiority. Nietzsche and Kirkland do everything in their power to tear down the West. And even Bloom's support for the Western Canon is built upon a foundation of virulent hatred for *dominant* defenses of the Western Canon, both the conservative view, which according to Bloom celebrates authors and texts that support Christian moral values, and the leftist view, which according to Bloom celebrates authors and texts from groups that have been oppressed by the powers that be. In that sense Bloom, like Nietzsche (and Heidegger), is a Strong Critic in the German Romantic tradition.

# 2

# The Casting of Civilizational Spells: Nietzsche as Precursor, Bloom as Ephebe

If the Orientalist civilizational spell pictures the Westerner as a scientist (and therefore smarter and better) and the Asian as a mystic (and therefore dumber and worse), the Occidentalist spell tends to flip that value hierarchy on its head: the Asian is a mystic (and therefore more natural and authentic, and better) and the Westerner is a scientist (and therefore more alienated from nature, and worse). This transvaluation of values is more or less what we will find in Russell Kirkland's idealization of Chinese Daoism and demonization of American self-centered secularism in Chapter 3. But what happens before the Western Occidentalist learns much about Asian religion? Graham Parkes' 1991 collection *Nietzsche and Asian Thought* is mostly prospective, focused on the influence Nietzsche had on Asian thought, rather than retrospective, about what Nietzsche knew about Asian thought; the three studies of his familiarity with Asian (mostly Indian) works, by Johann Figl (Parkes 51–63), Michel Hulin (64–75), and Mervyn Sprung (76–90), serve mostly to trace his tendency to generalize and pontificate about non-European thought from a position of relative ignorance. If we read his *Genealogy of Morals* as an Occidentalist critique of the West, his inability to set up a Kirklandian Ideal—a Chinese Daoism, say—as a utopian alternative to the West's pervasive slave morality condemns him to unrelenting negativity. Arguably the only positive figure in the book is the aristocratic Strong Man, the primordial warrior who killed and raped as he pleased—a rather horrific nostalgic projection back into the distant past that offers precious few resources for ethical orientations to the future.

Harold Bloom, whose Nietzschean ruminations in *The Western Canon* I interweave in this chapter with readings of Nietzsche's

*Genealogy*, does have the "Oriental" Jewish mysticism of the Kabbalah to set in admiring juxtaposition to the Western culture wars (conservative moralists vs. leftist multiculturalists) that he despises; tellingly, however, in *The Western Canon* he tends to fold Kabbalistic perspectives into his praise for Western canonical literary classics, rather than, Kirkland-style, setting up "Oriental" mysticism as a utopian alternative to the West.

Despite these differences, Nietzsche offers a signal theorization of the etiology of what Sakai calls the West's civilizational spells—and Bloom offers a revealing instantiation of those spells.

## 2.1 Nietzsche 1: Slave Morality as a Civilizational Spell

Friedrich Nietzsche doesn't use Sakai's term "civilizational spells," of course, but in almost every way he is the premier Western theorist of such spells—especially in *Zur Genealogie der Moral/On the Genealogy of Morals*, his "polemic" (*Streitschrift*: the book's subtitle) against the intergenerational survival of such spells in Germany, and more generally in the Judeo-Christian West.

Nietzsche (1887/92: 7) begins section 5 of his first essay by noting that "vielfach noch in jenen Worten und Wurzeln, die 'gut' bezeichnen, die Hauptnuance durchschimmert, auf welche hin die Vornehmen sich eben als Menschen höheren Ranges fühlten"/"through those words and roots which designate 'good' there frequently still shines the most important nuance by virtue of which the noble felt themselves to be men of higher rank" (Kaufmann 1967/89: 28). He gives numerous examples: the "good" are the powerful, the truthful, the courageous, the warlike, the godlike, the pure, and through those "goodness" words still *durchschimmert* "shines through" the lingering *Hauptnuance* "main nuance" of those personal qualities "felt" by a long-dead class; the "bad" are the cowardly, the base, the dark-haired. The character qualities that "linger" in these words tend to be either physical attributes or the bodily activities and behaviors that arise from those attributes:

> Der "Reine" ist von Anfang an bloss ein Mensch, der sich wäscht, der sich gewisse Speisen verbietet, die Hautkrankheiten nach sich ziehen, der nicht mit den schmutzigen Weibern des niederen Volkes schläft, der einen Abscheu vor Blut hat,—nicht mehr, nicht viel mehr! (I: 6; Nietzsche 10)

> The pure man was originally one who washed himself, who refused to eat certain foods entailing skin diseases, who did not sleep with the unwashed plebeian women, who held blood in abomination—hardly more than that. (Golffing 1956: 165)

> Die ritterlich-aristokratischen Werthurtheile haben zu ihrer Voraussetzung eine mächtige Leiblichkeit, eine blühende, reiche, selbst überschäumende Gesundheit, sammt dem, was deren Erhaltung bedingt, Krieg, Abenteuer, Jagd, Tanz, Kampfspiele und Alles überhaupt ... (I: 7; 11–12)

> The chivalrous and aristocratic valuations presuppose a strong physique, blooming, even exuberant health, together with all the conditions that guarantee its preservation: combat, adventure, the chase, the dance, war games, etc. (Golffing 167)

Those lingering "nuances" of master morality are lingering civilizational spells—spells whose atavistic power to bewitch the Nazis has rendered Nietzsche's admiration for them infamous. The interesting question to ask about that infamy, though, is not whether the racist spell of the "blonde Bestie" (Nietzsche 21)/Blond Beast would have bewitched the Nazis even without Nietzsche's praise (of course it would have) but whether the *frisson* of evil that we feel when we read or hear it is not evidence that we too are still in some way under its sway. The fact that its affective impact on us today tends to twitch somewhere between ideological indignation and uneasy historical accommodation/rationalization does not, in other words, necessarily indicate our calm liberation from that spell. It still has the power to stir up an ideological-becoming-emotional response.

Alongside those "noble" spells, of course, Nietzsche also and more famously identifies—and vilifies—the lingering civilizational spells associated with what he calls the *ressentiment* of slave morality, the revaluation of aristocratic values along lines better suited to the ascendancy of the downtrodden. Here terms for weakness are transformed into the new terms for "goodness":

> Die Ohnmacht, die nicht vergilt, zur "Güte"; die ängstliche Niedrigkeit zur "Demuth"; die Unterwerfung vor Denen, die man hasst, zum "Gehorsam" (nämlich gegen Einen, von dem sie sagen, er befehle diese Unterwerfung,—sie heissen ihn Gott). Das Unoffensive des Schwachen, die Feigheit selbst, an der er reich ist, sein An-der-Thürstehn, sein unvermeidliches Warten-müssen kommt hier zu guten Namen, als "Geduld," es heisst auch wohl die Tugend; das Sich-nicht-rächen-Können heisst Sich-nicht-rächen-Wollen, vielleicht selbst Verzeihung ("denn s i e wissen nicht, was sie thun—wir allein wissen es, was s i e thun!"). (I: 14; Nietzsche 29)

> Impotence, which cannot retaliate, into kindness; pusillanimity into humility; submission before those one hates into obedience to One of whom they say that he has commanded this submission—they call him God. The inoffensiveness of the weak, his cowardice, his ineluctable standing and waiting at doors, are being given honorific titles such as patience; to be *unable* to avenge oneself is called to be *unwilling* to avenge oneself—even forgiveness ("for they know not what *they* do—we alone know what *they* do"). (Golffing 180–1)

This is, clearly, a history of the revaluation not merely of *values*, but of *words*. It is, in that sense, a history not just of what words *mean*, nor merely of what words are *made* to mean through iterative use, but of the *power* of words, in the very specific sense of how those words and their meanings and their uses are charged with the power aspirations of a new ruling class, what Nietzsche calls the rule of *ressentiment*, or the "priestly aristocracy" (and what he will identify in the third essay as the ascetic tradition, or the "ascetic priesthood"). This is again the intergenerational survival of ancient civilizational spells: the speech acts of the ancient conquerors and their former slaves leave lingering traces in language, traces we can uncover millennia later, because through their speech acts they have, as Felman (1980: 128; Porter 1980/2003: 65) puts it, *written on the real*:

> Par opposition au pur movement, l'acte, suggère ici Mallarmé, est ce qui *laisse des traces*. Or, il n'y a pas de traces sans langage : l'acte n'est lisible comme tel (c'est-à-dire comme effet : effet de reel) qu'à l'intérieur d'un context dans lequel il *s'inscrit*. L'acte est donc une sorte d'écriture dans le réel ...
>
> Through its opposition to pure movement, the act, Mallarme suggests here, is what *leaves traces*. Now there are no traces without language: the act is legible as such (that is, as effect, as reality effect) only within a context in which it is *inscribed*. The act is thus a sort of writing on the real.

Through those traces, the words retain their civilizational spell down through the centuries—retain their power to *cast* an evaluative affective spell on the people who use them.

What these descriptions fail to specify, however, is where all this happens—what "the real" is that is written on; through what medium *die Hauptnuance [den Wörtern] durchschimmert* "the [words'] primary nuance shimmers through." In what sense is it possible for Nietzsche to detect in a *word* a lingering trace or "nuance" of some aristocratic value that is no longer openly displayed in or on *bodies*? For that matter, in what sense can the *histories* of rancorous priestly values be read in the "nuances shining through" words like kindness, humility, obedience to God, patience, or forgiveness? And finally: what kind of project is his polemical debunking of those histories? What exactly is he trying to do to the spell that those words continue to cast on us? Or, to put that differently: what counterspell is he trying to cast on us, in order possibly to free us from the Judeo-Christian slave-moral civilizational spell that holds us hostage?

## 2.2 Nietzsche 2: The Mnemotechnics of Pain

Nietzsche doesn't give a direct answer to these questions, but he does offer an intergenerational theory of *trained memory* that can be applied to the formulation of an answer:

> Ein Thier heranzüchten, das versprechen darf—ist das nicht gerade jene paradoxe Aufgabe selbst, welche sich die Natur in Hinsicht auf den Menschen gestellt hat? ist es nicht das eigentliche Problem vom Menschen? ... Dass dies Problem bis zu einem hohen Grad gelöst ist, muss Dem um so erstaunlicher erscheinen, der die entgegen wirkende Kraft, die der Vergesslichkeit, vollauf zu würdigen weiss. (II: 1; Nietzsche 41)

> To breed an animal with the right to make promises—is not this the paradoxical problem nature has set itself with regard to man? and is it not man's true problem? That the problem has in fact been solved to a remarkable degree will seem all the more surprising if we do full justice to the strong opposing force, the faculty of oblivion.[1] (Golffing 189)

By "Vergesslichkeit"/"the faculty of oblivion" Nietzsche means "ein aktives ... Hemmungsvermögen" (41)/"an active screening device" (189) that partly works like what Freud would later call primary repression to block from consciousness "was nur von uns erlebt, erfahren, in uns hineingenommen wird" (41)/"what we experience and digest psychologically" (189), but partly also to screen out purely physiological processes:

> von dem Lärm und Kampf, mit dem unsre Unterwelt von dienstbaren Organen für und gegen einander arbeitet, unbehelligt bleiben; ein wenig Stille, ein wenig tabula rasa des Bewusstseins, damit wieder Platz wird für Neues, vor Allem für die vornehmeren Funktionen und Funktionäre, für Regieren, Voraussehn, Vorausbestimmen ... (41)

> to protect us from the noise and agitation with which our lower organs work for or against one another, to introduce a little quiet or *tabula rasa* into our consciousness so as to make room for the nobler

functions and functionaries of our organism which do the governing and planning. (189; Golffing's translation modified)

We are, in other words, dealing here with brain function—and thus with body.

And when Nietzsche then goes on to write of the creation of "ein Gegenvermögen ... ein Gedächtniss" (41)/"an opposite power, that of remembering" (189), he grounds his genealogical ruminations in physiological processes as well, both metaphorically, in digestion and dyspepsia—"somit keineswegs bloß ein passivisches Nicht-wieder-los-werden-können des einmal eingeritzten Eindrucks, nicht bloß die Indigestion an einem ein Mal verpfändeten Wort" (42)/"This involves no mere passive inability to rid oneself of an impression, no mere indigestion through a once-pledged word with which one cannot 'have done'" (Kaufmann 58)—and literally, in the actual physical transformation of bodies to force us to remember.

Why is the faculty of remembering—of overcoming our natural physiological tendency to forget, to inhibit, to screen out—essential for promising? Because keeping a promise requires continuity, "ein aktives Nicht-wieder-los-werden-wollen, ein Fort- und Fortwollen des ein Mal Gewollten, ein eigentliches *Gedächtniss des Willens*" (42)/"an active *desire* not to rid oneself, a desire for the continuance of something desired once, a real *memory of the will*" (Kaufmann 58), which is to say, "remembering" not just mentally but behaviorally, physically, actionally, remembering with the acting body, so that even if the mental images of the promise are lost to oblivion, the body will remember and follow through.

Since this corporeal remembering also tends to be passed on from generation to generation, the conditioning of the human animal to remember its promises may serve to retain the "power" or somatic "charge" ("nuance") of words from generation to generation as well. Let's see how that works.

Nietzsche says that making humans "able to remember" so as to be "able to promise" requires "the preparatory task of rendering man up to a certain point regular, uniform, equal among equals, calculable" (II: 2;

Golffing 189). Nietzsche's original German for that list of adjectives is "nothwendig, einförmig, gleich unter Gleichen, regelmäßig und folglich berechenbar" (43), literally "necessary, uniform, like under likes, regular and therefore calculable." Walter Kaufmann (59) and Douglas Smith (1996: 40) stick as close as they can to the German with "necessary, uniform, like among like [Kaufmann]/an equal among equals [Smith], regular, and consequently calculable"—but "necessary" for *notwendig* does seem a bit strange. Necessary for what? Francis Golffing, accordingly, leaves it out. Carol Diethe (1994/2006: 409) takes an interesting stab at the list of adjectives by rendering it "undeviating [*notwendig*], uniform, a peer amongst peers, orderly and consequently predictable"—her own bracketed inclusion of Nietzsche's original German term signaling to the reader that there is a potential semantic problem there—and Michael Scarpitti (2013: 44–5) similarly gives us "reliable, uniform, like among his like, regular and consequently predictable."

Those last two, however, Diethe's "undeviating" and Scarpitti's "reliable," are tentative paraphrases of *notwendig* without a clear semantic etiology or trajectory from the German original to the paraphrase. Both in fact read like rough synonyms of *einförmig, regelmäßig, berechenbar*, and thus like extrapolations of the easy-to-understand list to cover the gap left by the semantic strangeness of *notwendig*. How then should we unpack *notwendig*? I suggest that Nietzsche means the adjective morphologically, in its root derivation from the implicit infinitive *sich an die Not wenden* "to turn/address/orient oneself to need," thus "need-oriented" or "need-addressed." *Die Not*, too, is need in the sense of affliction, destitution, emergency, hardship, privation, want—so that rendering us *notwendig* means making us susceptible of being turned toward what's missing, toward a lack or a want. *Wendig* is also physically agile, flexible, sinuous, able to turn in many different ways, and thus also figuratively mobile or versatile. If what is missing is memory, memory-as-continuity, memory-as-continuity-as-surety-for-promises—if the lack is generated physiologically, to protect our ability to plan things rationally, by the "faculty of oblivion"—then rendering us *notwendig* means reorienting our bodies toward remembering as the filling of a new physiological need. And since that reorientation is ideologically normative, and therefore a mobilization of group norms as pressure on individual group members to conform, we might want to think of *wenden* "to turn" as a channel of collective conation. So: *notwendig* as "need-conatized"? "Want-conatized"?

*Regelmäßig*, which four of the five translators (all but Diethe) dutifully (and correctly) render "regular," is morphologically "rule-measure-y," from *Regel* "rule" and *Maß* "measure," in the sense of rule-governed, regulated. This is, in other words, the process by which we are socially regulated, subjected to social regulation. Nietzsche says "regelmäßig und folglich berechenbar," rule-governed and *therefore* calculable, assessable, computable, estimable, evaluable, figurable, priceable, quotable, reckonable—the verb *berechnen* behind his *berechenbar* means to set a numerical value, either in general mathematical terms, to calculate or compute, to figure or reckon, or, in the specific realm of commerce, to estimate a cost, to price an item, to quote a price. Given Nietzsche's explicit theorization of an economic exchange of guilt for/from debt (section 2.5), and thus of morality circulating through commerce, this is a weighty and carefully chosen metaphor: it means that, once rendered uniform, like everybody else, somatically turned/conatized toward the filling of a lack or want, and regulated, the human animal is not just *predictable* (as Diethe has it) but *calculable*, available for reliable mathematical and specifically monetary calculations.

In sum, then, Nietzsche is looking to trace a genealogy of social control that has been designed collectively to give humans an embodied memory of the will, to overcome our physiological tendency to forget by imposing a uniform and *lasting* regulatory and valuational regime on our psychosocial functioning—one that has lasted, judging from Nietzsche's examples, hundreds and even thousands of years. What channel of social conditioning might make all that possible? For Nietzsche there is only one possible answer: pain.

"Wie macht man dem Menschen-Thiere ein Gedächtniss? Wie prägt man diesem theils stumpfen, theils faseligen Augenblicks-Verstände, dieser leibhaften Vergesslichkeit Etwas so ein, dass es gegenwärtig bleibt?"… Dies uralte Problem ist, wie man denken kann, nicht gerade mit zarten Antworten und Mitteln gelöst worden; vielleicht ist sogar nichts furchtbarer und unheimlicher an der ganzen Vorgeschichte des Menschen, als seine M n e m o t e c h n i k. "Man brennt Etwas ein, damit es im Gedächtniss bleibt: nur was nicht aufhört, weh zu thun, bleibt im Gedächtniss"—das ist ein Hauptsatz aus der allerältesten (leider auch allerlängsten) Psychologie auf Erden. Man möchte selbst sagen, dass es überall, wo es jetzt noch auf Erden Feierlichkeit, Ernst, Geheimniss, düstere Farben im Leben von Mensch und Volk giebt, Etwas von der Schrecklichkeit n a c h w i r k t, mit der ehemals überall auf Erden versprochen, verpfändet, gelobt worden ist: die Vergangenheit, die längste tiefste härteste Vergangenheit, haucht uns an und quillt in uns herauf, wenn wir "ernst" werden. Es gieng niemals ohne Blut, Martern, Opfer ab, wenn der Mensch es nöthig hielt, sich ein Gedächtniss zu machen; die schauerlichsten Opfer und Pfänder (wohin die Erstlingsopfer gehören), die widerlichsten Verstümmelungen (zum Beispiel die Castrationen), die grausamsten Ritualformen aller religiösen Culte (und alle Religionen sind auf dem untersten Grunde Systeme von Grausamkeiten)—alles Das hat in jenem Instinkte seinen Ursprung, welcher im Schmerz das mächtigste Hülfsmittel der Mnemonik errieth. In einem gewissen Sinne gehört die ganze Asketik hierher: ein paar Ideen sollen unauslöschlich, allgegenwärtig, unvergessbar, "fix" gemacht werden, zum Zweck der Hypnotisirung des ganzen nervösen und intellektuellen Systems durch diese "fixen Ideen"—und die asketischen Prozeduren und Lebensformen sind Mittel dazu, um jene Ideen aus der Concurrenz mit allen übrigen Ideen zu lösen, um sie "unvergesslich" zu machen. (II: 3; 45–6)

"How does one create a memory for the human animal? How does one go about to impress anything on that partly dull, partly flighty human intelligence—that incarnation of forgetfulness—so as to make it stick?" As we might well imagine, the means used in solving this age-old problem have been far from delicate: in fact, there is perhaps nothing more terrible in man's earliest history than his mnemotechnics. "A thing is branded on the memory to make it stay there;

only what goes on hurting will stick"—this is one of the oldest and, unfortunately, one of the most enduring psychological axioms. In fact, one might say that wherever on earth one still finds solemnity, gravity, secrecy, somber hues in the life of an individual or a nation, one also senses a residuum of that terror with which men must formerly have promised, pledged, vouched. It is the past—the longest, deepest, hardest of pasts—that seems to surge up whenever we turn serious. Whenever man has thought it necessary to create a memory for himself, his effort has been attended with torture, blood, sacrifice. The ghastliest sacrifices and pledges, including the sacrifice of the firstborn; the most repulsive mutilations, such as castration; the cruelest rituals in every religious cult (and all religions are at bottom systems of cruelty)—all these have their origin in that instinct which divined pain to be the strongest aid to mnemonics. (All asceticism is really part of the same development: here too the object is to make a few ideas omnipresent, unforgettable, "fixed," to the end of hypnotizing the entire nervous and intellectual system; the ascetic procedures help to effect the dissociation of those ideas from all others.) (Golffing 192–3)

Neurologists in our day might argue with Nietzsche over the exclusivity of this channel of pain for effective learning—pain does work wonderfully, of course, but really any physiologically intense experience will have the same effect, including terror, lust, and fun. The advantage pain has over all these other physiological channels of learning is that it is the easiest to impose on a whole population, systematically, uniformly, regularly, calculably. Fun and lust do not easily lend themselves to social regulation (though the entertainment industry tries its best); terror depends too strongly on surprise to be easily sustained. Pain is perfect.

What pain does specifically is to recondition the autonomic nervous system. It is possible to set up an experiment where, say, imperceptible electric shocks are administered to subjects whenever they draw a card from a certain pile; without making a conscious decision to do so, or even noticing the shocks, the subjects will soon stop drawing from that pile (Damasio 1994: 212–22). What stops us, in fact, is what Antonio

Damasio calls somatic markers, which are *stored* in the autonomic nervous system, thus transforming it, reconditioning it. As Damasio presents the somatic-marker hypothesis, in fact, the (continually-being-)reconditioned autonomic nervous system works *with* reason and our ethical sense to guide (not shackle) the decision-making process: Damasio's theory is not nearly as behaviorist as Nietzsche's seems here to be. Most likely, though, Nietzsche is exaggerating the robotic regulation of human memory through pain for shock effect:

> Diese Deutschen haben sich mit furchtbaren Mitteln ein Gedächtniss gemacht, um über ihre pöbelhaften Grund-Instinkte und deren brutale Plumpheit Herr zu werden: man denke an die alten deutschen Strafen, zum Beispiel an das Steinigen (—schon die Sage lässt den Mühlstein auf das Haupt des Schuldigen fallen), das Rädern (die eigenste Erfindung und Spezialität des deutschen Genius im Reich der Strafe!), das Werfen mit dem Pfahle, das Zerreissen- oder Zertretenlassen durch Pferde (das "Viertheilen"), das Sieden des Verbrechers in Öl oder Wein (noch im vierzehnten und fünfzehnten Jahrhundert), das beliebte Schinden ("Riemenschneiden"), das Herausschneiden des Fleisches aus der Brust; auch wohl dass man den Übelthäter mit Honig bestrich und bei brennender Sonne den Fliegen überliess. Mit Hülfe solcher Bilder und Vorgänge behält man endlich fünf, sechs "ich will nicht" im Gedächtnisse, in Bezug auf welche man sein Versprechen gegeben hat, um unter den Vortheilen der Societät zu leben,—und wirklich ! mit Hülfe dieser Art von Gedächtniss kam man endlich "zur Vernunft" !—Ah, die Vernunft, der Ernst, die Herrschaft über die Affekte, diese ganze düstere Sache, welche Nachdenken heisst, alle diese Vorrechte und Prunkstücke des Menschen: wie theuer haben sie sich be-zahlt gemacht! wie viel Blut und Grausen ist auf dem Grunde aller "guten Dinge"! (II: 3; 47–8)

> Germans have resorted to ghastly means in order to triumph over their plebeian instincts and brutal coarseness. We need only recount some of our ancient forms of punishment: stoning (even in earliest legend millstones are dropped on the heads of culprits); breaking on the wheel (Germany's own contribution to the techniques of punishment); piercing with stakes, drawing and quartering, trampling to death with

horses, boiling in oil or wine (these were still in use in the fourteenth and fifteenth centuries), the popular flaying alive, cutting out of flesh from the chest, smearing the victim with honey and leaving him in the sun, a prey to flies. By such methods the individual was finally taught to remember five or six "I won'ts" which entitled him to participate in the benefits of society; and indeed, with the aid of this sort of memory, people eventually "came to their senses." What an enormous price man had to pay for reason, seriousness, control over his emotions—those grand human prerogatives and cultural showpieces! How much blood and horror lies behind all "good things"! (Golffing 193-4)

All this pain to condition humans to remember *words*—specifically, speech acts: promises, negative promises, "I won'ts." If the inclination to forget is physiological-becoming-psychological, brain-becoming-mind, then the painful lessons that inculcate a rudimentary regulatory memory in us must be physiological-becoming-psychological as well, which is to say, somatic. Felman (1980: 128-9) calls the speech act "[une] production énigmatique et problématique du *corps parlant*, [qui] fait éclater dès lors la dichotomie métaphysique entre la portée du 'mental' et la portée du 'physique', l'opposition entre corps et esprit, entre matière et langage"/"an enigmatic and problematic production of the *speaking body*, [which] destroys from its inception the metaphysical dichotomy between the domain of the 'mental' and the domain of the 'physical,' breaks down the opposition between body and spirit, between matter and language" (Porter 1983/2003: 65). These physical-becoming-mental performances, ground zero for cultural participation, then build the icotic foundation for reason, rational control of the body, the human animal's most prized achievement—that which, we take pride in asserting, sets us off from the "lower" animals.

Another way of putting this is that everything we take to be "normal" and "natural" and "practical" and "commonsensical" in our lives seems so because we have been conditioned to naturalize it that way—and conditioned specifically in our corporeal functioning, our kinesthetic-becoming-affective experience of the world. When Nietzsche (60) says that—

"alle Zwecke, alle Nützlichkeiten sind nur A n z e i c h e n davon, daß ein Wille zur Macht über etwas weniger Mächtiges Herr geworden ist und ihm von sich aus den Sinn einer Funktion aufgeprägt hat" (II: 12)

- "all pragmatic purposes are simply symbols of the fact that a will to power has implanted its sense of function in those less powerful" (Golffing 210)
- "purposes and utilities are only *signs* that a will to power has become master of something less powerful and imposed upon it the character of a function" (Kaufmann 77)
- "every purpose and use is just a *sign* that the will to power has achieved mastery over something less powerful, and has impressed upon it its own idea [*Sinn*] of a use function" (Diethe 416)
- "all aims, all uses are merely *signs* indicating that a will to power has mastered something less powerful than itself and impressed the meaning of a function upon it" (Smith 58)
- "all ends and all utilities are only *signs* that a desire for power has overcome a less powerful force and has impressed upon it its own interpretation of a function" (Scarpitti 63)

—he means implanted/imposed/impressed in or on the *autonomic nervous systems* of those less powerful. *Aufprägen* is actually to imprint, impress, emboss, in the sense of stamping a coin: the will to power's "sense of a function" is "embossed" on the less powerful, the body significantly transformed in the image of power.

This metaphor was picked up again by Michel Foucault (1975; Sheridan 1977), in fact, in using Kafka's "In the Penal Colony" to metaphorize power as *inscribed on the body*, and after that tended to proliferate in poststructuralist theory, as part of the project to discursivize "the real." Judith Butler (1990/99: 166), for example, cites Foucault on Kafka's "In the Penal Colony" and comments:

> In a sense, for Foucault, as for Nietzsche, cultural values emerge as the result of an inscription on the body, understood as a medium, indeed, a blank page; in order for this inscription to signify, however, that medium must itself be destroyed—that is, fully transvaluated

into a sublimated domain of values. Within the metaphorics of this notion of cultural values is the figure of history as a relentless writing instrument, and the body as the medium which must be destroyed and transfigured in order for "culture" to emerge.

Yes, it is a metaphorics: history is not a writing instrument; the body is not a blank page. But what is it a metaphor *for*? Who or what is its tenor? Just "cultural values"? And how exactly does the metaphor work? What are the passageways by which cultural values are transported metaphorically into bodily inscriptions, and inscriptions—written texts—are transported metaphorically into or onto bodies? Is there any sense in which "history" or "culture" (or whatever we want to call the matrix of regulatory forces that impact our bodies) actually *has* a physical impact on our bodies? Nietzsche doesn't just write vaguely of cultural values "emerging" through these metaphorical processes; he says that civilization is collectively and emergently imposed on bodies through actual physical pain, through floggings, beatings, torture—and that pain physically aids memory, that the muscle memory of pain actually transforms the bodies and thus the social behavior of whole populations, and through these bodily transformations of social behavior transforms also the way those populations think, what they believe. This is not just a metaphorics; it is a protoneurological explanation of social control through somatic conditioning. Foucault studies how bodies are forced to stand and march in rigid military formation, or to sit in rigid rows and columns, backs straight, heads up, right arm raised in a specific way to signal a request for permission to talk, and by being thus forced to behave in disciplined ways actually *become* disciplined—rendered not only physically but ideologically "docile." These physical applications of force to bodies—and their neurological implications for socioideological regulation—are elided in Butler's otherwise powerfully somatic argument.

I'm actually simplifying Butler's argument, though, by ignoring the fuller context in which she presented it the year before *Gender Trouble* appeared, in "Foucault and the Paradox of Bodily Inscriptions" (1989: 603), as a reading of Foucault (1971; Bouchard and Simon 1977):

Indeed, I shall try to show that, for Foucault, not unlike for Kafka in *The Penal Colony*, the cultural construction of the body is effected through the figuration of "history" as a writing instrument that produces cultural significations—language—through the disfiguration and distortion of the body, where the body is figured as a ready surface or blank page available for inscription, awaiting the "imprint" (*ibid.*, 148) of history itself. Although Foucault appears to argue that the body does not exist outside the terms of its cultural inscription, it seems that the very mechanism of "inscription" implies a power that is necessarily external to the body itself. The critical question that emerges from these considerations is whether the understanding of the process of cultural construction on the model of "inscription"—a logocentric move if ever there was one—entails that the "constructed" or "inscribed" body have an ontological status apart from that inscription, precisely the claim that Foucault wants to refute.

In the revised version of this reading that she included in *Gender Trouble*, Butler stressed the metaphorical nature of Foucault's theorization of "construction" as "inscription"; here, however, the image of history writing on the body as surface seems to be somehow complexly literalized, metaphorically inscribed only on the surface and sending its tenor deeper into the interior of Foucault's thought about the construction of bodies. In other words, Butler seems to be arguing that the image of history as surface inscription reflects the *true nature* of (this part of) Foucault's thinking about the body—it's not just a surface metaphor for the Nietzschean *internalization* of mastery. "In a sense," she writes, "*Discipline and Punish* can be read as Foucault's effort to reconceive Nietzsche's doctrine of internalization as a language of inscription" (605). This reading would construe Foucault as *rejecting* the somatic theory I'm setting up here—which is in part a theory of somatic internalization.

Butler's textual cues for this reading of Foucault, however, are rather scant. They are almost all, in fact, right here, in the lines immediately following the above quote: "Within 'Nietzsche, Genealogy, History,' Foucault describes the body through a series of metaphors and figures, yet predominantly as a 'surface,' a set of multidirectional 'forces,' and as the scene or site of a cultural inscription. He writes: 'the body is the inscribed surface of events' (ibid.). The task of genealogy, he claims, is 'to expose a body totally imprinted by history' (ibid.)" (603). And Foucault does indeed write these things. Butler doesn't provide particularly full citations, of course—they lack a complicating context—but the fact that Foucault also elsewhere in the essay returns to the metaphor of surface inscriptions would seem to justify Butler's use of these two brief passages as summary representations of Foucault's entire argument: two pages later, for example, in a passage Butler does not cite, Foucault refers again to his claim that "descent qualifies the strength or weakness of an instinct and its inscription on a body" (Bouchard and Simon 150). Then again, what Foucault (156; emphasis added) actually writes there is that "la provenance désigne la qualité d'un instinct, son degré ou sa défaillance, et la marque qu'il laisse *dans un corps*": "the source designates the quality of an instinct ... and the mark that it leaves *in* a body."

But let's say for the sake of argument that *dans* there should be read as referring to the surface of the body and not its interior—that Donald Bouchard and our own Sherry Simon read the preposition correctly in English. Starting there, just how metaphorically should we take this talk of surface inscriptions? If an instinct is inscribed *on* a body, what exactly is the surface we're talking about? Butler (605) wants this to mean that Foucault is refusing to theorize the *inside* of bodies: "The prohibitive law is not taken into the body, internalized or incorporated, but rather is written *on* the body, the structuring principle of its very shape, style, and exterior signification." But surely instincts do have to be imagined as "taken into the body"? How are instincts channeled neurologically if not "inside" the body? This consideration does make it seem as if the image of an inscribable surface must be a metaphor for something else, in fact some sort of somatic internalization.

And what about the notion that "the body is the inscribed surface of events"? What does this mean? Butler seems to take it to mean something like "history inscribes events on the surface of the body," but that's not what Foucault says; he says that to the extent that we can think of events as having a surface, that surface *is* the body. "Writing on the surface of the body" would again seem to be a metaphor for something else—not necessarily somatic internalization, here, but neither must it necessarily be read to mean that Foucault takes the body to be a "blank page," which is the key to Butler's claim that Foucault's thinking about the body is "paradoxical."[2]

What Foucault in fact writes, more fully contextualized, is this:

> Le corps: surface d'inscription des événements (alors que le langage les marque et les idées les dissolvent), lieu de dissociation du Moi (auquel essaie de prêter la chimére d'une unité substantielle), volume en perpétuel effritement. La généalogie, comme analyse de la provenance, est donc à l'articulation du corps et de l'histoire. Elle doit montrer le corps tout imprimé d'histoire, et l'histoire ruinant le corps. (Foucault 154)

> The body is the inscribed surface of events (traced by language and dissolved by ideas), the locus of a dissociated Self (adopting the illusion of a substantial unity), and a volume in perpetual disintegration. Genealogy, as an analysis of descent, is thus situated within the articulation of the body and history. Its task is to expose a body totally imprinted by history and the process of history's destruction of the body. (Bouchard and Simon 148)

"Imprimé"/"imprinted," obviously, is an allusion to Nietzsche's printing/minting trope *aufgeprägt*—which again does not tell us just how metaphorically the image is to be taken. The image of the body as *surface d'inscription* "surface of inscription" (or "inscribed surface") that begins the quotation, and that Butler cites as evidence for her reading of Foucault in terms of surface inscriptions, is only the first of three metaphors Foucault offers: [1] surface, [2] *lieu*/locus, and [3] volume.

(1) As we've seen, the surface is not the surface of the body but the inscribed surface of events, which are "traced by language and dissolved by ideas": the body *is* a metaphorical event-surface, *is*

where verbal/ideational events are "inscribed." Clearly, in Foucault's modification of Nietzsche's printing trope the *surface d'inscription des événements* "event-surface of inscription" is a metaphor for *some* kind of transformative effect on the body, without regard for whether that effect remains on the surface or affects internal processes as well. (2) "Lieu de dissociation du Moi"/"locus of a dissociated Self" is nonrestrictive with regard to interiority—that "place" could be a surface or a bodily interior—but it's difficult to imagine (3) a "volume en perpétuel effritement"/"volume in perpetual disintegration" as anything other than a metaphor for interiority. *Effritement* is "crumbling," which suggests that the "volume" in Foucault's trope is a book, perhaps (as in its Latin derivation) a parchment scroll, but a scroll or a book has *contents*—it is not the same kind of image as a blank page. It is a structure with depth, with extension in three dimensions, not just width, like a two-dimensional plane or surface.

All this is still only to say that Foucault's thinking about the body in these metaphors is exploratory: that he has not, Butler to the contrary, locked himself into a conception of the body as inscribable surface or blank page; that there is considerable free play in the metaphoricity of his descriptions, and thus room *also* for a conception of history as somatic internalization *in* as well as inscription *on* the body.

But now let us turn back a page, to where Foucault first raises the connection between *la provenance* "descent" and the body. Note here the proliferation of "dans"/"in" prepositions: "Enfin la provenance tient au corps. Elle s'inscrit dans le système nerveux, dans l'humeur, dans l'appareil digestif. Mauvaise respiration, mauvaise alimentation, corps débile et affaissé de ceux dont les ancêtres ont commis des erreurs" (153)—"Finally, descent attaches itself to the body. It inscribes itself in the nervous system, in temperament, in the digestive apparatus; it appears in faulty respiration, in improper diets, in the debilitated and prostrate body of those whose ancestors committed errors" (147). This in fact is the first appearance in Foucault's essay of the metaphor of inscription—and clearly, no matter what we decide about *la marque qu'il laisse dans un corps* "the mark that it leaves in/on a body," here

Bouchard and Simon agree that *dans* has to refer to physiological interiority: "It inscribes itself *in* the nervous system, *in* temperament, *in* the digestive apparatus ... *in* faulty respiration, *in* improper diets, *in* the debilitated and prostrate body ..." Not on: in. It is quite clear here that Foucault is troping all these internalized physiological responses to the verbally saturated events of history *as* a "being inscribed"—that inscription is a metaphor for internalization, and indeed that the internalized tenor of the metaphor is precisely the bundle of neurological and generally physiological processes that we saw Nietzsche adumbrating as well. It is clear, in other words, that Foucault is following Nietzsche in theorizing the body not as surface but as somatic internalization.

## 2.3 Bloom 1: The Western Canon as a Tug-of-War Between Civilizational Spells

Now let us turn to a partially suppressed somatics of domination, with an eye to the somatic "spells" that continue to churn up aggressively conflicted affect right on the very surface of events—the scholar's body as the surface of the desired universalizing event. I am thinking of Harold Bloom (b. 1930), professor emeritus of English at Yale and author of highly regarded critical and theoretical works—culminating perhaps in *The Anxiety of Influence* in 1973 and *A Map of Misreading* in 1975, from which latter I borrowed the six tropes that I repurposed as tropes of translation in Robinson (1991). Always larger than life, always at the epicenter of polemical engagement, Bloom is arguably the most famous and most controversial literary scholar working in English; his 1994 book *The Western Canon*, which made many erstwhile fans of Bloom's work cringe with embarrassment, has also received considerable praise and numerous critical studies (see e.g., Schneidau 1995; Weisman 1996; Schultz 1996; Baumlin 2000; Redfield 2003). As we shall see, Nietzsche—and especially the Nietzsche of the *Genealogy*—is a major influence on Bloom's thought as well (see Ratner-Rosenhagen 2011: 274ff).

*The Western Canon* is subtitled *The Books and School of the Ages*—clearly a groping for the timelessness that is generally taken to be a prerequisite for universality. The fact that the canon that Bloom wants to stabilize and thereby ostensibly universalize is a *Western* canon—excluding "the East," or, as we used to say, "the Orient"—might be read as undercutting any claim he might lodge for universality; but we also know that for centuries, until not so very long ago, certainly in my lifetime, the West was taken (not just in the West) *as* the universe, Western values therefore as universal values, and the Western Canon therefore also as a universal canon. If as Bloom argues Shakespeare is the "Center of the Canon," then Shakespeare is the Center of World Literature:

> If we could conceive of a universal canon, multicultural and multivalent, its one essential book would not be a scripture, whether Bible, Koran, or Eastern text, but rather Shakespeare, who is acted and read everywhere, in every language and circumstance. Whatever the convictions of our current New Historicists, for whom Shakespeare is only a signifier for the social energies of the English Renaissance, Shakespeare for hundreds of millions who are not white Europeans is a signifier for their own pathos, their own sense of identity with the characters that Shakespeare fleshed out by his language. For them his universality is not historical but fundamental; he puts their lives upon the stage. (Bloom 1994: 38)

Bloom knows this, not because he was a celebrity English professor at Yale, but because he is a Western intellectual, and Western intellectuals just *know* these things about the rest of the world. Don't ask them how they know; they just do. Their knowledge is objective, and their objectivity is universal.

The bone of contention for Bloom comes down to a fairly simple question: what *is* a literary canon? The traditional view, from which he (partly) tries to distance himself, is that it is the stable collection of great works from the past—on the model of the Biblical canon, namely, the collection of works that together make up the Bible. To the extent that the Biblical canon is understood mystically, as the collection of works *written by the Holy Spirit to be included in the Bible*, or that was *revealed by God as intended to be included in the Bible*, the model derived from it is analogical, and somewhat difficult to apply to the canonization of literary classics: the analogue of the Holy Spirit would be genius, perhaps, and the analogue of revelation might be the mystique of literary appreciation; but then why does the literary canon keep changing? Why is it not etched in stone, unchanging for all time, like the mystical "received" conception of the Bible? In some sense the application of the model of the Biblical canon to literary canonization demands a more secular, institutional understanding of the formation of the Biblical canon: it was negotiated over many centuries by committees of churchmen reading the texts and deciding which best supported official Church doctrine.

But even that institutional historicization of Biblical canon-formation has tended to be mystified through lingering doctrinal reference to the supernatural origins and aims of the Bible:

[1] There can only be one Bible.
[2] The (1) one Bible can only consist of a limited number of books.
[3] What (2) limits the books to be included is a criterion of doctrinal adherence.
[4] The (3) doctrines that (2) limit inclusion are true.
[5] The (4) truth of those (3) doctrines is not local or temporary but stable and universal.

The application of this model to traditional efforts at literary canonization requires some shifts and adjustments, but remains analogically recognizable:

[1'] The literary canon is relatively stable. Since new works of genius can be written at any time, it has to be open to change; but genius (the literary equivalent of the Holy Spirit) is rare, and its literary products are rare, and so change must be rare as well.
[2'] The (1') genius-based stability of the literary canon requires a very high degree of selectivity. The gates must not be opened to any old piece of writing that someone likes a lot.

[3'] What (2') limits inclusion in the literary canon is recognizable greatness. To be eligible for canonization, a literary classic must be truly great, truly a product of undeniable genius.

[4'] The (3') understanding of literary greatness or genius that (2') limits inclusion in the literary canon is quasi-mystical—one *just knows it*—but also therefore objective.

[5'] The (4') quasi-mystical objectivity that (1'-3') stabilizes the literary canon is not local or temporary but universal.

Something like (1'-5'), as I say, is the conservative understanding of literary canon-formation that Bloom (partly) challenges. He is powerfully attracted to the (3') mystique and even the mysticism of (1') literary genius—in fact identifies with it himself—and therefore also to (2') strict exclusivity, and indeed to the elitist ethos of exclusivity; he also seems to believe wholeheartedly in the (4') objectivity and (5') universality of canon-formation. His is an esoteric rather than an Enlightenment scientific universalism, but there are nonetheless surprising and striking parallels between his irritation at the cultural relativists that have usurped literary criticism from him and Andrew Chesterman's irritation at the cultural relativists that critique his Eurocentrism.

The one point on which he deviates sharply and proudly from the conservative (crypto-scriptural) view of the canon is in the matter of what constitutes literary genius: his dark-Romantic/Nietzschean/Gnostic/Kabbalistic understanding of genius as emerging out of pain, and specifically the agonistic intensification of pain-drenched memory, diverges strikingly from what he takes to be the slave morality of traditional Christian views. I want to put that deviation on hold for discussion in section 2.4; for now, though, note that what initially makes his *Streitschrift*/polemic interesting and relevant to a Nietzschean account of civilizational spells is that he extends that critique of "slave morality" both to the conservative moralists among the traditional canonizers *and* to the cultural relativists that seek to undermine and undo the civilizational spells that haunt canonization.

For Bloom, in other words, literary-critical slave morality is equally reprehensible *in everyone but himself*, whether it supports or attacks the canon: whether the evil at which it tsks its collective moralizing tongue is the political radicalism that the traditionalists on the Right loathe or the racism, sexism, colonialism, and generally the "Eurocentrism"—even the insistence on drawing clear civilizational boundaries around "the West," and thus "the Western Canon"—that the (multi)cultural relativists on the Left loathe. Like Chesterman on relativism in TS, Bloom assumes that the relativists are actually universalists in disguise, seeking to expand the canon to include women and people of color—all those who have been excluded in advance by Eurocentric/colonialist/patriarchal civilizational spells—and protests that this kind of expansion actually serves to *destroy* or *overthrow* the canon. Ironically, overthrowing (rather than expanding) the canon is precisely what the cultural relativists have in mind: to them the canon, and generally the hierarchical project of canon-formation, and thus the exclusive valuing, interpreting, and teaching of only a small group of dead white male writers deemed canonical, is a sick and twisted practice haunted by civilizational spells.

As Bloom reads that counterhegemonic project, however, it is itself haunted by the civilizational spell that Nietzsche calls slave morality:

[Contra 1'] The leftist rabble resent the notion of "genius" ("mastery" as the natural expression or emanation of "the master") that limits and stabilizes the canon as a tool of hegemonic oppression.

[Contra 2'] The leftist rabble require the canon to be flexible enough to include whatever writing they want to celebrate at any given time.

[Contra 3'] The criterion for such leftist celebration is identity-politics resentment (slave morality): they want us to include any writer who is female or a person of color (ideally a woman of color) whose writing is all about her resentment of white sexist/racist power.

[Contra 4′] The leftist rabble who seek to expand and thereby (accidentally) destroy the canon think they're objective, but they aren't. They are actually seeking to overthrow objectivity.

[Contra 5′] The quasi-objectivity mobilized by the leftist rabble for the expansion(-cum-destruction) of the canon pretends to be universalist but is actually only local, and purely affect-driven (resentment, and generally slave morality).

So contemptuous, in fact, is Bloom of the "leftist" view that a literary canon is just an elitist social construct, organized by those civilizational spells, that he vituperates the proponents of this view throughout *The Western Canon* as "the School of Resentment"—all-but-explicitly invoking Nietzsche's attack on *ressentiment* as slave morality. While repeatedly invoking Nietzsche's authority on pain-driven memory (see section 2.4), however, Bloom does not make the connection between the positions he attacks on both the Right and the Left and slave morality, or between his own position and Nietzsche's "Strong Man" or "Blond Beast," the master who is above all such moralistic concerns:

> I am not concerned, as this book repeatedly makes clear, with the current debate between the right-wing defenders of the Canon, who wish to preserve it for its supposed (and nonexistent) moral values, and the academic-journalistic network I have dubbed the School of Resentment, who wish to overthrow the Canon in order to advance their supposed (and nonexistent) programs for social change. (1994: 4)

He is indeed "not concerned" with that debate in the very specific sense that he is not taking sides in it, and indeed is setting himself well above the fray; but in actual fact he is *obsessively* concerned with the debate, in the sense that he hates both sides, despises both sides, despises the whole debate with such a passion that he cannot leave it alone, but keeps fiercely recurring to it. In particular the left-wing detractors that he calls "The School of Resentment" are the thorns in his flesh, the mosquitoes in his ear—the constant goad to his Olympian academic demeanor. As a result, he has a hard time getting through a paragraph without viciously lashing out at them. "Though heralded as a piece of serious academic criticism," as James S. Baumlin (2000: 24) notes of *The Western Canon,* "the book modulates into a modern Jeremiad, presenting an unstable mixture of analysis, lamentation, exhortation, satire, confession, personal invective, and prophecy seeking its unity (and appealing to its readership) less through argument than through the voice and personality of its author." The very thought of his opponents on the Left makes Bloom see red: he calls them "lemmings" (4, 16, 18), "the new commissars" (16), "social engineers" (18), "the academic rabble" (27), and, most rebarbatively and repetitively, "resenters." But he can't help taking shots at the Right either. His "lack of concern" in that paragraph seems mainly to be a concern for image-management: as he attacks the left-wing position he does not want to be simply assimilated to the right-wing position.

Because he is constantly overheating on these issues, running too hot to slow down and give complex thought to the implications of his polemics, it's often not quite clear what he means. When he refers to the Right's "supposed (and nonexistent) moral values," for example, does he mean that the Right has no moral values, or that moral values simply do not exist? When he refers to the Left's "supposed (and nonexistent) programs for social change," does he mean that the Left has no programs for social change, or that there is no such thing as a program for social change? Or does he mean that those things exist, but when the Right defends the canon it is not actually applying moral values, and when the Left attacks the canon it is not actually pursuing a program for social change? Never mind: Bloom can't be bothered with such quibbles. The main thing is that the Right and the Left are equally wrong-headed. He can't quite put his finger on *how* their different wrong-headednesses might be equated; apparently it didn't occur to him to invoke Nietzsche's slave morality, which does seem to be what he's groping for. The Right hasn't been explicitly moralistic since the attack on that approach launched by the New Critics in the 1930s and 1940s—the conservatives in the National Association for Scholars are basically aging New Critics—but a good argument might be made for the claim that their supposed objectivity in elevating certain works to greatness and diminishing others is nevertheless an atavism of slave morality. And the "supposed (and nonexistent) programs for social change" pursued by the Left ("all six branches of the School of Resentment: Feminists, Marxists, Lacanians, New Historicists, Deconstructionists, Semioticians" [527]) are patently informed by an atavistic slave morality as well: a concern for the downtrodden and excluded, a channeling of anger and resentment at oppression into ostensibly objective principles of inclusion and exclusion, etc. The Strong Argument, it seems to me—the kind that might have been made by the Strong Critic—is not that those social programs are "supposed (and nonexistent)" but that they are displaced forms of slave morality. Nietzsche of course associated slave morality with the "ascetic priesthoods" of both Judaism and Christianity; it is definitively the *ressentiment*/resentment/rancor felt by the powerless toward their oppressors and converted by them upon their rise to power into a passive-aggressive moral high ground that retributively tramples the values associated with power (Nietzsche's aristocratic Strong Man, Bloom's Strong Poet) in the name of "love" and "forgiveness." The idea would appear to be that the New Critics vanquished the Christian literary moralists on the Right, but just scant decades later found themselves vanquished in turn by Marxist and other "identity-politics" literary moralists on the Left—with new ideological justifications for their moral crusade, but beneath the jargon and the high-powered argumentation preaching the same pernicious slave morality, trying to deny the Strong Poet the right to take what he wants:

> Our educational institutions are thronged these days by idealistic resenters who denounce competition in literature as in life, but the aesthetic and the agonistic are one, according to all the ancient Greeks, and to Burckhardt and Nietzsche, who recovered this truth. (6)
>
> Pragmatically, the "expansion of the Canon" has meant the destruction of the Canon, since what is being taught includes by no means the best writers who happen to be women, African, Hispanic, or Asian, but rather the writers who offer little but the resentment they have developed as part of their sense of identity. (7)

The Strong Poet competes for literary laurels, and wins them through "aesthetic strength" (29); the School of Resentment or School of Slave Morality would banish such competition in the name of collaboration or cooperation, which Bloom tropes contemptuously as "quilt making" (7).

The rhetorical danger that Bloom would have incurred by invoking slave morality as a Nietzschean term of reprobation, of course, would have been to draw excessive attention to Nietzsche's Romantic glorification of the master—the feudal lord, the warrior who killed and took and raped as he pleased, the Strong Man—and thus by extension to the problematic ideological implications of his own celebration of the Strong Poet. And while Bloom might be inclined in his heart of hearts to scorn the widespread association of Nietzsche's Strong Man with Nazism (Nietzsche was Nietzsche, not a Nazi, and what the Nazis did with him is irrelevant, and only leftist lemmings would make a *cause célèbre* out of that association, etc.), and thus of his own Strong Poet with rape, murder, and ruthless domination, even he is probably pragmatic enough not to want to risk it.

Still, it would have made his combined attack on the Right and the Left far more coherent, had he dared (or thought of it).

Certainly it seems beyond question that by resentment Bloom means something like Nietzsche's *ressentiment,* and that he has modeled his argument loosely on Nietzsche's. What makes both Nietzsche's polemic against Judeo-Christian moralism and Bloom's polemic against identity-politics moralism so powerful, of course, is that both Jeremiahs indulge liberally in the resentment they condemn in others. It doesn't matter that Nietzsche and Bloom both feel overwhelmingly superior to the moralizing descendants-of-slaves they attack; the Judeo-Christians for Nietzsche and the leftist literary activists for Bloom not only control the institutions but have spread their pernicious morality through the hearts and souls of the culture, so that, as Bloom complains, "I feel quite alone these days in defending the autonomy of the aesthetic" (10). He is the only aestheticist left, the last remaining dinosaur, his entire species teetering in his person on the verge of extinction:

Our legions who have deserted represent a strand in our traditions that has always been in flight from the aesthetic: Platonic moralism and Aristotelian social science. The attack on poetry either exiles it for being destructive of social well-being or allows it sufferance if it will assume the work of social catharsis under the banners of the new multiculturalism. Beneath the surfaces of academic Marxism, Feminism, and New Historicism, the ancient polemic of Platonism and the equally archaic Aristotelian social medicine continue to course on. I suppose that the conflict between these strains and the always beleaguered supporters of the aesthetic can never end. We are losing now, and doubtless we will go on losing, and there is a sorrow in that, because many of the best students will abandon us for other disciplines and professions, an abandonment already well under way. (18)

And so yes, he feels resentful too. The identity-politics leftists have stolen literary criticism out from under him, and from under people like him. No words are too harsh, therefore, for these high-minded "new commissars" who "resent literature" (521) and "the aesthetic value of literature" (518). No opportunity to attack them, to impugn their motives and trample their values as they have trampled Bloom's, must be passed up. If it strikes readers as ironic that Bloom resentfully attacks his opponents for their resentment, that like Nietzsche Bloom too moralizes vitriolically against the moralizers, so be it. These matters are far too important for him to worry about petty considerations like rhetorical *ethos*, presenting the reader with a calm and consistent persona as subliminal backing for his claims.

If we follow Sakai's lead, then, and read both Nietzsche's *Genealogy* and Bloom's *Western Canon* as articulations/exemplifications of Western civilizational spells, we might want to say that there are (at least these) two: the master-spell and the slave-spell. Each of them would be based not on current mastery and slavery, of course, but, as in Nietzsche, on the distant past: these would be *intergenerational* spells. The master-spell would dispose those it haunts to wield power-over, to compete, to dominate, to subjugate without compunction; the slave-spell would dispose its victims to be inclusive, to participate in power-with, to collaborate, to encourage and empower, to defend the downtrodden. The master-spell would precondition a Social Darwinist meritocracy and/or plutocracy; the slave-spell would precondition an egalitarian democracy, or even a utopian communist anarchy. In a colonial context, the master-spell would reassure and embolden the colonizer who conquers, enslaves, and dehumanizes the colonized; the slave-spell would disquiet the colonizer who refuses (Memmi 1957; Greenfield 1965/91: 19–44).

On that head, then, three notes:

First, while Nietzsche attributes *ressentiment* to the slave-spell alone, the resentful tone of both Nietzsche's *Genealogy* and Bloom's *Western Canon* suggests that there is a resentment that is endemic to each spell. The descendants of former slaves, currently haunted by the slave-spell, have inherited resentment from previous generations—this is Nietzsche—but the descendants of former masters, currently haunted by the master-spell, have also inherited a sense of entitlement from previous generations, and as a result bitterly resent their reduced circumstances in the present. Harold Bloom, professor emeritus of English at Yale, an academic celebrity, resents the academic Left not only for imposing their values on literature departments, and so peripheralizing him and hundreds of others like him, but for being *unworthy* of their current ascendancy. They are, after all, under the slave-spell. Their values are the (transvalued) whingeing of former slaves: championing the excluded and vilifying anyone who dares voice the master-spell that celebrates strength, power, victory.

Second, the Western powers often seem to channel both the master-spell and the slave-spell into one and the same foreign policy—as when they "export democracy" through ruthless military and economic domination. The slave-spell urges them to empower the "natives," to educate them, to cultivate their creativity and initiative, to make them as close to equal to their colonizers as "humanly" (read: "colonially") possible; the master-spell grows impatient with their slow progress toward full equality and democratic freedom, their apparent reluctance or inability to emulate their obvious superiors, and puts draconian laws and other institutions in place to force the people their ancestors enslaved to be "free" (free to vote for the corrupt puppets chosen to rule them by their erstwhile foreign masters; free to spend their slave wages on a Big Mac with fries and a Coke). The simultaneous channeling of the slave-spell and the master-spell into foreign policy creates a powerful double-bind: be as smart and strong as I am; know that you can never be as strong or as smart as I am; resent my undeserved ascendancy; know that I do actually deserve it (because I'm naturally smarter and stronger than you); know that I will despise and punish you not only for your failure to ascend to my heights but for your resentment of your own failure-in-advance; know also that I am (partly) ashamed of my own master-spell, and will indignantly deny it if challenged. And so on.

And third, I am emphatically not suggesting that in celebrating the literary "mastery" of the Strong Poet Bloom is actually celebrating rape, murder, or ruthless military and economic domination—any more than Nietzsche is. I am suggesting that Bloom, like Nietzsche, is under a civilizational master-spell, which in Sakai's terms "haunts" his study of great writers like a ghost. Nor, obviously, do I literalize all the supernatural tropes invoked by Sakai and the other CTS theorists. No spells, no ghosts, no enchantments. Only the deep intergenerational survival of icotic/ecotic orientations.

> *Icosis*: socioecological plausibilization, from Greek *eikos* "plausible," *ta eikota* "the plausibilities." Derived from Aristotle's insistence that, given a choice between a claim that is true but implausible and a claim that is plausible but untrue, we will tend to favor the latter, because plausibility is the somatic mark of normative communal acceptance. A somatic theory of the social construction of truths, realities, and identities. First derived from Aristotle in Robinson (2016a), though it first appeared in print in Robinson 2013b (which was written later but published earlier).
>
> *Ecosis*: the socioecological becoming-good of the community, which is also the becoming-communal of goodness-norms. From Greek *oikos* "household, community," the source of the English words *ecology* and *economy*. In Attic Greek *eikos* and *oikos* were pronounced so similarly that many Greek writers punned on them. Also most fully derived and defined in Robinson (2016a).

## 2.4 Bloom 2: The Canon as Memory as Pain

I mentioned early in section 2.3 that Bloom seems to accept everything about the traditional "mystical" understanding of canon-formation except its conception of the nature of literary genius, which for him emerges out of pain, and specifically the agonistic intensification of pain-drenched memory. In asserting this view he explicitly, though rather vaguely, attributes it to Nietzsche (with my bracketed numbers for discussion):

> The issue is the mortality or immortality of literary works. [1] Where they have become canonical, they have survived an immense struggle in social relations, but those relations have very little to do with class struggle. [2] Aesthetic value emanates from the struggle between texts: in the reader, in language, in the classroom, in arguments within a society. [3] Very few working-class readers ever matter in determining the survival of texts, and left-wing critics cannot do the working class's reading for it. [4] Aesthetic value rises out of memory, and so (as Nietzsche saw) out of pain, the pain of surrendering easier pleasures in favor of much more difficult ones. [5] Workers have anxieties enough and turn to religion as one mode of relief. [6] Their sure sense that the aesthetic is, for them, only another anxiety helps to teach us that [7] successful literary works are achieved anxieties, not releases from anxieties. [8] Canons, too, are achieved anxieties, not unified props of morality, Western or Eastern. (38)

To begin with (1) the "immense struggle in social relations" that canonized literary works have survived and (2) the "struggle between texts" as which Bloom glosses (1): what exactly is that struggle? He seems to think, first of all, that his multiculturalist opponents are all not only leftists but vulgar Marxists who want to reduce everything to the class struggle; and, second, that (3) the disenfranchisement of the working class in canon-formation somehow proves him right and them wrong. Even apart from the fact that the disenfranchisement of the working class is a strange basis for the claim that the class struggle is irrelevant, and even setting aside the question of whether (multi-)

cultural relativists in literary studies are all grimly intent on forcing all canon-formation into the Procrustean bed of the class struggle, there remains the question of what kind of struggle he is referring to. He seems to mean something like what Northrop Frye (1957/73: 18) calls the "stock exchange" of literary value: "That wealthy investor Mr. Eliot, after dumping Milton on the market, is now buying him again; Donne has probably reached his peak and will begin to taper off; Tennyson may be in for a slight flutter but the Shelley stocks are still bearish." Richard Halpern (1997: 117) notes that Frye's image "not only satirizes the seeming capriciousness of canonical revision but implicitly engages the relation between aesthetic value and exchange-value"—a useful bridge from Bloom's Gnostic aestheticism forward to Nietzsche's somatic economics of legal punishment in section 2.5—but in what sense precisely does Bloom locate that struggle "*in* the reader, *in* language, *in* the classroom, *in* arguments within a society"? What is this "in-ness"? Is it anything like Foucault's "Elle s'inscrit *dans* le système nerveux, *dans* l'humeur, *dans* l'appareil digestif …"? Or does each of those locations (readers, languages, classrooms, arguments) have its own peculiar kind of in-ness? What kind of medium is each kind of in-ness for that struggle?

It is difficult for me to understand the "struggle between texts," whether in the reader or in the classroom, in "language" (whatever that is) or an argument, as anything other than a *felt* struggle, a phenomenological struggle that is constructed imaginatively by readers and teachers and students and fought in the realm of affect. Indeed Bloom himself is enough of a Freudian to know that the Agon he celebrates is not abstract or intellectual but powerfully libidinal, which is to say, in my terms, somatic. The Bloom of *The Anxiety of Influence* knew that "the autonomy of the aesthetic" (1994: 10)—had he been inclined to theorize literary history in such vainglorious terms back in the 1970s—is in fact not particularly autonomous, at least in the rationalist sense of autonomy, in which reason makes executive decisions and the rest of the organism obeys. To the extent that "the aesthetic" is a libidinal Agon, it is not something that individuals control. If anyone controls it, it is groups, though never perfectly, and never consciously, rationally, with their (super)egos; but again, Bloom doesn't want to think about any of that. In order to cling to his Gnostic conception of "the aesthetic" as born in solitude (see Baumlin 24), he mystifies it, refuses to theorize it.

Bloom's thinking is almost everywhere muddled, making it difficult to map his theoretical modeling, but it seems clear that for him the claim that (2) "Aesthetic value emanates from the struggle between texts" lays the groundwork for the rather more energetic claim that (4) "Aesthetic value rises out of memory, and so (as Nietzsche saw) out of pain." This sequence would appear to indicate that the struggle between texts *generates* (or at least channels) pain, which in turn generates (or organizes/stabilizes) memory, which generates aesthetic value. Just how that works he doesn't say; but it seems to have something to do with (5) the feelings of anxiety that the working class experience, presumably in response to the precarity of the material and affective conditions of their lives, which as we've seen for Bloom does not make (3>1) the class struggle relevant to canon-formation. The working class, he says, (5>6) typically turns to religion rather than art for relief from their anxieties, because art just makes them more anxious. This is a stereotype, of course: simplistic, not a particularly nuanced depiction, but plausible, culturally plausibilized, and therefore "true" in the icotic sense. The interesting question, though, is why Bloom singles out the working class as his Nietzschean canary in the coal mine—why it is specifically the working class whose "sure sense that the aesthetic is … only another anxiety helps to teach us that successful literary works are achieved anxieties, not releases from anxieties." Why is it a social class that is selected to do this teaching, and why is it that social class in particular? If not only (7) a literary work but (8) a literary canon *is* "an achieved anxiety"—if "achieved anxiety" is its stable inner nature, its ontology—surely the implication is that it successfully and reliably (which is how I read "achieved") channels anxiety to and/or from *everybody*? What then is special about the signaling role played by the working class?

Bloom is not particularly forthcoming on this point, important and even pressing as it appears to be for him; but it seems reasonable to suggest that the anxieties that he believes are "achieved" in literature emerge out of class tensions, especially perhaps the pressures of upward mobility:

- the commodification and consumption of art—"the aesthetic"—is controlled by the upper classes and their (outsourced) servants in the professoriate, especially say academics like Richard Florida (2002/14, 2008);
- the middle classes tend to seek social legitimation in part by learning to "appreciate" art, almost always by attending university and taking classes from people like Harold Bloom, but that project of upward class mobility is a notable (but perhaps socially somewhat less manifest) source of stress and anxiety for them as well;
- that substantial portion of the working class that lets the precarity of the material and affective conditions of their lives keep them out of university will never "matter in determining the survival of texts."

But of course, that for Bloom is not a class struggle. What else it might be, I'm not sure.

The question remains, however: what is the "pain" Bloom means? We know what kind of pain Nietzsche means as a goad to memory: savage corporal punishment. We know what Foucault does with that goad, in the disciplining of docile bodies. But what is the pain out of which aesthetic value arises? Bloom glosses it as "the pain of surrendering easier pleasures in favor of much more difficult ones," and seems to associate it (denyingly) with class anxieties; presumably it is Freud's *Unbehagen* "malaise" or "unpleasure" of civilization, in the title of *Das Unbehagen in der Kultur/Civilization and its Discontents*. The fact that Bloom is an avowed (though of course proudly heretical) Freudian, and the fact that Freud too learned this model from Nietzsche, suggest that we're on the right track; and certainly "the pain of surrendering easier pleasures in favor of much more difficult ones" would mark a "high" or "advanced" level of the civilization process that Nietzsche tracks. By the time teachers are inflicting the anxieties and pains of learning about literature on students, they no longer need to enforce their lessons with ghastly corporal punishments; their students have been prepared for subtler channels of (affective) pain by centuries of (progressively less) physical pain. Nietzsche's model of the intergenerational (and so cumulative) transmission of pain-based memory should also remind us not to scorn the pain and anxiety of classroom learning about literature. The "memory" that is inculcated in this way is not just individual memory (remembering the characters and themes of a Shakespeare play for the quiz) but collective, civilizational memory, and channels far more traumatic suffering out of the distant past than just the local individualized fear of appearing stupid.

For Bloom "the pain of surrendering easier pleasures in favor of much more difficult ones" seems specifically to have something to do with the literary estrangement effect that has been so important to the Romantic and post-Romantic tradition: asking "what makes the author and the works canonical," he reports his discovery that "the answer, more often than not, has turned out to be strangeness, a mode of originality that either cannot be assimilated, or that so assimilates us that we cease to see it as strange" (3). But what *is* literary strangeness, exactly? What happens when we attempt and fail to assimilate it to our "canon" of everyday familiarity, and what happens when it "so assimilates us that we cease to see it as strange"? Bloom would not be happy to learn that Marx was interested in the same familiarization/habitualization phenomenon (see Robinson 2008: 190–94; 2017: section 1.2); such phenomenologies would appear to be no respecter of ideologies. (Unfortunately for Bloom's anti-leftist ideological affiliations, he and Marx work the same post-Romantic tradition.) For Viktor Shklovsky, drawing on the aesthetics of Broder Christiansen (1909) and the phenomenological/vitalist thought of Henri Bergson (1889; Pogson 1910), estrangement works somatically: the reader or writer *feels* a certain literary effect as strange, as alien to the familiar canon of the everyday; as s/he continues to be exposed to it, by reading or writing it, it becomes increasingly familiar, "so assimilates us that we cease to see it as strange," necessitating further estrangements in order once again to "делать камень каменным" (Shklovsky 1925/29: 11)/"make the stone stony." As I showed at length in Robinson (2008), this constant homeostatic regulation of our sense of reality through the hypermimetic artistic titration of strangeness is the formalist definition of the aesthetic, radically apolitical in Shklovsky (and thus presumably more attractive to Bloom), highly politicized in Brecht (and thus presumably less attractive to Bloom, as indeed it was to the East German Marxists of Brecht's day). Brecht's idea, of course, was that familiarity dulls us to our own best interests, and thus serves social power; the Brechtian artist can best serve the Marxist cause by waking readers and theatergoers up, using the estranging strategies of epic theater. This latter conception of literature (and of "the aesthetic") seems to Bloom the polar opposite of his own; in fact it is a powerfully politicized version of his own view, which he like Shklovsky and Brecht borrowed from the Romantics. Bloom wants to deride the sociopolitical agenda of Brecht's followers among his colleagues as absurd and regrettable, based purely on resentment, resentment qualitatively different from his own; in fact the main difference between Bloom's and Brecht's conceptions of literary estrangement is that Bloom doesn't care about awakening the anxious disenfranchised working class to their own best interests. Both men believe equally in the salutary aesthetic effects of the "difficult pleasures" of feeling oneself being estranged from the familiar, from all that feels secure but has a deadening effect on one's experience of the world –from what Shklovsky, drawing on Bergson, called automatization or habitualization, or "algebraization." Brecht simply wants to harness those effects for the political galvanization of the working class. Bloom's tendency to heap rather vicious and nonunderstanding scorn on that inclination mostly reflects his own disinclination to think through the etiology and implications of his own theories. (More on estrangement in section 2.7, where Bloom cites Shklovsky admiringly.)

Out of this same mystification comes Bloom's insistence that the canon is "the relation of an individual reader and writer to what has been preserved out of what has been written" (17). If the canon has anything at all to do with aesthetic standards, as he repeatedly suggests it does, it cannot be purely a relationship between individuals and "what has been preserved out of what has been written": individuals don't create or maintain standards, and they can only enforce them effectively if they are part of a larger collective supporting them. Nor can the canon be purely individualistic if it is the constantly emerging result of a libidinal Agon between and among texts: agons are by definition fought transindividualistically. What I suggest Bloom means is that it *feels as if* the Canon is "the relation of an individual reader and writer to what has been preserved out of what has been written"—regardless of how collectively it comes to be, each individual *experiences* it (as-if-) individualistically. Again, this is Nietzsche's insight: the internalization of mastery makes it seem to each individual as if s/he *wants* to live and feel and think and behave in accordance with social power. Nietzsche's notion of the internalization of mastery would appear to be none other than what Bloom euphemizes as pain-based memory: Nietzsche's theory is specifically that social power uses pain to enforce a collective normative memory ("mastery") in the individual. The specifically left-leaning twentieth-century versions of this Nietzschean theory that Bloom attacks in Gramsci and Foucault and their followers are once again entirely congruent with Bloom's own insistence that "Aesthetic value rises out of memory, and so (as Nietzsche saw) out of pain"; Bloom is only able to ignore that congruence by mystifying "memory" and "pain" out of the specific etiology of communal-becoming-state power to which Nietzsche traced it.

The interesting question for a somatic theory of literary interpretation, though, is *how* the individual relates to "what has been preserved out of what has been written." If the literary canon *is* that relation, as Bloom claims it is, it is not a thing, an object: it is a collective phenomenology, a shared psychosocial construct. The traditional view, of course, is that the canon is simply "what has been preserved out of what has been written"; Bloom's innovation lies in psychologizing it, phenomenologizing it, bringing it off the library shelves and the syllabi and placing it in the individual's relational *sense* of what has been preserved, and specifically in the individual's *memory* of the sense of what has been preserved, and ultimately in the individual's *pain/anxiety* that organizes the memory of the sense of what has been preserved. The literary canon is, yes, in a sense, *what we remember*— what is preserved in and through individuals' relational memories. That is Bloom's brief. But Nietzsche insists that the role pain plays in organizing and enforcing those memories is collective, authoritarian, directed to the (individualized) internalization of (collective) mastery. Bloom wants to ignore this, but his own (inchoate but Nietzschean-identified) pain-based model of memory urges us to ask *how* we relate. How are individual responses to literature organized into collective conceptions? After all, *the canon* is not each individual's idiosyncratic memory; for it to be *the canon*, it must be collectively organized in some way. (Unless of course the "greatness" that leads to the canonization of a given text is an objective textual property that individuals simply register more or less accurately—the conservative NAS view that Bloom's insistence on the phenomenology of "relationality" is designed to undo.) And how are collective conceptions internalized as individual relations to what has been preserved?

 I broached the social neuroscience behind somatic theory briefly in section 2.2; suffice it to say here that the somatic "relationality" that makes the normativization of individual group members' responses and subsequent reticulation of normativized group body states to individuals involves the mirror neuron system, specifically the unconscious mirroring of other people's body language, producing a simulation of their inner body states that *feels real*—indeed feels like one's own. This is the etiology of the phenomenology that Bloom describes, according to which the individual's relation to what has been preserved from the past is a purely individualized event: phenomenologically, it not only *feels* like one's own, it *is* one's own (it is generated inside one's own body, and is not phenomenologically marked as a representation of someone else's body state); but it is also neurologically a mimesis, a new individual iteration of the normativized shared orientations, inclinations, motivations, evaluations that are currently being reticulated through the group. Those orientations (etc.), which I call icoses, are for Nietzsche—and presumably also for Bloom—collective regulatory channels of pain, specifically regulatory reactivations of ancient embodiments of pain (fear, anxiety, guilt, and so on) that mobilize literary and other aesthetic knowing for a productive tension between normativity ("standards") and counternormativity ("estrangement").

## 2.5 Nietzsche 3: Guilt and Debt

Note further that as Nietzsche presents it, the "person" who finally has a memory imprinted in or on his/her body is *man* "one":

> Mit Hülfe solcher Bilder und Vorgänge behält *man* endlich fünf, sechs "ich will nicht" im Gedächtnisse, in Bezug auf welche *man* sein V e r- s p r e c h e n gegeben hat, um unter den Vortheilen der Societät zu leben … (II: 3; Nietzsche 47–8; italics added)

> With the help of such images and processes *one* finally keeps five, six "I will nots" in memory, in regard to which *one* has given his p r o m- i s e, in order to live under/among the benefits of society … (translation DR; italics added)

> *Periperformativity*: the ratification of performatives by the community. Coined and theorized by Eve Sedgwick (2003: 67–91) in terms of the "they" that ratify/verify/enforce the "I/you" performative act. She begins with "I dare you," which only works if there are they-witnesses, and moves to "I now pronounce you man and wife," and the problem of gays asked to witness/ratify heterosexual marriage by sitting in the church. The notion that the quasipersonal "one" is the quintessential periperformative pronoun is first developed in Robinson 2016c and 2017; the significance of periperformativity for icosis/ecosis is explored in Robinson 2015a and 2016d.

*Man* "one" is a periperformative composite—here a composite of billions of individuals over dozens of generations. Implicit in those efforts is also a collective "teacher" of these lessons: in Nietzsche's formulation, evolving (pre-)European cultures with all their local differences are somehow inexplicably united in their determination to "teach" their members "five or six 'I won'ts'"—proto-civilizational spells. If it is the pedagogical-becoming-physiological-becoming-psychological imposition of "remembering" on "forgetting" that makes possible a regulated speech act of promising, then, the "real" on which these traces are written, the medium through which the nuances shine, is the collectivized "individual" body of Europe(ans), the *interpersonal-becoming-intergenerational body-becoming-mind* that keeps (peri-)performing the pain-trained speech acts generation after generation. A "main nuance" would then be the somatic (under)ground of a word, the sublexical surge of interpersonal-becoming-intergenerational body "in" a word; a word "carries" the glow of that nuance in the Bakhtinian sense of being "saturated" with it, saturated with the intergenerationally embodied dialogues in which it has been used for as long as it has been used, the "dynastic" tonalizations with which it has been iteratively icotized (or "itericotized"). Of course all that is to say that the tonal saturations of a word are "carried" not by the word itself but by the bodies of the people who use them, speak and hear them, tonalize and retonalize them—but the partial collectivization of those bodies at once singularizes their plurality and pluralizes any given individual's singularity. For Bakhtin (1934–5/1975: 153–60; Emerson and Holquist 1981: 342–8) the внутренне убедительное слово/*vnutrenne ubeditel'noe slovo*/"internally persuasive word" is saturated with random experiential tonalizations, with whatever tonalizations one's interlocutors happen to give it; this process is very like what Pierre Bourdieu calls *habitus*. The авторитарное слово/*avtoritarnoe slovo*/"authoritarian word" for Bakhtin is saturated with power tonalizations, "nuances" charged with "power over," with "hegemony," with "rule," with a master-spell—and this is the kind of word Nietzsche wants to explore.

How then do the "I won'ts"—the promises that the body of Europe(ans) has learned through horrific pain to remember and to keep, which I called proto-civilizational spells—grow up to be full-fledged civilizational spells? I suggested in section 2.1 that the nuances of words are civilizational spells; but surely those spells are also both more and less than such nuances. More, in the sense that civilizational spells would encompass larger phenomena (say, ideologies, moralities, mythologies) than the nuances of individual words; but also less, in the sense that only the nuances of certain words—the ideological, moral, and mythological ones—would resonate with civilizational spells. What Sakai calls civilizational spells are an icotic *organization* of the somatics of language—specifically, in CTS terms, an icotic organization of the somatic heterolinguality of human social address, and thus of the somatics of translation.

Even if we back off from the idealized image of the perfect collectivization of those bodies—*man* "one" as a single aggregate intergenerational body-becoming-mind—and isolate for scrutiny the mere fact that all those cultures for all those centuries systematically inflicted pain on recalcitrant bodies, the degree of unity in even that fairly diffuse "program" or "project" is remarkable. Why always pain? Why what Katharina Rutschky (1977) calls *die schwarze Pädagogik* "the black pedagogy" (often translated as "the poisonous pedagogy"; see also Miller 1990), steeped in the mortification of other people's flesh? The medieval term "mortification" suggests Christian ideologies of the evil of flesh, of course—the carnal urges, above all, lust and gluttony, as driven by the devil—and it may be that all those millions of "teachers" who inflicted pain as the channel of their teaching were simply applying Christian theology to their pedagogical task; but we know that most adults who inflict pain on children and other recalcitrants could not articulate the Christian theology behind their impulse to hurt. It seems more likely that pain-as-discipline (to subsume Nietzsche's thinking into Foucault's) was and continues to be an ecosis, a kinesthetic-becoming-affective-becoming-conative-becoming-cognitive project of large masses of people over many generations—an ecological (collectively constructed and guided) and moral (ecotic or becoming-good) directionality or entelechy that was deeply felt and only rarely became cognitive. (In some sense Nietzsche's *Genealogy* is the perfect fulfillment of the becoming-cognitive, as is Foucault's *Discipline and Punish*: the verbalization/theorization of an impulse that for most of its history has diffidently refrained from full cognitive articulation.) In important ways pain was neither only the target of this project, nor only its primary pedagogical method, but the project's dynastic through-put: the beaten child grows up to beat his or her children, not only out of revenge, as Nietzsche tends to assume, but out of the ecotic normativization of hurting others, the deep-seated feeling that, even if it is unpleasant to inflict pain on children, it has to be done. And such is the power of that normativization, it is rarely even unpleasant: the child's flesh has ecotically always already become one's own recalcitrance, that part of oneself that resists control and so provokes sudden irrational anger, punitive anger that *must* be vented as physical-becoming-emotional-becoming-verbal abuse.

More: in the ecotic mobilization of the tension between normativity and counternormativity, the individual is conditioned to generate not only the regulatory standards but the recalcitrant to-be-regulated estrangement of standards—both rule and the unruly, punishment and defiance, norms and the impulse to deviate from norms. The individual is enculturated as a microcosm of societal mastery-over-rebellion, which is to say, as both mastery's punitive triumph over rebellion and as the undying urge to rebel, in symbiotic circularity.

As an ecosis, pain-as-discipline is aimed not at understanding but at becoming-good, the becoming-good of the whole community; in his determination to understand that process, and to articulate his understanding as a "genealogy of morals," Nietzsche's essay is not just becoming-cognitive but itself icotic, an intervention into ecosis so as to turn the becoming-good into a becoming-true. The famous history Nietzsche constructs deriving *guilt* from *debt*, based on the etymological fact that German uses the same word (*Schuld*) for both, is specifically an *icotic* history—not only a history of icosis, but a history whose effect on the reader is icotic as well. And since an icosis is specifically a somatic ecology, the circulation of felt becoming-normative pressures through a group, the effect of his debunking of the value-derivation of "guilt" from "debt" is to ground it in the body: in *pleasure and pain*. The commercial experience of owing something to a creditor, he argues, only gets transformed into *guilt*, into the theology of *ressentiment*, by being itericotized as guilt *painfully* in the debtor's body and *pleasurably* in the creditor's body:

> Namentlich aber konnte der Gläubiger dem Leibe des Schuldners alle Arten Schmach und Folter anthun, zum Beispiel so viel davon herunterschneiden als der Grösse der Schuld angemessen schien:— und es gab frühzeitig und überall von diesem Gesichtspunkte aus genaue, zum Theil entsetzlich in's Kleine und Kleinste gehende Abschätzungen, zu R e c h t bestehende Abschätzungen der einzelnen Glieder und Körperstellen. ... Machen wir uns die Logik dieser ganzen Ausgleichungsform klar: sie ist fremdartig genug. Die Äquivalenz ist damit gegeben, dass an Stelle eines gegen den Schaden direkt aufkommenden Vortheils (also an Stelle eines Ausgleichs in Geld, Land, Besitz irgend welcher Art) dem Gläubiger eine Art Wohlgefühl als Rückzahlung und Ausgleich zugestanden wird,—das Wohlgefühl, seine Macht an einem Machtlosen unbedenklich auslassen zu dürfen, die Wollust "de fair le mal pour le plaisir de le faire", der Genuss in der Vergewaltigung ... (II: 5; 50-1)

The creditor, moreover, had the right to inflict all manner of indignity and pain on the body of the debtor. For example, he could cut out an amount of flesh proportionate to the amount of the debt, and we find, very early, quite detailed legal assessments of the value of individual parts of the body. ... Let us try to understand the logic of this entire method of compensations; it is strange enough. An equivalence is provided by the creditor's receiving, in place of material compensation such as money, land, or other possessions, a kind of *pleasure*. That pleasure is induced by his being able to exercise his power freely upon one who is powerless, by the pleasure of *faire le mal pour le plaisir de la faire*, the pleasure of rape. (Golffing 196)

In other words, the abstract *monetary* equivalencies of debt and repayment are displaced onto the body, given bodily form, both in the pain suffered by the debtor and in the pleasure taken by the creditor in the debtor's pain. This bodily displacement too is subjected to the regulatory regime of competing-becoming-universal equivalencies (Liu 1999: 19): there must be a legislated correspondence between the monetary value of the debt (the numerical abstraction) and the somatic value of the debtor's pain (the regulated corporealization) in order for the creditor to count the somatic value of his pleasure in that pain as adequate compensation for the debt. This means that the creditor is compensated for the unpaid debt at three removes, through four equivalencies: *monetary to monetary value* (amount of money loaned → amount of money unpaid), *monetary to somatic value* (amount of money unpaid → amount of pain suffered), *somatic to somatic value* (amount of pain suffered → amount of pleasure enjoyed), and *somatic to monetary value* (amount of pleasure enjoyed → amount of money loaned). For a schematic representation of this circulation, see Fig. 2.1. There the "monetary to somatic" equivalence down the right-hand side of the diagram involves the surrogate confiscation of the unpaid amount in or through the debtor's bodily pain; and the "monetary from somatic" equivalency up the left-hand side of the diagram derives compensation for the creditor through a reverse calculus of that same confiscatory equivalency on the debtor's side.

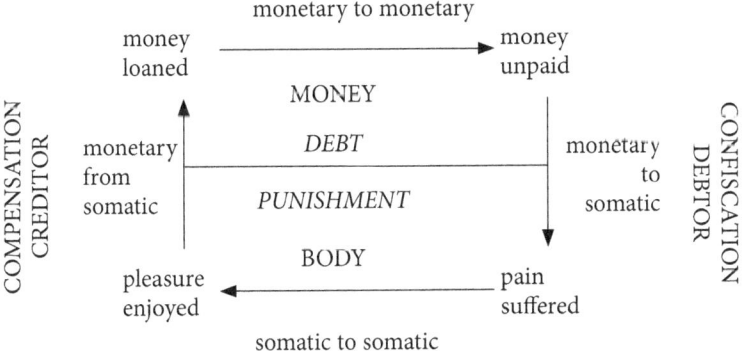

**Figure 2.1** The monetary-somatic exchange of debt and punishment

But of course these equivalencies are difficult to calculate precisely. The bodies that suffer pain and enjoy pleasure cannot be imprinted or embossed or rendered calculable in the precise way a coin can. What happens instead, as Bakhtin would suggest, is that the word "debt" off the top half of the diagram is increasingly *saturated* with body, with a somatics of compensatory pleasure and pain: the linguistic traces of bodily pleasure and pain in punishment from the bottom half—and, later, of guilt and satisfaction, the moral equivalents of punishment—are "written" on the real of the speaking body, "imprinted" or "embossed" in or on the speaking body as event-surface, "inscribed," which is to say, ecotically somatized.

## 2.6 Nietzsche 4: The Desomatization of Somatic Codes

My question in this section, as I promised in the opening paragraphs of section 2.1, is "why is it so easy to deny that one is under such a spell?" Sakai's metaphor—the spell—suggests an easy answer to the question: one of the things that happen to you when you're under a spell is that by definition you have no idea that you're under a spell. Everyone who has ever watched a Disney movie knows that when a good character is under a wicked witch's spell, s/he may do horrible things without the slightest inkling that doing those things is in any way out of character—and, when the spell is lifted, may have only the vaguest memory of doing things that s/he now (of course) knows were very wrong.

But that is only a metaphor; and my use of Disney cartoons to illustrate the metaphor further trivializes it by association. Surely the functioning of civilizational spells, or whatever we wish to call them, is more complex in the real world? Let us take another look at Chesterman (2014: 83–4):

> Now, the relativists are surely right in pointing out that some of our current Western assumptions in TS look doubtful in the face of evidence from translation practices that have so far been little studied,

whether in the West (e.g. the study of non-professional translation) or elsewhere. But then the Popperian response would be: let us then test these assumptions on whatever relevant data we can find, wherever we find some, and the more widely the better. Conversely, ideas that originate in non-Western cultures should also be tested, on any relevant data available, in whatever culture, to check whether they apply more generally. If the assumptions and ideas are supposed to be valid for translation universally, we can test them anywhere. To repeat: there is no particular geographical virtue in privileging an idea because it comes from the West or the non-West. To do so would take us back to Nazi or Stalinist science (see further Fuller 2003, 182–3).

Almost certainly, there, Chesterman assumes that he is *not* under a civilizational spell. He is simply applying to a perceived problem the principles of science, as articulated by Karl Popper, who, as Chesterman (82) reports, according to Fuller (2003) lost the famous 1965 University of London debate with Thomas Kuhn (1962/70) but should have won. Among "the assumptions and ideas [that for Chesterman here] are supposed to be valid for translation [studies] universally" would be at least the following:

[1] It is possible for humans to identify other people's assumptions and ideas as stable objects for testing (*it is not a civilizational spell to believe in the accurate analytical perception of objects in the real world, even in areas fraught with social and ideological complexity, like what is going on inside other people's heads, and even when cultural lenses may make it difficult to notice, appreciate, or otherwise objectify certain phenomena*).

[2] It is natural and therefore expected for humans to want to establish the universality of (1) the assumptions and ideas they encounter (*it is not a civilizational spell to believe in universal truths, or in the "natural human" desire to establish universal truths*).

[3] It is natural and possible for humans to seek (2) universal verification of the "assumptions and ideas" in (1) by stabilizing social and other phenomena as "data" on which to test them (*it is

not a civilizational spell to believe in the ideal separability of data from hypotheses and variables).

[4] It is natural and possible for humans to devise neutral and therefore objective tests that will (2) universally verify or falsify (1) specific assumptions and ideas when applied to (3) stabilized data (*it is not a civilizational spell to believe in testing as an objective process that reliably and universally distinguishes truth/factuality from falsehood/counterfactuality*).

[5] It may be perverse, but is nevertheless *humanly* and *naturally* perverse, for uncritical thinkers to fall short of the natural tendencies outlined in (1–4), and so to be subject to civilizational spells—for example, to fall into the error of believing that "there is [some] particular geographical virtue in privileging an idea because it comes from the West or the non-West."

[6] In case these people are not rational enough Popperians to be convinced by the simple statement that (5) they are wrong, the emotional scare tactics of associating their beliefs with Hitler and Stalin may do the trick (*it is not a civilizational spell to believe in simple binaries in which Hitler and Stalin are evil and whatever is presented rhetorically as their opposite is by implication good and right and wonderful*).

Now obviously I believe that the assumptions and ideas in (1–6) are indeed products of a particular set of Western civilizational spells; I surmise that in Chesterman's mind that belief shunts me over into (6) the Hitler-and-Stalin camp. I would dearly like to suggest that Walt Disney would agree with me that Andrew Chesterman is actually under an evil spell, and that, if that spell could be somehow removed, he would freely and with some relief admit that he was "not himself" while writing that position piece; unfortunately, I think that Walt Disney would probably have agreed wholeheartedly with Chesterman, and that both Disney and Chesterman might be inclined to turn the tables on me and assert that *I* am the one under a spell for challenging (1–6) obvious truths.[3]

A more pessimistic observer than I might want to insist that, as in a David Lynch film—I'm thinking especially of *Mulholland Drive* (2001)—it is in the end impossible to undo the impression each side has that the other is under a spell, and establish the true nature of reality once the spells have been removed, because such overlapping mind-bending spells constitute what we take to be reality and cannot be removed.

While such a nightmarish world view might in fact appear to be the logical conclusion of Kantian Idealism—the philosophical orientation that conditions Kuhn to reject Popper and me to reject Chesterman—it is striking that Friedrich Nietzsche, in almost every way the most radical post-Kantian philosopher in the nineteenth-century German Idealist tradition, and the thinker who set the stage for a whole panoply of twentieth-century assaults on calm scientific objectivism, was not willing to follow Lynch and others down that rabbit hole. *On the Genealogy of Morals* is in fact Nietzsche's most concerted attempt to track *reality*—specifically, the real-world ways in which the "spells" of ideology and power have shaped policies and punishments, and in which those policies and punishments have shaped Western civilization.

Indeed in addition to theorizing the shaping influences those spells have had on who we are and how we act and why we take our assumptions to be universal truths, Nietzsche also tracks the influence of those spells on our inclination to deny such things—our tendency to disembody and desituate our knowing, to universalize. He shows, for example, how the heavily somatized system of equivalencies that surrounded the punishment of debt became a *code*, a legal code whose iteration strikingly resembles that of a language, a linguistic code:

> Man hat keinen noch so niedren Grad von Civilisation aufgefunden, in dem nicht schon Etwas von diesem Verhältnisse bemerkbar würde. Preise machen, Werthe abmessen, Äquivalente ausdenken, tauschen—das hat in einem solchen Maasse das allereste Denken des Menschen präoccupirt, dass es in einem gewissen Sinne d a s Denken ist; ... (II: 8; Nietzsche 58)

No grade of civilization, however low, has yet been discovered in which something of this relationship has not been noticeable. Setting prices, determining values, contriving equivalences, exchanging—these preoccupied the earliest thinking of man to so great an extent that in a certain sense they constitute thinking *as such*; ... (Kaufmann 70)

This sounds rather as if Nietzsche were describing language, speech acts as assessments of pleasurable/painful values, which are then introjected back *into* the speech acts and thus *become* "d a s Denken," or, as Walter Kaufmann translates that, come to "constitute thinking *as such*." Unlike code theories of language in the "Saussurean"/structuralist[4] tradition, however, which normatively naturalize abstract linguistic codes as the *a priori* reality of language, Nietzsche theorizes the "legalinguistic" code itericotically, as repeatedly impressed on or implanted in bodies by a collective will to power:

Überall, wo Gerechtigkeit geübt, Gerechtigkeit aufrecht erhalten wird, sieht man eine stärkere Macht in Bezug auf ihr unterstehende Schwächere (seien es Gruppen, seien es Einzelne) nach Mitteln suchen, unter diesen dem unsinnigen Wüthen des Ressentiment ein Ende zu machen, indem sie theils das Objekt des Ressentiment aus den Händen der Rache herauszieht, theils an Stelle der Rache ihrerseits den Kampf gegen die Feinde des Friedens und der Ordnung setzt, theils Ausgleiche erfindet, vorschlägt, unter Umständen aufnöthigt, theils gewisse Äquivalente von Schädigungen zur Norm erhebt, an welche von nun an das Ressentiment ein für alle Mal gewiesen ist. Das Entscheidendste aber, was die oberste Gewalt gegen die Übermacht der Gegen- und Nachgefühle thut und durchsetzt—sie thut es immer, sobald sie irgendwie stark genug dazu ist—ist die Aufrichtung des G e s e t z e s, die imperativische Erklärung darüber, was überhaupt unter ihren Augen als erlaubt, als recht, was als verboten, als unrecht zu gelten habe: indem sie nach Aufrichtung des Gesetzes Übergriffe und Willkür-Akte Einzelner oder ganzer Gruppen als Frevel am Gesetz, als Auflehnung gegen die oberste Gewalt selbst behandelt, lenkt sie das Gefühl ihrer Untergebenen von dem nächsten durch solche Frevel angerichteten Schaden ab und erreicht damit auf die Dauer das

Umgekehrte von dem, was alle Rache will, welche den Gesichtspunkt des Geschädigten allein sieht, allein gelten lässt—: von nun an wird das Auge für eine immer u n p e r s ö n l i c h e r e Abschätzung der That eingeübt, sogar das Auge des Geschädigten selbst (obschon dies am allerletzten, wie voran bemerkt wurde). (II: 11; 65–6)

Wherever justice is practiced and maintained one sees a stronger power seeking a means of putting an end to the senseless raging of *ressentiment* among the weaker powers that stand under it (whether they be groups or individuals)—partly by taking the object of *ressentiment* out of the hands of revenge, partly by substituting for revenge the struggle against the enemies of peace and order, partly by devising and in some cases imposing settlements, partly by elevating certain equivalents for injuries into norms to which from then on *ressentiment* is once and for all directed. The most decisive act, however, that the supreme power performs and accomplishes against the predominance of grudges and rancor [*die Gegen- und Nachgefühle*, lit. "the against and towards feelings"]—it always takes this action as soon as it is in any way strong enough to do so—is the institution of *law*, the imperative declaration of what in general counts as permitted, as just, in its eyes, and what counts as forbidden, as unjust: once it has instituted the law, it treats violence and capricious acts on the part of individuals or entire groups as offenses against the law, as rebellion against the supreme power itself, and thus leads the feelings of its subjects away from the direct injury caused by such offenses; and in the long run it thus attains the reverse of that which is desired by all revenge that is fastened exclusively to the viewpoint of the person injured: from now on the eye is trained to an ever more *impersonal* evaluation of the deed, and this applies even to the eye of the injured person himself (although last of all, as remarked above). (Kaufmann 75–6)

Note here what this passage is *not* saying: it is not suggesting that the somatics of *ressentiment*, grudges, rancor, revenge, and injury is simply replaced with a disembodied code of law—with law as abstract sign system. Rather, the code is progressively *itericotized* as disembodied, depersonalized, distanced, abstracted—"the eye is trained to an ever more *impersonal* evaluation of the deed"—and the itericosis proceeds somatically, "lead[ing] the feelings of its subjects away from the direct injury caused by such offenses." Nietzsche here has *lenkt das Gefühl*, guides or steers or directs the feeling, governs or regulates the feeling: steers or regulates bodies somatically. It's no accident, in fact, that Nietzsche's strongest metaphors for this process are kinesthetic:

- *das Objekt des* Ressentiment *aus den Händen der Rache herauszieht* "takes the object of *ressentiment* out of the hands of revenge"
- *lenkt sie das Gefühl ihrer Untergebenen von dem nächsten durch solche Frevel angerichteten Schaden ab* "leads the feelings of its subjects away from the direct injury caused by such offenses"
- *wird das Auge für eine immer u n p e r s ö n l i c h e r e Abschätzung der That eingeübt* "the eye is trained to an ever more *impersonal* evaluation of the deed"

It's also no accident that that last metaphor uses (re)vision to figure not (re)cognition but the iterative rechanneling of the somatics of the grudge, of rancor, of *ressentiment* into the circulation of value. Our sense of sight, for two and a half millennia our richest source of metaphors for the spatializing movement of abstract thought, here points us metaphorically back toward *feeling*, toward an orientation of the body in action, toward the somatics of the speech act.

Notice also that *die stärkere Macht* "the stronger power" or *die oberste Gewalt* "the supreme power," the grammatical subject of all these transitive verbs—*suchen* "seek," *ein Ende machen* "put an end to," *herausziehen* "take out," *an Stelle setzen* "substitute," *erfinden* "devise," *aufnötigen* "impose," *erheben* "elevate," *tun* "perform," *durchsetzen* "accomplish," *behandeln* "treat," *lenken* "lead," *erreichen* "attain"— cannot possibly be the state. The state may *"seek* a means of putting an end to the senseless raging of *ressentiment* among the weaker powers that stand under it" ("in Bezug auf ihr unterstehende Schwächere (seien es Gruppen, seien es Einzelne) nach Mitteln *suchen*"), but it cannot attain that means simply by criminalizing revenge. The legal agency that Nietzsche specifically cites as the means that the "supreme power" institutes in order to achieve its ends can indeed declare some things permitted and therefore just and other things forbidden and therefore unjust; can indeed *Übergriffe und Willkür-Akte Einzelner oder ganzer Gruppen als Frevel am Gesetz, als Auflehnung gegen die oberste Gewalt selbst behandel[n]* "treat[] violence and capricious acts on the part of individuals or entire groups as offenses against the law, as rebellion against the supreme power itself." But that political "act" does not directly bring about the desired end. The "thus" Kaufmann adds to *lenkt sie das Gefühl ihrer Untergebenen von dem nächsten durch solche Frevel angerichteten Schaden ab*—"thus leads the feelings of its subjects away from the direct injury caused by such offenses"—in fact *mis*leads, insofar as it makes the leading of feelings sound like the simple automatic consequence of the institution of the law. So does the *erreicht* "attains" of *erreicht damit auf die Dauer das Umgekehrte von dem, was alle Rache will, welche den Gesichtspunkt des Geschädigten allein sieht* "in the long run it thus attains the reverse of that which is desired by all revenge that is fastened exclusively to the viewpoint of the person injured"—insofar as it makes the direct object of that verb (*das Umgekehrte von dem* "the reverse of that which …") sound like another simple automatic consequence of the law. Leading the feelings of subjects is an ecotic process that can only be achieved by indirection, by circulating regulatory impulses through groups, and hoping that the groups do indeed continue to circulate them, and to enforce them. *Das Umgekehrte von dem, was alle Rache will, welche den Gesichtspunkt des Geschädigten allein sieht* "The reverse of that which is desired by all revenge that is fastened exclusively to the viewpoint of the person injured" is such an intensely localized process that it is rather obvious that no state power could ever hope to accomplish it through direct action. As Nietzsche has it, *only* the injured party's viewpoint sees what revenge desires; Kaufmann tropes that "only-ness" as a "fastening," and that seems like a justified addition to Nietzsche's image, except that neither Nietzsche nor Kaufmann gives us any clue as to what force might have "fastened" revenge's desires to the injured party's viewpoint, and therefore what *das Umgekehrte* "the reverse" might entail. It would presumably, in Kaufmann's trope, involve first the "unfastening" of (thoughts/feelings of) revenge in each individual—both the person injured and his or her family members and friends—from that individual's viewpoint, and then the gradual "reversal" of the desires previously attached to those thoughts and feelings. It would, in other words, consist in what is commonly known as the winning and changing of hearts and minds: achievable at best by effective rhetoric or other propaganda, but even then involving the itericotic marshaling of group opinion for the incremental modification of group truths (see Robinson 2016a).

Specifically, the somatics of *ressentiment* is icotically re(peri-)performed or "steered by crowd remote control" through an evaluative binary switch into "good" and "bad," "right" and "wrong," into *was überhaupt unter ihren Augen als erlaubt, als recht, was als verboten, als unrecht zu gelten habe* "what in general counts as permitted, as just, in its eyes, and what counts as forbidden, as unjust." *Ressentiment* reperformed (through millions of incremental disaggregated social encounters) as icotically "permitted" becomes progressively depersonalized, disembodied, cognitivized, abstracted, thus tending to support legalinguistic unification; *ressentiment* reperformed as icotically *verboten* "forbidden" is itericotized *als Frevel am Gesetz, als Auflehnung gegen die oberste Gewalt selbst* "as offenses against the law, as rebellion against the supreme power itself." Note that the *Frevel am Gesetz* "offense against the law" there invokes Schleiermacher's charge that anyone attempting to write brilliantly and originally in a foreign language would be *frevelhaft* wicked, like a witch going doubled like a ghost. A *Frevel* in German is a crime or iniquity, a sin or blasphemy; originally it was an act of sacrilege, linked with taboo. This polarization of *ressentiment* has the consequence that the body itself is increasingly performed/icotized as rebellious, not just against the law but against the ancient religious mystification of the law as instituted and enforced by an implacable deity. The *Frevel am Gesetz* "offense against the law" is somatic-becoming-social, first and most deeply felt as a mystical terror—a spell, but a priest-spell rather than a master- or slave-spell—and only gradually "modernized" as jurisprudence, codified in the law books as a disembodied propositional abstraction.

Note further that the association of obedience with impersonal cognitive disembodiment eventually makes not only the somatics of *ressentiment* but *all* somatics rebellious. It is not merely that a grudging, rancorous, resentful demand for or bodily/behavioral orientation toward revenge is itericotized as rebellion, but that *all* bodily or behavioral responses to power, including submissive ones, are increasingly itericotized forbiddingly. At first cringing and groveling are the appropriate socio-kinesthetic responses to power; but as power is progressively codified, legalized, cognitivized, abstracted icotically out of the realm of bodily domination and submission—out of the realm of the pound of flesh, out of the realm of the pleasure the creditor takes in the debtor's physical pain—as that abstraction comes increasingly to be felt as an internal imprint, impress, emboss, the "stamp" of approval as inward limitation and guide—submission is gradually reitericotized as a cognitive event, as a simple mental (re)cognition of the superior power of/as law. The defendant's submissive body in a court of law should sit still or (when called upon to receive judgment) stand tall, calm, untroubled; should not draw attention to itself in any way. The voice and lips that carry the required speech acts of submission should not waver or tremble. Those speech acts should be tonalized neutrally, without the tiniest hint of cringing, let alone of sarcasm or defiance.

This is still, clearly, a somatized code, or what Nietzsche (II: 7; 56) calls a *Logik des Gefühls* "logic of feeling": any code that specifies how the bodies of not only defendants but judges, attorneys, jurists, and audience members must behave in a court of law (for example) remains powerfully somatic *in* its very denial of the somatic channel of its dissemination, especially given that the code-as-imprint is felt rather than written down, marked not graphologically but somatically. What is enforced in this most "modern" version of the code Nietzsche describes is not the *absence* of the body but the somatic *suppression* of the body: the itericotic "banishment" of a somatics of domination and submission through the enforcement of a specific neutralized or bureaucratized somatics of domination and submission, one that makes it possible for everyone present (and absent) to pretend that no bodies *are* present.[5]

## 2.7 Bloom 3: The Western Canon, Universalized

For reasons that we explored in section 2.3—the master-spell that haunts him with the notion that he is entitled to respect that he is not getting—Bloom is no better at desomatizing his resentment toward the slave-moralists than Nietzsche is. But in one sense he succeeds quite well at disembodying and so (rhetorically) universalizing his project: he manages to elide the socioaffective contribution made to the stabilization of the Western Canon by *translators*. He identifies twenty-four canonical authors—Shakespeare, Dante, Chaucer, Cervantes, Montaigne, Molière, Milton, Goethe, Wordsworth, Austen, Whitman, Dickinson, Dickens, Eliot, Tolstoy, Ibsen, Proust, Joyce, Woolf, Kafka, Borges, Neruda, Pessoa, and Beckett—along with one canonical critic (Dr. Johnson) and one canonical thinker (Freud). Of these he reads twelve in translation, occasionally naming the English translators he has read in italics and parentheses after the passages he cites. Dante is translated from the Italian; Cervantes, Borges, and Neruda from the Spanish; Montaigne, Molière, and Proust from the French; Tolstoy from the Russian; Goethe, Kafka, and Freud from the German; Pessoa from the Portuguese. Beckett of course first wrote several of the works Bloom discusses in French, then translated them himself into English; for Bloom they are simply works in English. But then for Bloom the Western Canon would appear to be fundamentally an English-language canon. Even though it wasn't completely written in English, it is enough to read it in English. This should remind us of Lydia H. Liu (1999: 22) noting that "the English language of the late twentieth century would be the closest analogue to the gold of the preceding era": global English as the linguistic and cultural gold standard of our day. *Of course* the

Western Canon was written in English! *Of course* it should be discussed in English! As Lewis E. Harrington (2006: 42) translates Morinaka Takaaki:

> It is probably unnecessary to point out that the theoretical discourses of various genres today are not exempt from English-language imperialism [*Eigo teikokushugi*]. The condition for thought today is, in short, that every kind of thought must presuppose that it will be translated into English [as in fact this thought was—DR's comment]. Regardless of the region or language in which it is enunciated, to the extent that it attempts to maintain communicability, thought cannot reject being mediated by English. This may already be a global condition, and if so, then the survival of theoretical discourse can even be said to be determined by whether or not it accepts being mediated by English.

Two centuries ago the German Romantics argued as if with one voice that the canon of world literature should be written in German, by translators, so that the German language might become the "allgemeines Organ der Mitteilung für die gebildeten Nationen" (Schlegel 1803/1965: 36)/"speaking voice of the civilized world" (Robinson 1997/2002a: 221). The right to speak for *die gebildeten Nationen* "the developed nations" (the West, but only the *best* of the West: no Finnish or Bosniak or Basque classics), in other words, should be taken away from French, the *lingua franca* of the day (so to speak), and given to German. By the end of the second millennium after the birth of the Universal Western Savior Jesus Christ, English has first dibs. English is the new gold standard. (Jesus Himself, after all, spoke the sixteenth-century English of William Tyndale, Myles Coverdale, and King James's revisers/translators.) The various translators Bloom cites are not *interpreting* the great Western classics into their own idiosyncratic English; there aren't competing translations, each with its own unique construction of a given classic. The commensurability between the source texts and the translations Bloom cites is so perfect that the distortive effects translating might conceivably have had on the canon that he wants to stabilize as *the* Western Canon never come up. The Canon is what it is—in English.

Here's an interesting sidelight on that: Bloom famously has a photographic memory for poetry. Once he has read a poem, he remembers it verbatim forever. There are stories of him as an undergrad at Cornell, back in the late 1940s, rising heavily up out of his desk at the back to correct some professor—I heard it told about Meyer Abrams (1912–2015)—who had just misquoted some poem. All those decades that he was writing about English and American poetry—Shelley, Blake, Emerson, Yeats, Stevens, and so on—that photographic memory stood him in good stead. It was relatively easy for him to track allusions through a series of revisionary readings by poets, because he remembered so much of their work, accurately. But what happens when he reads a poet in translation? Does his photographic memory work as well then? Does his memory flash-freeze the translation as "the poem" forever?

For example, he reads Neruda as "superbly translated by John Felstiner" (1994: 482), and does with Felstiner's translation some of the things he has been doing most of his career with Anglo-American poetry:

> Felstiner remarks that Whitman informs the pathos of Neruda's voice in the poem: "the plasmic human sympathy, the welcoming of materiality and sensuousness, the awareness of common lives and labor, the openness toward the human prospect, the poet's volunteering himself as a redeemer." I regard that last image as the most crucial, though in Neruda one of the most troublesome, because Whitman's Emersonian gnosis is very different from Neruda's Manichaean Communism. A direct juxtaposition of the close of "The Heights of Macchu Picchu" and *Song of Myself* presents both poets at their strongest, and does not favor Neruda:
>
> > *(tell me everything, chain by chain,*
> > *link by link, and step by step,*
> > *file the knives you kept by you,*
> > *drive them into my chest and my hand*
> > *like a river of riving yellow light,*
> > *like a river where buried jaguars lie,*
> > *and let me weep, hours, days, years,*

*blind ages, stellar centuries.*
*Give me silence, water, hope.*
*Give me struggle, iron, volcanoes.*
*Fasten your bodies to me like magnets.*
*Hasten to my veins to my mouth.*
*Speak through my words and my blood.)*

*I depart as air. ... I shake my white locks at the runaway sun,*
*I effuse my flesh in eddies, and drift it in lacy jags.*

*I bequeath myself to the dirt to grow from the grass I love,*
*If you want me again, look for me under your boot-soles.*

*You will hardly know who I am or what I mean,*
*But I shall be good health to you nevertheless,*
*And filter and fibre your blood.*

*Failing to fetch me at first keep encouraged,*
*Missing me one place search another,*
*I stop somewhere waiting for you.*

Both poets address multitudes, with Neruda's metaphors a blend of High Baroque Quevedo and magical realism or surrealism: river of riving yellow light, buried jaguars, and the "struggle, iron, volcanoes" that animate the dead workmen, who in turn magnetize both Neruda's language and his desires. That is credible pathos, intense and strenuous, but less persuasive than the gentle authority of Whitman's lines, which are uncannily patient and receptive. (482–4)

When he writes that "a direct juxtaposition of the close of 'The Heights of Macchu Picchu' and *Song of Myself* presents both poets at their strongest, and does not favor Neruda," by "Neruda" he means Felstiner's Neruda; "both poets" refers to Whitman in the English original and Neruda in Felstiner's English translation. Never mind the issue of relative aesthetic "quality," though that is always primary for Bloom—never mind whether Festiner's Neruda is "as good as" Neruda's Neruda in Spanish, and therefore, say, whether a comparison of "Alturas de Macchu Picchu" and *Hojas de Hierba* in Eduardo Moga's 2014 translation might in fact favor Neruda: the point is that for Bloom Neruda *just is* a poet who is read in English. The poetic images in "river of riving yellow light, buried jaguars, and the 'struggle, iron, volcanoes'" are "Neruda's metaphors." Bloom doesn't even need to put quotation marks around the first two, because, presumably, they aren't language at all, not quotable passages from the poem, let alone from an English translation of the poem: they're *images*. They're autonomous objects, put in "the poem" by Neruda himself. Bloom of course has zero motivation to go check Neruda's original Spanish and compare it with Felstiner's rendition:

> como un río de rayos amarillos,
> como un río de tigres enterrados,
>
> (Neruda 1950)

> like a river of yellow rays,
> like a river of buried jaguars,
>
> (literal translation DR)

> like a river of riving yellow light,
> like a river where buried jaguars lie,
>
> (Felstiner 1980: 195)

Felstiner's interpretive contribution to that second line is obviously minimal—he replaced the passivizing *de*/"of" with the more active "where ... lie"—but in his hands the *rayos amarillos*/"yellow rays" have become the striking "riving yellow light." The fact that "river of riving" (approximating the assonance of "río de rayos") is a poetic effect achieved not by Neruda but by Felstiner, however, is not in any way relevant to Bloom. The poetic product of his work is just an image, stabilized in English by the act of translation and the act of printing, but an image that in Bloom's mind doesn't depend for its stability on that history. It just *is*. And it just is Neruda's. Comparing those stable images to the ones he finds in Whitman, Bloom is able to identify Neruda's images as "credible pathos, intense and strenuous, but less persuasive than the gentle authority of Whitman's lines, which are uncannily patient and receptive." This is poetry stabilized, objectified, universalized—in English, but without any need to notice how it all came to be in English, because to notice that, to pay attention to it, would be to historicize it, and to feel the complexities of that series of shifting articulations, and thus to deuniversalize it.

Or consider this moment in Bloom's chapter on Tolstoy, where he identifies Tolstoy's ability to awaken in the reader a sense of strangeness in everything about which he writes as the prime source of his literary greatness:

> Victor Shklovsky, a major modern Russian critic, noted that "the most common strategy in Tolstoy is one of refusing to recognize an object, of describing it as if it were seen for the first time." This technique of strangeness, combined with Tolstoy's tonality, results in the reader's happy conviction that Tolstoy enables him to see everything as if for the first time, while also giving him the sense that he has seen everything already. To be both estranged and at home seems unlikely, but that is Tolstoy's all but unique atmosphere. (336)

This obviously evokes the estrangement strategy that we've seen Bloom borrowing from (post-)Romantic/modernist artistic theory and practice. The creation of a sense of strangeness/foreignness/alienation, in German *Befremdung/Entfremdung/Verfremdung*, is the high ideal of both the Romantic and post-Romantic poetry on which Bloom based his *Anxiety of Influence/Map of Misreading* theorizing; and it was one of the key concepts of the post-Romantic and especially modernist/formalist theorization of literature, in a historical trajectory I trace in Robinson (2008) from the German and English Romantics to Shklovsky to Brecht. What Bloom calls a "technique of strangeness" is actually a technique of awakening a *feeling* of strangeness, or what Shklovsky (1925/9: 11) calls a прием остранения/*priyom ostraneniya*/"estrangement device" (Lemon and Reis [1965: 12] call it a "technique of defamiliarization"; Sher [1990/8: 6] calls it an "enstrangement device"). Given Bloom's career-long grounding in the (post-)Romantic tradition, it is not surprising that he finds Shklovsky on Tolstoy and invokes his key concept as a basis for canonization.

The point to mark here, though, is that once again we find a foreign author writing in English. When Shklovsky wants to "note" something about Tolstoy, he notes it in English. That of course is a tendentious way of observing that Bloom doesn't flag the Shklovsky quotation—"the most common strategy in Tolstoy is one of refusing to recognize an object, of describing it as if it were seen for the first time"—as an English translation from Shklovsky's Russian, leaving us to wonder whether Shklovsky was "a major modern Russian critic" who wrote in English. After all, that is practically the global norm these days. By the end of the second millennium the English language is the academic gold standard. Bloom calls Shklovsky a "major *modern* [rather than modernist] Russian critic," and doesn't give his years of birth and death (1893–1984), leaving open the possibility that Shklovsky is our contemporary, living and working in the age when most academic publishing is in English.

Bloom doesn't bother to cite his sources, either, which further dehistoricizes the conversation into which he is dipping his oar. Indeed it takes some detective work to track the Shklovsky quotation down. Could it be this, for example, from his most famous article on estrangement, "Искусство как Прием" (translated by Lemon and Reis as "Art as Technique," by Benjamin Sher as "Art as Device") from 1917?

> Прием остранения у Л. Толстого состоит в том, что он не называет вещь ее именем, а описывает ее, как в первый раз виденную, а случай—как в первый раз произошедший ... (1917/1929: 11)

> Tolstoy makes the familiar seem strange by not naming the familiar object. He describes an object as if he were seeing it for the first time, an event as if it were happening for the first time ... (Lemon and Reis 1965: 13)

> The devices by which Tolstoy enstranges his material may be boiled down to the following: he does not call a thing by its name, that is, he describes it as if it were perceived for the first time ... (Sher 1990/1998: 6)

Unless we assume that Bloom is quoting badly from memory, however—his photographic memory doesn't work with prose—that probably isn't his source. It's close, but not close enough. A Google search for the actual quotation turns up screen after screen of academic blog posts and lecture notes/study guides prepared by professors for their students, all using it but without citing their sources, either. I finally track it back to Victor Erlich's (1975: 82) English translation of Shklovsky's "Параллели у Толстого" (published in the journal "Жизнь Искусства"/*Zhizn' Iskusstva*/"The Life of Art," 1919, later included in "Ход коня"[6]/*Khod konya* [Shklovsky 1923: 115-25], translated as *Knight's Move* [Sheldon 2005: 73-8]) as "Parallels in Tolstoy." Bloom is writing in the early 1990s about the canonical works of Tolstoy, not about modernist theories of estrangement, so it seems reasonable that he should stumble upon Shklovsky in a lesser-known article with Tolstoy's name in the title, rather than the famous 1917 article, which Benjamin Sher had just retranslated as "Art as Device" in 1990.

It is also interesting to note that Erlich (1914–2007) was Bloom's older Yale colleague—sixteen years Bloom's senior. He defended his Columbia dissertation on Russian Formalism in 1955, the same year Bloom defended his Yale dissertation on Shelley; both of them were hired at Yale that same year, Erlich in Russian, Bloom in English. Erlich translated the piece Bloom quotes for his Yale University Press anthology *Twentieth-Century Russian Literary Criticism* (81–5). It seems reasonable to conjecture that Bloom knew Erlich as a colleague, perhaps had a conversation or two with him about twentieth-century Russian literary critics around the time Erlich's anthology was published, and went looking for it again nearly two decades later when he decided to write a chapter on Tolstoy in *The Western Canon*.

In a sense Erlich and Bloom brought very different backgrounds to Yale. Erlich was born in Russia, in 1914, but was taken to Poland in 1917 when his parents fled the Russian Revolution; he later fled the Nazis out of Poland, first to Lithuania, then through Russia and Japan to the United States, where he arrived in 1942. Bloom was born and raised in the United States, in the Bronx. One should, however, resist the temptation to binarize the two, Erlich the cosmopolitan polyglot who translated, Bloom the monolingual American who reads everything in English: both, after all, were born into scholarly Jewish families who raised them speaking Yiddish and reading literary Hebrew. Even growing up in the Bronx, Bloom didn't learn English until he was six. Regardless of where they were physically born, where they grew up geographically, culturally they were born and raised in the learned Jewish diaspora, saturated in interculturality and loss.

There is no good reason to assume, therefore, that Bloom *believes* Shklovsky wrote in English, let alone that he is some sort of stereotypical monolingual American who never thinks in or about foreign languages. Writing "Shklovsky ... noted that 'the most common strategy in Tolstoy ...'" is a *convention*. It's easier, of course. It saves the monolingual reader—and author, and editor—time and effort. No one has to slog through all the bibliographical details in Cyrillic script:

Шкловский В. Параллели у Толстого.—«Жизнь Искусства», 1919, 22-23 ноября, № 299-300.

But it's not just a pragmatic solution; it's also *the way things are done*. It is so much the standard academic convention to cite a translation in English, without flagging it as a translation, and thus to give the impression that its source author originally wrote it in English, that my discussion over the last few paragraphs of the observation that for Bloom "Shklovsky writes in English" may well strike some readers— those who aren't translation scholars—as petty academic pedantry, a TS scholar's pet peeve.

Of course Bloom published the book not with one of the university presses that published his earlier academic work, but with Harcourt Brace. He wanted to appeal to the widest possible audience, have the greatest possible impact, make the most possible money. Citing sources, tracking histories of influence and dissemination, comparing translations with each other and with the source text: all that drops away before the mandates of global capitalism, in this case the profit-driven conventions of "international" publishing based in New York City, in English, for the entire world's educated readership. We can blame the elision of translation on trade publishing.

And yet not only are translation histories often elided in studies of translation published by prestigious university presses; I've done it myself. It's a *norm*.

Bloom achieves this normative deforeignized/universalized state not only by quoting Shklovsky's Russian Formalist voice in Erlich's deforeignized English, and not only by omitting the historicizing markers of having been translated—indeed of possibly having been translated misleadingly—but by adding an "at-homeness" to the idealized/universalized reader's response to Tolstoy's "tonality": "This technique of strangeness, combined with Tolstoy's tonality, results in the reader's happy conviction that Tolstoy enables him to see everything as if for the first time, while also giving him the sense that he has seen everything already. To be both estranged and at home seems unlikely, but that is Tolstoy's all but unique atmosphere." I assume that the reader is to read "Tolstoy" there in his (not her) mind's ear English-style, with the stress on the first syllable, *TOLE-stoy* (Tólstoy), not Russian-style, with the stress on the second syllable, *tall-STOY* (Tolstóy). Thus when I read Bloom's claim that there is a unique "tonality" or "atmosphere" in "Tolstoy's" writing that makes "the reader" feel at home in it, I surmise that he is specifically referring to *Tólstoy's* rather than *Tolstóy's* writing. Bloom (and the idealized/universalized male reader-avatar that he projects) is, in other words, feeling at home not in Tolstóy's writing in Russian, but in a translator's rewriting of Tolstóy in English as Tólstoy. He may even be feeling at home in the writing of more than one translator, giving him the impression that his feeling of at-homeness stands surety for the stability and continuity of "the" "tonality" or "atmosphere" of the writing across translations, and thus that what he is feeling at home in is not (just) a translation or two or three but *Tólstoy* (as if that English writer-avatar were "the" Russian writer Tolstóy).

Note further that Bloom's notion that "the reader" feels at home in Tólstoy's writing is something that *he* adds to Shklovsky—or rather, perhaps, Shklovsky's notion that Tolstóy estranges everything is something that Bloom adds to his experience of being at home in Tólstoy's writing (in English translation). Whichever way we want to run that, Bloom identifies his resulting "happy conviction" that he is having it both ways—"estranged and at home"—and first projects it onto "the reader," who is just coincidentally male, then celebrates it as "Tolstoy's all but unique atmosphere." He presents this "atmosphere," in other words, not as an effect of domesticating translations, and certainly not as his own personal response to (English translations of) Tólstoy (and of Shklovsky on Tólstoy); nor is it even the response of every possible empirical reader of English translations of Tólstoy and of Shklovsky on Tólstoy. It is "~~Tólstoy~~>Tolstoy." There is such a perfect commensurability between "Tólstoy" and every possible English translator of Tolstóy, and perhaps even between "Tólstoy" and every possible target reader of those translations, that translational equivalence can be stabilized and so universalized into a guarantor of the canonicity of a purified/delocalized "Tolstoy."

Add to all that, of course, the icotic/ecotic processes I have been teasing out of Nietzsche: the "perfect commensurability" that guarantees canonicity is a periperformative crowd effect. *One* loves Tolstoy, *one* admires Tolstoy as a canonical writer, because *one* is the aggregate of a normative crowd of readers who unconsciously, icotically, make sure that Tolstóy is read in a certain way in Russian and translated in a certain way into Tólstoy in English—and even if some renegade translator were to buck this trend, were to impose a counter-hegemonic Tólstoy on Tolstóy, those translations too would still be read in the icotic way in English, as *Tolstoy*. This is not a mechanical process, and therefore very far from an inevitability: there could well be a culture that icotized "Tolstoy" as a mediocre writer, just as, say, "Edgarpo" is lionized as a great writer in French translation but "Edgar Allen Poe" is relegated to minor status in the United States. But locally, wherever a given writer is canonized, lionized, icotized as a universal classic, s/he seems *naturally* or *inherently* great. That feeling of naturalness, of the "inevitability" of canonization, is the premier byproduct of icosis.

## 2.8 Configuration?

Of course Bloom would vigorously contest my icotic model as too collectivist, therefore too leftist. When I visited him in his home in 1983, and told him about the dissertation I had just finished on (anti-) apocalyptic American literature—published as Robinson (1985)—and its central character, Edgar Allan Poe, he was casually dismissive of Poe, insisting that Poe *just is* a minor writer; and dismissive also of the French readers who thought Poe was so great, comparing them to the French film buffs who lionized Jerry Lewis. "They aren't reading Poe," he pronounced; "they're reading Baudelaire, or Mallarmé, or whomever." By translating Poe into French, this implies, the great French nineteenth-century writers were creating a radically *new* Poe, and the target of French readers' admiration was not the actual American Poe, who remains inexorably minor, but their creation.

In Sakai's terms, in other words, for Bloom there was no cofiguration at work in the creation of Poe's French reputation. The American Poe did not shape the creation of the French Poe in any way—could not have done. Certainly Baudelaire could not have understood some deeply buried greatness in Poe that his American readers—up to and including Harold Bloom—had never seen. In the regime of homolingual address as Sakai theorizes it, the French are *by definition and by default* incapable of reading American literature with more discernment than American readers.

In one sense, of course, Bloom's identification of the contribution made by translators to the dissemination and reputation in other languages of works originally written in English, in order to distinguish that contribution from the (apparently intrinsic) literary value of the originals, is radically at odds with his suppression of the contribution of translators to the (apparently intrinsic) literary value of works that he reads in English translation. But that discrepancy is only logical, based on the (abstract logical) notion that one should treat originals and translations in the same way, no matter which language they were originally written in and into which language they were translated. The sense in which these mirror-image conceptions of originals and translations are *not* at odds is the one Sakai stresses: in the regime of homolingual address things written in one's own native language are qualitatively different from things written in a foreign language, and cannot be treated in the same way. The English language is Bloom's homolingual realm and regime. He has mastered it, understands it perfectly, precisely by dint of the homolingual (icotic) police work constantly being done along the boundary between English and all other languages. Once a foreign work has been admitted to the realm of English, it *is* English. It has been ideally deforeignized, and so is ready to circulate as local, as familiar, as an instantly recognizable thing.

It is also telling that this deforeignization of translated works clashes with the post-Romantic ethos of foreignization, which Bloom explicitly and repeatedly celebrates. Bloom resolves that clash by exclaiming admiringly at "Tolstoy's" knack for estranging everything while also making "the [male] reader" feel completely and comfortably "at home" in his writing. That this homey scene is a generalization and indeed universalization of Bloom reading Tólstoy in homey (deforeignized) English translation is, of course, something that only a leftist/multiculturalist/relativist translation scholar would be rude enough to point out.

Two years after I had that conversation in New Haven with Bloom (see also Robinson 1988), Jefferson Humphries (1985) brought out his Lacanian reading of the cofigurative construction of French and American literature, *Metamorphoses of the Raven: Literary Overdeterminedness in France and the South Since Poe*, tracking not only the cofigurative creation of a French Poe but, via the influence of the French Poe on French Symbolisme, the cofigurative creation of a

Symbolist tradition of Southern Gothic writing in the United States. Many of the great Southern writers in the early twentieth century were reading French Symbolisme avidly; early in their careers Allen Tate and William Faulkner were also translating it into English. No wonder that Faulkner, like Poe, was for decades ignored in America and lionized in French—that Faulkner remained in print throughout the thirties and forties only in French translation, and that it was largely in response to French admiration for Faulkner that American critics began to take another look, and to discover Faulkner's greatness. The iterations of Lacan's Schema L that Humphries keeps jerry-building throughout his book effectively psychologize not individual writers or translators or readers but something like a collective cofigurative agent that inhabits and keeps restlessly transforming the relationship between France and the American South.

That Harold Bloom was disinclined to accept this sort of cofigurative model of literary value in the early 1980s, and seemed still to be rejecting it in the early to mid-1990s, as Sakai began to theorize it, is not surprising; it remains for the most part ideologically counterintuitive today as well, two decades later. The critical project to which we turn in Chapter 3, Russell Kirkland's 1997 condemnation of American translations of the *Laozi*, is equally hostile to the notion of cofiguration—and yet provides even stronger evidence of the role cofiguration plays in the shaping of intellectual and aesthetic traditions than does Bloom's mystification of canon-formation.

# 3

# East and West: Toward an Intercivilizational Turn

And now let me bring this book to a close with a case study that offers the ideal illustration not only of Sakai's theory of cofiguration at its fiercest intercivilizational pitch, but of the fiercest and most puritanical *denial* of intercivilizational cofiguration as a factor in the global transmission of texts. Russell Kirkland's 1997 diatribe against American translations of the *Laozi* or *Daodejing* is exemplary in its anti-cofigurative purism, but equally exemplary, I argue, in its parading of apparently undeniable evidence of cofiguration.

## 3.1 An East-to-West Countertradition as a Cofigurative Regime of Translation

My brief in this final chapter, picking up on hints that I began to drop in section 1.2, is that there is a powerful Western dissident tradition that has been intensively and extensively influenced by Asian "theory"—the Asian philosophy that (as Sakai [2010: 441] reports) the founder of phenomenology, Edmund Husserl, claims never existed:

- G. W. Leibniz (1646–1716) reading not only everything translated from and written about China in Europe but corresponding extensively with Joachim Bouvet (1656–1730), the French Jesuit missionary to China who shared with Leibniz the belief that ancient Chinese thought formed part of the *philosophia perennis*;
- Ralph Waldo Emerson (1803–82) reading avidly not only in the Daoist and Confucian classics in English and French translations[1]

but in Emanuel Swedenborg (1688–1772) and the German Romantics, who were also avidly reading the Chinese classics;
- Charles Sanders Peirce (1839–1914), declaring primary fealty to Emerson and Schelling, developing out of Chinese-influenced German/American Idealism a strain of pragmatism that shaped several generations of influential thinkers (James, Royce, Dewey, Whitehead, Burke, etc.);
- Martin Heidegger (1889–1976) reading extensively not only in Nietzsche but the Kyoto School, Zen Buddhism, and Daoism;
- and so on. (see Robinson 2015a: §3.7 and section 3.3.2 below for a more detailed history)

Esoteric, Romantic, pragmatist, phenomenological: what did all these China-influenced strains of Western thought have in common? Certainly they were not all the same, but there were some family resemblances:

- they were all oppositional, rejecting and seeking to overturn hegemonic trends: state religion, especially repressive moralisms and patriotisms; mercantilism, commercialism, capitalism; technology and the increasing mechanization of life; and (*pace* Chesterman) scientific materialism, derogated by William Blake as "the tyranny of the five senses";
- they were all philosophically Idealist, believing that Mind is the only true reality, and that matter is an illusion (or, for Peirce, mind consolidated by habit);
- they all valued intense experience, the *feeling* of direct contact with a god, the sublimity of nature, artistic imagination and creativity, or life in the body;
- they all sought fuel for their oppositional imaginations from foreign and ancient sources, especially the Neoplatonists (Plotinus, Porphyry, Iamblichus, etc.), the pseudepigraphic writings attributed to Hermes Trismegistus, the Sanskrit Vedas, and the Daoist, Confucian, and Buddhist classics.

> *Regime of translation.* As I noted in the Preface, I'm deploying this Sakai coinage icotically, to refer descriptively to a socioaffective ecology—without the negative valence as illusion that Sakai imposes on it. Yes, technically, regimes of translation are illusions, but technically in a post-Kantian purview so is everything else; the icotic signpost is that some illusions are *constructed collectively and felt deeply as objective realities.* Valencing those latter—icoses—*negatively* as illusions betrays a lingering objectivist/positivist orientation. Sakai (1997: 51) defines the regime of translation as "an ideology that makes translators imagine their relationship to what they do in translation as the symmetrical exchange between two languages"; he argues that national languages are born out of such regimes. Cf. the ideological process or project that Bakhtin (1934–5/75: 83) describes as imagining, and seeking to bring about, a unified language: "Единый язык не дан, а, в сущности, всегда задан"/"A unified language is not a given [*dan*], but, in fact, a project that is undertaken [*zadan*]."

In what sense can this oppositional movement, or series of movements, be understood as a cofigurative regime of translation? Listing stylistic and generic differences within what has come to be called "Japanese," for example, including syntactic and semantic borrowings from Chinese and various regional dialects, Sakai (1997: 16) notes that "what characterizes the emergence of the national language is that generic differences that can be represented cofiguratively in the regime of translation are all subsumed under the generality of the national language; these genres have to be perceived as the species within the genus of the Japanese language." "Cofiguration" in his terminology is the interactive process by which source and target cultures create each other *as* separate and coherent cultures, through translation, and construct "translation" as that "symmetrical exchange between two languages."

What makes this notion useful for the study of intercivilizational encounters is that it involves both sides in the constitutive history, thus enabling a more nuanced account of unequal power relations than the victimization schema in which the more powerful party is simply the active perpetrator and the less powerful party is simply its passive victim. Orientalism, for example, is a hierarchical cofigurative schema in which "the Occident" and "the Orient" mutually cofigure each other in a relationship of inequality, the West coming to embody superiority not unilaterally, merely through the imposition of its military and economic might and subjective will on Asia, but interactively, subjugated Asia working collaboratively with the West to enforce the desired hierarchies. This is the critical shift engineered by Sakai's keyword "cofiguration": Orientalism is *cocreated*, in relationship. This emphatically does not mean that Asia participated in that relationship as an equal partner. Nor does it mean that Asia "wanted" it, or in the early centuries necessarily even understood it. But it does mean that it is through participation in that relationship that "Eurocentrism, characteristic of modernity, is most powerfully manifest in narratives by non-Western intellectuals" (Sakai 50).

## 3.2 The Occidentalist Attack on "Immature, Self-Centered Western Minds"

Let us, then, take a close look at a case study of cofigurative Occidentalist translation criticism—specifically, a radical attack on American *Laozi* translations. There have been several such attacks in recent years, beginning perhaps with Steve Bradbury's 1992 article "The American Conquest of Philosophical Taoism," and continuing more recently with Paul R. Goldin's 2002 article "Those Who Don't Know Speak: Translations of the *Daode Jing* by People Who Do Not Know Chinese"; I propose to focus my analysis on an unpublished 1997 lecture (available in .pdf on the Web) delivered at the University of Tennessee by an eminent Sinologist named Russell Kirkland, emeritus professor of religion (with a special focus on Asian religions) at the University of Georgia.

## 3.2.1 Kirkland on Distortions of Daoism

Professor Kirkland has devoted most of the last three decades to an activist recuperation among Western readers of what he argues is the original religious or "liturgical" form of Daoism. To that end he has negatively targeted both the Western tendency to read the *Laozi* as easy popular mysticism and the Chinese and Western tendency to split religious Daoism off from philosophical Daoism, in what he takes to be the misguided attempt to "save" the latter from the "peasant superstitions" of the former. Kirkland's 2004 book *Taoism: An Enduring Legacy* was a kind of culmination of those efforts; despite debilitating visual impairment beginning in the year after that book came out, however, and a stroke in 2012, leading to his disability retirement in 2014, he has continued to work on Daoism, and is currently editing a four-volume collection of articles on Daoism for Routledge's Critical Concepts in Religious Studies series.

One of the arms of his recuperation of religious Daoism has been to trace the actual history of Daoist texts in China, in order to underscore two interconnected points: first, drawing on the work of Kobayashi Masayoshi (小林正美, b. 1943) (1992, 1995) and others, he argues that the religious 道教 *daojiao* or Daoist tradition was not a superstitious "folk" bastardization of a classical philosophical movement but rather a post-classical product of elite thinkers and statesmen in the Liu-Song dynasty (mid-fifth century CE), which *created* the classical philosophical movement by reading the 《老子》 *Laozi* and the 《莊子》 *Zhuangzi* as its precursors. And second, he argues that the creation of the *Laozi* in Warring States China was a deliberate marketing ploy devised by "delocalizing" an older oral religious tradition, drawing on a philosophical vocabulary and poetic style borrowed mostly from the (fourth-century BCE?) 《內業》 *Neiye*.

In other words, according to Kirkland the *Laozi*, or the "*Tao Teh King*" or "*Tao Te Ching*" so beloved of Western translators, adapters,[2] and pop-mystical readers, is not the founding Daoist text that it has long been taken to be. This demystificatory plank—the plank he develops at book length in Kirkland (2004)—is perhaps the primary one in Kirkland's activist platform, as it shunts the *Laozi* onto a side track and gives Daoist religion historical and ideological pride of place.

The second arm of Kirkland's recuperative agenda, however, is an attack on those Western translations, and on the Western individualistic Protestant/Enlightenment/Romantic mentality that has consumed those translations with great enthusiasm. This latter is my focus in this chapter. Bracketing the whole question of 道教 *daojiao*'s Chinese history, I want to suggest that Kirkland collapses several centuries of Western intellectual (and social, etc.) history into far too monolithic a whipping boy—and that a more nuanced account of that history will offer us not only new tools for thinking about the reception of ancient Chinese philosophy in the West, but new tools for thinking about translation as configuration.

Here is a representative passage from Kirkland's unpaginated 1997 lecture:

> As the contemporary Chinese interpreter Tu Wei-ming has frequently noted, both Western intellectuals and modern Chinese intellectuals are heirs to the sensibility of the European Enlightenment of the 18th century. That sensibility was rooted, in turn, in the Protestant Reformation, and was shaped by the secularism of intellectuals who were moved by reflections upon Newton. Later, the Enlightenment sensibility was refocussed by the ideals of the 19th-century Romantics, so that Westerners—for nearly two centuries now—have assumed that the locus of all legitimate values can and must be sought only within the individual. For instance, most Americans today will generally tell you that "religion" is essentially a "personal" matter, that it is the prerogative of the individual to "decide for her/himself" what to believe. (The implication, of course, is that there is no higher truth than the autonomous individual subjectivity, that there is really nothing true or real or valid or good except "me.")

Note the reigning assumptions there: that [a] the ideological value-system that Western translators have imposed on the *Laozi* is purely Western, emerging out of the Protestant Reformation, the

European Enlightenment, and the German and English Romantics, and continuing to dominate Western thought about "religion" as "essentially a 'personal' matter" still today; and [b] that the tendency among Chinese scholars to read the text along the same lines is a product of Western influence. The subtext, of course, is that [c] the only legitimate approach to this text is to unearth from beneath the rubble of Occidental misreadings the true, authentic, original *Chinese* meaning and significance of the *Laozi*, namely, its true religious core. Cofiguration is the enemy; bliss lies in a purified myth of origins.

As Kirkland continues:

> Rather than learning to understand Taoism as it was actually taught and practiced by Taoists in traditional and modern China, Americans have been conditioned to understand "Taoism" in terms of an appealing vision of personal simplicity and a so-called "harmony with nature," both delightfully free of any unpleasant cultural baggage. Who amongst us, for instance, would fall in love with a Taoism that involved actual moral principles to which one must subjugate one's free will, or a real higher power that has priority over our own desire for individual autonomy? In the Western imagination, the Taoism of China has been ignored in favor of a Taoism of our own devising, just as an immature, self-centered man might avoid getting "bogged down" in the realities of an actual living woman, preferring a fantasy woman who never argues, never says no to his wishes, and never thinks or acts for herself. The "Taoism" of such writers as Huff and Le Guin constitutes precisely such a fantasy. And not only does such a fantasy have nothing to do with the actual facts of Taoism, but it would never have existed had it not been for the Protestant revolt against church authority in matters of truth, the teachings of Jean-Jacques Rousseau about returning to a simpler life, and the 20th-century reaction against the dehumanizing effects of the Industrial Revolution. No aspect of the fantasy Taoism created by immature, self-centered Western minds has any basis in the facts of Taoism in China.

Add here to (a–b–c), then, another assumption: that [d] religion, *real* religion, is characterized by "actual moral principles to which one must subjugate one's free will, [and] a real higher power that has priority over our own desire for individual autonomy." None of that "secular Chinese philosophy" blather, on the one hand, or that pathetic "superstitious" folk polytheism on the other. Daoism has a "real higher power." It's practically monotheistic. We Westerners fail to see this in Daoism because we are "immature [and] self-centered," people who smugly believe that

1. there is no God: [there is] only an impersonal reality called "Tao," and it doesn't have a will that I have to respect above my own personal desires;
2. there is no true moral authority outside of myself: anyone who says otherwise is trying to oppress me;
3. "Truth" is whatever I say it is. (Kirkland)[3]

## 3.2.2 Problems in Kirkland's Attack

What strikes me as a signal kind of cognitive dissonance in this attack, and therefore as a useful wedge to insert into Kirkland's argument, by way of opening up a CTS perspective on his claims, is this notion that the Western love of the *Laozi* is an expression of typical Western selfish individualism—for isn't it the usual assumption that the powerful attraction of the *Laozi* (and other "Eastern" "mystical" texts) for Western readers lies precisely in their *anti*-individualism? Would the casual (educated) reader not want to protest that Kirkland has it exactly backwards when he avers that for these people "there is no higher truth than the autonomous individual subjectivity, [so] that there is really nothing true or real or valid or good except 'me'"? Isn't the *Laozi*'s pull for its countercultural fans not the *celebration* of self but the siren call of the *surrender* of self? Like Kirkland, Red Pine (1996/2009: xi–xii) too draws on the research of 杜維明 Du Weiming (b. 1940), but specifically in his case to argue that the *Laozi* is not a sophisticated religious scripture but a primitive paean to the moon:

> However, the heart of Tu's thesis is not linguistic but textual, and based on references within the *Taoteching*. Lao-tzu says the Tao is between

Heaven and Earth, it's Heaven's Gate, it's empty but inexhaustible, it doesn't die, it waxes and wanes, it's distant and dark, it doesn't try to be full, it's the light that doesn't blind, it has thirty spokes and two thirteen-day (visible) phases, it can be strung like a bow or expand and contract like a bellows, it moves the other way (relative to the sun, it appears/rises later and later), it's the great image, the hidden immortal, the crescent soul, the dark union, the dark womb, the dark beyond dark. If this isn't the moon, what is it?

Pine (xii) adds that "the symbol the Taoists have used since ancient times to represent the Tao, ☯, shows the two conjoined phases of the moon"—but (and Pink Floyd 1973 is germane here) especially the dark side of the moon, "the dark union, the dark womb, the dark beyond dark." ("The dark beyond dark" is Pine's [2] translation of 玄之又玄 xuanzhiyou xuan in the *Laozi*'s famous first chapter.) Would one not want to protest, invoking Pine, that capitalism, scientism, liberal humanism, democracy, and the other hegemonic ideologies of the West for the last two or three centuries are the ideological/political/economic/social formations that idolize the individual in the rational light of day, the bright sun, the "me in the spotlight," losing its religion? Surely, this protester might continue, the translators, adapters, and fans of the *Laozi* in Western languages are the counterculture who *reject* those hegemonic ideologies, and celebrate a mystical surrender of self to the dark but benevolent forces of the universe, and specifically a surrender grounded in a Laozian 無爲 *wuwei*, which they translate as "non-action." Capitalism as the rational but bureaucratized action of the self in the service of enlightened self-interest; "Daoism" as mystical non-action in the service of the mystical impersonal dark.

Of course "Red Pine" is the pseudonym of an American Sinologist named Bill Porter (b. 1943), so perhaps that vitiates his claims—even though he spent two decades of his life (his thirties and forties) in Taiwan and Hong Kong, mostly living in and studying at Buddhist monasteries. (His pseudonym is an English translation of 赤松 Chi Song [赤=red, 松=pine], the name of a famous Daoist 仙/仚/僊 *xian* "immortal/sage/shaman.")

I will suggest as we proceed, however, that this initial protest against Kirkland's attack is superficial, and ultimately will not withstand close scrutiny: what in his opinion is individualistic is not so much American "Taoism" per se as it is the American insistence on being free to *choose* "Taoism." In other words, his attack is not really on that fairly narrow group of "mistranslators" or "pseudotranslators" (as he calls adapters) and countercultural readers of the *Laozi* that are the explicit targets of his diatribe, but more broadly on American freedom of religion in general—indeed on individualistic American culture as a whole, in both its liberal-secular and patriotic-Protestant guises.

Ultimately, of course, at the broadest possible level, it is an Occidentalist attack on "immature, self-centered Western minds." Kirkland's Occidentalism is manifest in his zeal not only to restore to Daoism its "original" "authentic" Chinese religiosity but to castigate the West for its "colonialist Orientalism" (Kirkland)—its egregious superimposition of its own homegrown secular individualism on top of the authentic Chinese religious tradition that it ignores-cum-tramples. Of the seven Occidentalist tendencies listed on p. 32, the four that are *least* obviously germane to a critical analysis of Kirkland's discourse are what Buruma and Margalit (2005) identify as Occidentalism's (a) rural orientation to farms and families; (c) ascetic orientation to abstinence (though his accusation of "immaturity" seems to hint at a Western tendency to value the instant gratification of desire); (d) heroicizing orientation to honor and death; and (e) organic orientation to nature and the natural. As Buruma and Margalit note, not all Occidentalisms display all seven orientations, because not all Occidentalisms are the same. What marks Kirkland's lecture as a channel of Occidentalist extremism is a combination of (b) his strong preference for—even outright obsession with—religion as ritual and submission to moral authority, and antagonism toward any other kind of religion as secularizing; (d) his tendency to launch vicious attacks against anything that even vaguely smacks of individualism; and (g) his passionate condemnation of foreigners' failure to appreciate authentic Chinese Daoism.

The wedge of cognitive dissonance that I identified at the head of this section concerned Kirkland's apparently counterintuitive attribution of Westerners' love of the *Laozi* to secular individualism. The Occidentalist rejoinder to that protest would be that any expression that falls short of liturgically purified religious extremism is secular extremism. (There is no middle ground between extremes.) As Buruma and Margalit characterize the ideology, (b) Occidentalist Catholics attack Protestants as secularizers (too individualistic, too anti-ritual), but so too do Occidentalist Orthodox Russians attack Roman Catholics as secularizers (too intellectual, too concerned with theology, not ritualistic enough); but then Occidentalist believers in non-Western religions also attack all Western religious believers as secularizers. And by the same token, (d) the Occidentalist would indeed tend to see Western mystics who believe in the surrender of the self as individualists, not only because *they* decide to surrender self (rather than being ritualistically prompted to do so by a religious group), but also because they are Westerners, and therefore *by definition* individualistic (and hence inexorably selfish, isolated, alienated, etc.).

In that light, Kirkland's attack on mystics as individualists makes perfect sense. It doesn't have to be empirically accurate; it is an ideological stance. It is Occidentalism.

The lecture's (g) nativist assault on "foreigners"'' misunderstandings of the *Laozi* is obviously also relevant, especially as I will want to challenge Kirkland's rejection of configuration below. In his view the Western "misreadings" of the *Laozi* that he identifies were not in any way influenced by Chinese thought. As Orientalisms they weren't even shaped by Western stereotypes of the East. They were organized by no configurative schema, "authored" by no East-West "coauthorship" (in Lydia Liu's [1999: 21] term) of the West's superiority and the East's inferiority. They were entirely the product of the West's ignorance of things "Oriental"—the West's colonial insistence on substituting its own phantasmatic projections for actual knowledge and understanding.

Before we begin to explore the configurative history of *Laozi* (mis-)translations, however, another apparent cognitive dissonance in the story so far: despite what we might (erroneously) want to read as his condemnation of all American Laozianism as incapable of understanding the true authentic core of Daoist religion, Kirkland is himself an American, a Southern boy, born and raised (and still living) in Georgia, and addressing his diatribe to an audience at the University of Tennessee.

But this dissonance is again only apparent. The American South, after all, is historically the Occidentalist region in the United States, decidedly rural, religious, collectivist, nativist, and still inclined to heroize the Confederacy; and as Buruma and Margalit also note, in the West the Orientalist-Occidentalist conflicts tend to take the form of liberals vs. conservatives. The ethos of "progress" or "modernity" tends to mean precisely the clutch of attitudes and practices that conservatives attack as "liberal" and Occidentalists attack as "Western."

A case in point: a puzzled undergraduate student of mine at the University of Mississippi once asked me in class what I meant by "conservative Christians." It took me a moment to figure out what the question implied: not that he didn't know what the collocation implied, but that he took it to be a tautology, like "tall skyscraper" or "free gift." When I told him that there are liberal Christians and even Marxist Christians, nearly all the students joined him in launching a barrage of skeptical questioning—which the one Californian in the class watched in amazement. The gist of their skepticism was that no true Christian could ever be a liberal, because liberals are all agnostics, let alone a Marxist, because Marxists are all raging atheists.

The acid test for Kirkland: would any "true Christian," or true Occidentalist, ever consider Ralph Waldo Emerson—an ordained Unitarian pastor at Boston's Second Church—a Christian, or religious in any sense of the word? I doubt it. He was too liberal, too progressive, too open-minded—not to mention that as a Unitarian he didn't believe Jesus was the son of God.

The acid test for me: would any "true academic," dedicated to open-ended and self-critical inquiry, ever accord a passionate Occidentalist *or* Orientalist respect as an academic? This is the ongoing challenge for multiculturalism: how open-minded is open-minded enough, and when does open-mindedness devolve into a fatuous superficial appreciation of everything?

Regardless of what we think of Kirkland's lecture at the University of Tennessee, though, it offers a useful springboard for debate on both (section 3.3) translation history and (section 3.4) the TS/CTS dynamic.

## 3.3 Three Historical Stages of *Laozi* Translation

Recall the broad historical sweep of Kirkland's finger-pointing at the secularizing individualism of the West: the Protestant Reformation > Newton > the eighteenth-century Enlightenment > the Romantic period. That's roughly three and a half centuries, from the early sixteenth to the mid-nineteenth century; the two centuries that Kirkland counts cover the *aftermath* of this longer early period, roughly the nineteenth and twentieth centuries, beginning with High Romanticism at the turn of the nineteenth century. Kirkland apparently takes this omnibus Protestant/Enlightenment/Romantic nexus of easy secular individualism from Bradbury (1992), which he praises as one of the first attempts to break the stranglehold this monolithic historical era apparently has on the Western mind: "Bradbury cites, in particular, the great influence of the 1944 pseudo-translation by the poet Witter Bynner. He says, 'Like many Americans attracted to Taoism, Bynner is an advocate of an enlightenment narrative of religion,' and Bynner reads so much 'Emersonian individualism' into the *Tao te ching* 'that Bynner's Taoism is nothing other than a patchwork of Yankee transcendentalism'" (Kirkland; Bradbury 34). "Pseudo-translation," by which Kirkland means an adaptation written by someone with no knowledge of the source language, is a bit unfair: Bynner (1881–1968) was an American poet who spent first nearly a year in China studying Chinese intensively, then eleven years collaborating with Jiang Kanghu (江亢虎, 1883–1954) on a series of translations of Tang Dynasty poems. Bradbury's dismissive phrase "Yankee transcendentalism" seems to caricature the Transcendentalism of Emerson and Thoreau and their friends as a kind of homespun low-church ("Yankee") pragmatism that is fundamentally antagonistic to religion in the high-church sense of ornate cathedrals, a hierarchical priesthood, a liturgical language alien to the parishioners, ancient rituals, and so on.

But—surely there is more one might say about five centuries of Western intellectual and social history than this omnibus condemnation?

I won't attempt to do justice to that history here; a full account of the three main stages of *Laozi* translation that Kirkland singles out—the Protestant Reformation, eighteenth-century esotericism, the Romantics—would have to be undertaken at book length. I propose here to focus my fairly cursory attention on the plenitude with which, *contra* Kirkland, those three stages proliferate evidence of Sakai's cofigurative regimes of translation.

### 3.3.1 Christianity

The story of the early Christianizing translations of the *Laozi* is well known, of course—so well known in fact that I assume Kirkland did not intend to exclude those translations from his attacks, so much as simply to focus his attention elsewhere. The problems that those translations pose for his polemic are that [a] they distort what Kirkland proclaims as "the true Daoist meaning" of the original Chinese text just as egregiously as the esoteric/Romantic translations and adaptations that he attacks, and [b] are often done by Protestants, but [c] have absolutely nothing to do with the mysticism that he attacks as quintessentially Western secularism and individualism.

Much of the work that has been done on early Jesuit translations in particular is fascinating, especially perhaps Claudia von Collani's (1981, 1985, 2008, 2012) studies of the "figurists" among the Jesuits, notably Leibniz's correspondent (see section 3.3.2 below) Joachim Bouvet (1656–1730). Bouvet famously adapted four-fold hermeneutic strategies[4] from medieval theology in order to read the Chinese characters figuratively or "anagogically," so that, for example, the Confucian keyword 仁 *ren*, first translated into English as "benevolence" by David Collie in 1828, was broken down into its component parts, 人/亻 *ren* "human" and 二 *er* "two," and interpreted to mean "the second man" or "the second Adam" or Jesus Christ. As a Jesuit, Bouvet was an intellectual Christian theologian, of course, and certainly the four-fold hermeneutic that he applied to the Chinese characters can easily be condemned as an intellectual analytic that could be (and typically was) employed rather willfully, and therefore apparently randomly, by the individual theologian. It would, in other words, be easy enough for an Occidentalist like Kirkland to attack even Bouvet's readings not only as Orientalist (which they certainly were) but as individualist secularism. But Bouvet was himself something of a theological mystic who believed in the *philosophia perennis*—the notion that all world religions were but expressions of a single universal religion, which for Bouvet happened to have been first revealed to the world in the Hebrew Bible—and the anagogical level of four-fold interpretation to which he gravitated was for him (as it was for a thousand years of Church Fathers) explicitly the highest and most mystical expression of God's Will. Attacking this kind of interpretation as "individualistic"—an expression not of God's Will but of the individual interpreter's will— would thus be a way of dressing ideological disagreement (bias) up as the orthodox condemnation of heterodoxy.

But let me adduce an example that is less well known: G. G. Alexander's *Lao Tsze: The Great Thinker With a Translation of His Thoughts on the Nature and Manifestation of God* from 1895. As a counterexample to Kirkland's omnibus condemnation, Alexander has the dual advantage of being (see point b in the first paragraph of this section, above) a devout Protestant (an Anglican major-general in the British Army[5]) and of citing in his Preface the arguments in favor of Christianizing translations by other Protestant translators (see points a and c) who did not in the end highlight their more sectarian preferences in their actual translations.[6] In other words, Alexander's Protestantism would take a run at resisting Kirkland's reduction to secular individualism.

Here, then, to begin with, is Alexander's expansive Christianizing rendition of the first chapter of the *Laozi*:

> God (the great everlasting infinite First Cause from whom all things in heaven and earth proceed) can neither be defined nor named.
>
> For the God which can be defined or named is but the Creator, the Great Mother of all those things of which our senses have cognizance.
>
> Now he who would gain a knowledge of the nature and attributes of the nameless and undefinable God, must first set himself free from all earthly desires, for unless he can do this, he will be unable to penetrate the material veil which interposes between him and those spiritual conditions into which he would obtain an insight.
>
> Yet the spiritual and the material, though known to us under different names, are similar in origin, and issue from the same source, and the same obscurity belongs to both, for deep indeed is the darkness which enshrouds the portals through which we have to pass, in order to gain a knowledge of these mysteries. (1895: 55–6)

In defense of this translation in his Preface, Alexander (xi-xii) writes:

> I am aware that in having rendered the character, the phonetic form of which is "Tâo," by the word "God;" instead of leaving it untranslated, as has been done by many previous translators, I have laid myself open to very severe criticism. But it was only after much deep and anxious consideration that I did so. I found that the various substitutes which had been suggested, or, in one or two instances, used, only imperfectly expressed the sense of a character, which apart from the signification attached to it by Lâo-tze, may be said to have—when taking into account its employment in combination—a greater variety of meanings than that of almost any other character in the Chinese language. Moreover, I was deeply impressed with the insufficiency of the various methods by which the several "translators" sought to evade or overcome this, their chief difficulty, by refusing to employ the single word, which, according to my view, forms the keynote, not only to a portion, but to the whole of Lâo-tze's thoughts. I fancied I could detect a certain timidity in dealing with this matter, for even those who considered they had found in the pages of the Tâo-tī-King, the recognition of a triune God, shrank from employing the one term which

would have best enabled them to enforce their views. This is especially the case with von Strauss, who, in his able and exhaustive work on the Tào-tī-King, after having entered fully into the reasons why the only legitimate rendering of the character "Tâo" must be "God," still follows the example of many others and leaves it untranslated.

Where Red Pine finds the moon, G. G. Alexander finds "a triune God." Later in his Preface Alexander adds what seems to us now like a pretty significant proviso: "at the same time, it has to be remembered, that the belief in a great traditional First Cause, which he was endeavouring to re-establish, was founded on a purely abstract idea of an overruling deity, and we must refrain as much as possible from seeking to bring it into harmony with the idea of God which belongs to our own beliefs" (xvii). This principle, unfortunately, seems rather at odds with the rather aggressively "harmonizing" arguments quoted above—as also with the quasi-apologetic nature of his note to Chapter LIII: "As used in the beginning of this chapter, the character 'Tâo' is evidently used for the 'Path' or 'Way,' meaning, of course, 'God's path,' 'God's way'" (126–7). A note to readers who don't do Chinese: the primary meaning of the character 道 dao is "road, way, path"; its radical 辶 chuo, on which the 首 shou head sits, means "to walk." 道 dao is still in common use today in the sense of "road" or "street"; it is found on many quite mundane street signs. Given Alexander's insistence in the Preface that as a translation of 道 dao the word "God" "forms the keynote, not only to a portion, but to the whole of Lâo-tzse's thoughts," it is a bit inconvenient for him to have to admit here that 道 dao also seems to mean, apparently just in this one place, something other than "God." But of course he could have gotten around that by quoting Jesus from John 14 to the effect that he himself is "the Way, the Truth, and the Life"; and the key passage in LIII, which he translated as "though the Great Way is very easy, the people love to follow the by-paths," is arguably close (though in fact opposite in eschatological effect) to Jesus's metaphor in Matthew 7:13-14: "Go in through the narrow gate, because the gate to hell is wide and the road that leads to it is easy, and there are many who travel it. But the gate to life is narrow and the way that leads to it is hard, and there are few people who find it" (Eugene Nida's *Good News* translation).

What is significant about this Protestant translation in the context of Kirkland's accusations is that it is [a] arguably "mystical," but within the confines of orthodox Christian doctrine (*not secular*); [b] grounded in what Alexander argues is a *communal* understanding of the text, the community, of course, being Western theologically oriented translators, who all *know* that 道 *dao* is actually best translated as "God," but resist the ostensibly natural and linguistically-and-theologically correct impulse to use that translation for fear of criticism from secular quarters (*not individualist*); and, above all, [c] so attentive to the actual classical Chinese meanings and usages that it is influenced by the Chinese source text's imagery: despite Alexander's Trinitarian bias, for him 道 *dao* as the triune God-the-Creator is not the Father but "the Great Mother of all those things of which our senses have cognizance" (*not purely Westernizing*).

*Pace* Kirkland, in other words—who actually only lumps Protestantism in with his omnibus condemnation of immature Western secularizing/individualizing ignorance in passing, without citing specific examples—this Christian translation is not evidence of the blanket imposition of Western ignorance utterly submerging the Chinese text. Rather, it is a cofigurative mish-mash of Western Christian and Chinese Daoist elements, in the apparent service (this is never made explicit) of something like the *philosophia perennis*, the notion that Daoist texts too refer to the same "universal" (i.e., crypto-Christian) mystical truths as the Judeo-Christian Bible.

The difference between my take on these matters and Kirkland's, of course, is that for him *any* mixture of the religious and secular is to be condemned as purely secular, any mixture of the communal and individualist is to be condemned as purely individualist, and any mixture of the Chinese and Westernizing is to be condemned as purely Westernizing, while for me the middles he excludes between purified binary poles are where complex human reality dwells. From my perspective the impulse to condemn such inevitable cofigurative mixtures as corruptions of a homolingual Chinese purity blocks our understanding of cofigurative regimes of translation; from his perspective, almost certainly, my tolerance for such mixtures blocks our understanding of purified Chinese Daoism.

### 3.3.2 Esotericism

"Esotericism" is my rough approximation of the middle segment in Kirkland's omnibus period, "the Enlightenment," which did, as he notes, draw heavily on the radicalizing thought of the Protestant Reformation—but which also drew, as he fails to note, on the radicalizing esoteric thought of the Renaissance, the tradition that fed most transformatively into German Idealism and Romanticism. If one tracks, say, the individualistic middle-class work ethic of Reformation Lutheranism, Anglicanism, Moravianism, and Calvinism into the Enlightenment, and thence into "Yankee transcendentalism," one does obtain a kind of coherent through-put tradition that supports Kirkland's caricature; but if one then adds the esoteric lines of force that the Enlightenment channeled out of the Renaissance and into Idealism and Romanticism, the result looks quite different, and to my mind considerably more interesting (and harder to dismiss as cheap pop-mysticism).

The most notable representative of the esoteric strain in the Enlightenment may have been G. W. Leibniz (1646–1716)—who, contrary to Kirkland's caricature of that strain as blinkered by Western ignorance of China, drew extensive and intensive inspiration from ancient Chinese thought. The esotericism that eighteenth-century thinkers channeled out of Renaissance alchemy, magic, and Kabbalah into Romanticism was not, in other words, some homegrown Western heresy, steeped in immature, selfish Western secularism and individualism; it was shaped cofiguratively with Chinese religion and philosophy. Leibniz's most direct connection with China was his detailed correspondence with Joachim Bouvet, but as Mungello (1977, 1982) shows, he also read everything that had been published about and translated from China in the

West and channeled it into the esotericism that was the signature of his late work. The primary form that his esotericism took was, as for Bouvet, Agostino Steuco's (1497–1548) theory of a "perennial philosophy" (see Schmitt 1966), the supposed universal source from which all religious traditions draw; as Perkins (2004: 9) notes, the reports Bouvet sent back to Leibniz from China were steeped in "ancient theology and hermetism," the belief that in Chinese thought was preserved the eternal wisdom of Creation before the Flood. The article Bouvet wrote and sent to Leibniz in 1700 on the 易經 *Yijing* "Book of Changes," for example, argues that the book contains "many precious remains of the debris of the most ancient and most excellent philosophy taught by the first Patriarchs of the world to their descendants, since corrupted and almost entirely obscured by the course of time" (quoted in Perkins). Leibniz's late Idealist metaphysical treatise *La Monadologie*[7] (1714) in particular reflects this *philosophia perennis*: the monads are eternal and indecomposable centers of force, each of which mirrors the entire harmonious panpsychic universe in a ceaseless unfolding. Again: not secular, not individualist, not purely Western. Leibniz may have been a Protestant (a devout Lutheran), but only the most crabbed dogmatism would take that religious preference as a basis for the blanket condemnation of his late mystical work as secular Western individualism.

The Swedish mystic Emanuel Swedenborg (1688–1772) also drew heavily on ancient philosophical texts from China. The Swedish East India Company, founded in 1731 by Jacobite Freemasons and pro-French Hats to profit from the Asian trade, did very well at that, and in fact secretly employed Swedenborg as their intelligence agent (Schuchard 2011); but a side effect of their (overt) mercantile and (covert) political missions was a surge of interest in Indian and Chinese philosophy as well, and much of that popularity is evidenced in Swedenborg's esoteric writings. One of his claims, in fact—later incorporated into the rites of Swedish Freemasonry—was that the Jewish Kabbalah was a reformulation of a much earlier revelation to Chinese "Yogis." Most of what Swedenborg knew about Chinese thought seems to have come from the reports of Moravian missionaries.

And to anticipate section 3.3.3: Henry James Sr. (1811–82), father to William (the psychologist and philosopher, 1842–1910), Henry (the novelist, 1843–1916), and Alice (the diarist, 1848–92), was a devoted Swedenborgian. All of the Transcendentalists, including Emerson (1803–82), Thoreau (1817–62), and Bronson Alcott (1799–1888), read Swedenborg avidly (and Emerson wrote a chapter of *Representative Men* on him), as did Transcendentalist-influenced writers like Walt Whitman (1819–92) and Herman Melville (1819–91). Stephen R. Palmquist (2000: chs. II and X) argues persuasively that Immanuel Kant (1724–1804) developed his "Copernican hypothesis"—his realization that space and time are a subjective projection, not stable properties of an objective world—while reading and responding to Swedenborg. If Palmquist is right, the driving philosophical force behind all influential Idealisms and most (post-)Romanticisms over the past two-plus centuries is grounded in Kant's critical reading of Swedenborgian mysticism, which was steeped in Freemasonry, Rosicrucianism, the Kabbalah, and ancient Chinese thought. As I'll show in section 3.3.3, it is precisely this Kantian Copernican hypothesis, channeled from Swedenborg by Kant to German Idealism, and by the Romantics and Transcendentalists from the German Idealists into major turn-of-the-century thinkers from Peirce to Whitehead, that has made the esoteric strain of Romantic thought philosophically so transformative.

So ubiquitous is this esoteric orientation in the dominant mode of *Laozi* translation over the last century and a half, it is a bit difficult to illustrate textually. It is highly indicative, for example, that Herbert Giles (1845–1935)—the influential Sinologist whose revision of Thomas Wade's (1818–95) system of Chinese romanization, "Wade-Giles," is the basis of the spelling *Tao Te Ching*—was an Anglican back-slider (agnostic anti-cleric) with esoteric (Masonic) leanings. But his translation in *The Remains of Lao Tzu: Re-Translated* (1886: 6)—"The way which can be walked upon, is not the eternal WAY: the name which can be uttered is not its eternal NAME," etc.—is not strikingly different from dozens of other well-known translations by prominent Sinologists,[8] or even from dozens of equally well-known renditions by what Kirkland derogates as "pseudo-translators," like the 1944 Witter Bynner adaptation that we saw Steve Bradbury attacking above. More striking, perhaps, are adaptations done by the most famous esoterics, like Aleister Crowley and Timothy Leary:

> The Tao-Path is not the All-Tao. The Name is not the Thing named.
> Unmanifested, it is the Secret Father of Heaven and Earth; manifested, it is their Mother.
> To understand this Mystery, one must be fulfilling one's will, and if one is not thus free, one will but gain a smattering of it.
> The Tao is one, and the Teh but a phase thereof. The abyss of this Mystery is the Portal of Serpent-Wonder. (Crowley 1918)

> That Which Is Called The Tao Is Not The Tao
> The flow of energy . . . . .
> Here . . . . .
> It . . . . .
> Is . . . . .
> Nameless . . . . .
> Timeless . . . . .
> Speed of Light . . . . .
> Float . . . . . beyond fear . . . . .
> Float . . . . . beyond desire . . . . .
> Into . . . . . this Mystery of Mysteries
> through this Gate . . . . . of All Wonder
> (Leary 1966: 55)

And yes, it is true that Crowley and Leary "translated" the *Laozi* without knowing Chinese—these are actually radical adaptations of existing translations. But does that mean that they imposed on the text a "purely" Western bolus of immature, selfish ignorance? Of course it doesn't. At a bare minimum they are picking up semantic/conceptual/imagistic influences from the translations they're consulting. Even Timothy Leary, who lets his imagination run freest with the text, gives us "Nameless" for 無名 *wuming* (without name), "beyond desire" for 無欲 *wuyu* (without desire), "this Mystery of Mysteries" for 玄之又玄 *xuanzhiyou xuan* (mystery within mystery), and "through this Gate

... of all Wonder" for 眾妙之門 zhong miao zhi men (wonder's gate). More than that, however, their whole orientation to the text, their whole attribution of mystical power to the *Laozi*, was shaped by several centuries of esoteric translations of the *Laozi* into English and other Western languages. For Kirkland the fact that that tradition has also had a significant shaping effect on Chinese scholars of the *Laozi*, as Du Weiming notes, is not an occasion for rejoicing, or even rethinking; but in Sakai's terms the whole multi-century enterprise is so overwhelmingly cofigurative that it is oppressively oversimplistic to attribute it all to the ideologically conditioned ignorance of the West.

### 3.3.3 Romanticism

If as T. E. Hulme (1911/24) famously quipped Romanticism was "spilt religion," the twentieth-century countercultural versions of the esoteric mysticism in section 3.3.2 were undoubtedly—Kirkland is quite right here—spilt Romanticism. What makes that "easy mysticism" so attractive to the counterculture is undoubtedly—again, Kirkland is right—the secular-but-spiritual resistance it channels to both patriotic church Christianity (what in the U.S. has been called "the American religion") and capitalism. There is, in other words, a very broad swath of Western "Laozianism" that embraces a mystical reading of the *Laozi* precisely because it stands in opposition to the dominant Christian-cum-nationalistic-cum-capitalistic ideology. Strongly as I have argued against various specific claims Kirkland makes, I would not want to be read as rejecting his views wholesale. At this broad aggregate level, he is on target.

What his blanket attack on this Western "Laozianism" misses, however—in addition to the cofigurative histories covered in sections 3.3.1 and 3.3.2—are the strains of post-Romanticism that have been, and continue to be, shaped powerfully by Kant's Copernican hypothesis. There are several such strains, the most famous perhaps running from Hegel to the poststructuralists, and typically known as "Continental philosophy"; I propose to focus my attention instead on another, with significant contributions by Emerson and Emersonians, namely the tradition of American pragmatism founded by Charles Sanders Peirce, including at least William James, Josiah Royce (1855–1916), John Dewey (1859–1952), C. I. Lewis (1883–1964), Kenneth Burke (1897–1993), and arguably Alfred North Whitehead (1861–1947) as well. Yes, Bradbury and Kirkland are right that Emerson has been popularized for a certain jingoistic American individualism; but to focus on that exclusively and completely ignore the transformative philosophical work inspired by his thought is to treat intellectual history as sheer political spin and demagoguery.

As is well known (see Christy 1963, Cheng 2000: 219n1), Emerson and Thoreau were super-consumers of translated Daoism and Ruism:

- They read the Daoist classics in Guillaume Pauthier's French translations and the Ruist classics in Joshua Marshman's 1809 translation *The Works of Confucius* and David Collie's 1828 translation in *The Chinese Classical Work Commonly Called the Four Books* (both of which Emerson had in his library and Thoreau found there upon first staying in the house in 1841)
- Emerson published a selection (translated by Thoreau from Pauthier's French) of "Sayings of Confucius" in the 1843 *Dial*
- Thoreau quoted extensively from Mengzi in *Walden* (1854)

What is interesting about those dates is that Charles Sanders Peirce was born in 1839 in Cambridge, Massachusetts, into a family that was powerfully drawn to Transcendentalist thinking. His father Benjamin Peirce (1809–1880), professor of astronomy and mathematics at Harvard and one of the most respected mathematicians of his day, was a member of the Saturday Club, along with Emerson, Longfellow, Holmes, and others; and many of the "mystical" ideas about cosmic evolution (as "love") that Charles (1992-8: 1.285-371) published in *The Monist* in the early 1890s were heavily influenced by a talk Benjamin gave in Baltimore in 1880, a few months before his death, with his son Charles in attendance, arguing that the universe is evolving from the void to order: "Passing through innumerable transformations, it terminates in a system, whence disorganization has been wholly eliminated, and where vast multitudes of individuals, each a perfect organism in itself, are combined in indestructible harmony. In the beginning, it has the unity of monotony; in the end, it has the unity of complete organization" (quoted in Brent 1993: 131–2).

The lines of force running from the Daoist (and Ruist) classics through Joshua Marshman (1768–1837, a Baptist missionary), Jean-Pierre Guillaume Pauthier (1801–73, a French Orientalist), and David Collie (who died in 1828 in his late thirties, third headmaster of the Ying Wa College [英華書院], the world's first Anglo-Chinese college), to Emerson in the early 1840s, to Thoreau in the 1840s and 1850s, to Peirce in his father's house all through his childhood and early adulthood, to James, Royce, Dewey, and Lewis—and thus the East-West cofigurative enterprise that continued to channel esoteric thought through Romanticism into philosophical pragmatism—are clear. What is less clear is how that cofigurative enterprise shaped Alfred North Whitehead, the philosophical precursor most commonly cited by Roger T. Ames and David L. Hall in their translation of the *Laozi* (2003: 30–1) and elsewhere. But those lines of force are there as well: Whitehead's process philosophy was heavily influenced by Peirce, James, and Dewey; and Charles Hartshorne (1897–2000), who worked as Whitehead's TA at Harvard for a semester in 1925, not only expanded Whitehead's process philosophy into an influential process theology, but along with Paul Weiss was one of the first two editors of Peirce's *Collected Papers* (1931–58). Notoriously difficult as Whitehead's philosophy is—Ames and Hall specifically draw on *Process and Reality* (1929)—it opens much more readily when viewed through the various lenses of Daoism, American Transcendentalism, and Peircean semeiotic.

As we began to see in section 3.1, one of the most obvious reflections of Ames and Hall's Emersonian/Peircean/Whiteheadian "Romanticism" is their insistence on translating 道 *dao* not as "the Way" but as "way-making," as an activity or process rather than as a quasideific force. "Experience," they write (77), "is processual, and is thus always provisional. Process requires that the formational and functional aspects of our experience are correlative and mutually entailing." The only reason that 道 *dao* might be indescribable or unnamable is that it's never finished—it's always in process. Any description or name bounds it, gives it a fullness or completeness that is inappropriate to an ongoing process. It would be like writing a biography of a living person: any narrative one might devise for it would impose an arc toward an end that is necessarily invented because premature. Fitting function to formation means building incompletion into functionality, leaving a strategic open-endedness that is receptive to the new, to surprise. In any process there are patterns, trends, and it is always a great temptation to convert those patterns or trends into a single stable essence, and convince oneself that one understands, that one "has" it, has the thing's "number." We feel that temptation because the unknowability of the future is disturbing to us, not least because that unknowability limits our ability to impose a stable meaning on the past. If the past becomes meaningful as a process extending infinitely into the unknowable future, the past must remain a sketch. Clarity must be indefinitely deferred. But, we think, if only we could draw a big white line at the present moment, or a few moments *before* the present moment, if only we could only cordon the past off from the future, we could package the past as a stable thing, an object, and so accurately describe it, name it. That, according to Ames and Hall (77–8), is the temptation against which Laozi warns. They continue:

> Our new thoughts shape how we think and act. And how we are presently disposed to think and act disciplines our novel thoughts. While the fluid immediacy of experience precludes the possibility of exhaustive conceptualization and explanation, enduring formal structures lend the flow of experience a degree of determinacy that can be expressed productively in conceptual language. The relative persistence of formal structures permits us to parse and punctuate the ceaseless flow of experience into consummate yet never really discrete things and events.

We *can* impose order on experience—and that is almost always a useful exercise. "The ceaseless flow of experience" is difficult to manage without such imposed order. The important thing to remember, though, is that the order we impose on experience is not the *truth* of that experience. It's a makeshift, a stopgap, a workaround.

The first thing we note about the Ames and Hall translation is that it is a secularizing application to the *Laozi* of a Western philosophical tradition emerging out of Romanticism, and thus apparently another product of the kind of "immature, self-centered Western mind" that Kirkland says typically distorts the text beyond all recognition. I am certain that Kirkland would condemn Ames and Hall's translation just as vehemently as he did Bynner's: even though Ames is a world-renowned Sinologist, he is confessedly influenced by Western philosophical thought, and he and David Hall impose on the "true" "authentic" Chinese core of the *Laozi* a demystification that makes it not a deeply religious text but a kind of pragmatic self-help book, organized around the development of productive habits.

The second thing we note about it, however, is that this "radical" reading/translation of the text emerges out of very much the same kind of cofigurative enterprise—indeed as a continuation of the *same* cofigurative enterprise—as the Christian and esoteric translations. From Kirkland's perspective that doesn't help at all: for him there is a single right way to read the *Laozi*, based on his construction of a 1,500-year-old religious tradition, and all other ways, including Ames and Hall's, are simply wrong. I have no illusions that he would suddenly find things to praise about the Ames and Hall translation, simply on the basis that it was influenced by Alfred North Whitehead. But he should, I submit, admit that his condemnation of all non-religious American translations and adaptations as shaped *only* by American individualism and secularism is a bit simplistic. The intellectual and ideological currents that shape this and other *Laozi* translations are cofigurative.

What is striking about the Ames and Hall translation is not, I suggest, that it is so powerfully transformative—though it is that—but that it didn't happen sooner. If Emerson and Thoreau were reading the

Daoist classics in the 1840s, and Peirce father and son were preaching a vitalist version of Emersonian thought in the 1880s and 1890s, and Whitehead published *Process and Reality* in 1929, why did it take *Laozi* translators until 2003 to channel that strain of post-Romantic thought into their understanding of the Chinese text?

That is a rhetorical question: the answer, I think, is not difficult to find. Again, the assault launched by Bradbury, Goldin, Kirkland, and others on the proliferation of (section 3.3.2) pop-mystical readings of the *Laozi* is partially on target: reading/translating/adapting the text that way is attractive not only because it feels vaguely rebellious but because it's *easy*. And while the Ames and Hall translation is not as difficult as Whitehead, it is far more difficult than something like this, by Ron Hogan (2002), who has no Chinese:

> If you can talk about it,
> it ain't Tao.
> If it has a name,
> it's just another thing.
> Tao doesn't have a name.
> Names are for ordinary things.
>
> Stop wanting stuff;
> it keeps you from seeing what's real.
> When you want stuff,
> all you see are things.
>
> These two statements
> mean the same thing.
> Figure them out,
> and you've got it made.

By contrast, this is how Ames and Hall (2003: 77) translate the first chapter:

> Way-making (*dao*) that can be put into words is not really way-making,
> And naming (*ming*) that can assign fixed reference to things is not really naming.

> The nameless (*wuming*) is the fetal beginnings of everything that is happening (*wanwu*),
> While that which is named is their mother.
> Thus, to be really objectless in one's desires (*wuyu*) is how one observes the mysteries of all things,
> While really having desires is how one observes their boundaries.
> These two—the nameless and what is named—emerge from the same source yet are referred to differently.
>
> Together they are called obscure.
> The obscurest of the obscure,
> They are the swinging gateway of the manifold mysteries.

While the Romantic impact on *Laozi* translations has not been anywhere near as universally deleterious as Bradbury and Kirkland claim, in other words, if it had been *more* salutary along the lines I have been suggesting, the kind of Emersonian/Peircean/Whiteheadian process thinking that Ames and Hall channel into their translation would have been old hat by now—the accepted way of translating the *Laozi* for say the last six or seven decades—and we would have been looking for ways of getting past that tired old orthodoxy. Instead, it is not only quite recent but a single stand-alone act of resistance to the (3.3.2) pop-mystical orthodoxy.

## 3.4 First Conclusion: Civilizational Spells, Again

Sakai's talk of "civilizational spells," of groups being "haunted" by the reflex to believe things in the face of apparently incontrovertible counterevidence, seems to align him with the Occidentalist camp, perhaps—insofar as we take his use of "magical" or "supernatural" tropes like spells and haunts to reflect an esoteric preference for the world of spirit and mind over the world of material objects. They don't, of course: they're tropes. But does that mean that we exempt Sakai himself from participation in—being "haunted" by—civilizational spells?

The Enlightenment/modern/scientist/universalist camp has no better tropes for this phenomenon, of course, because the civilizational spells that haunt them do not permit them to believe in such things as strange compulsions that defy reason, logic, and scientific method. Their model for ideology is propositional: there is a certain set of propositions that a group of people holds rationally to be true (until they are convinced otherwise). To the extent that this camp's "haunt" permits its members to entertain such notions as strange compulsions, it inclines them toward mechanistic explanations borrowed from the "science" of psychology (Freud's scientizing adaptation of Nietzsche's Occidentalism): there is this or that psychological mechanism that causes people to behave irrationally.

Marxist ideology theory, likewise a radical adaptation of an Occidentalist philosophy—Hegel's—is an awkward attempt to straddle the modernist/anti-modernist divide: with its "modern" atheistic rejection of magical/religious/supernatural explanatory models it gravitates toward materialist/mechanistic explanations, but tends to reject the immaterial mechanisms of psychoanalysis, and has been unable to generate its own mechanistic explanation of people's irrational attachment to "outdated" ideologies (those no longer supported by the current material conditions). Ideology for Marxists tends to be a rather airy propositional (super)structure to which its adherents adhere for mysterious reasons.[9] But because universalist science tends to operate through the mystification of its complicity with global capitalism and technologism, Marxists also tend to coopt the anti-modern/oppositional ideologemes of Occidentalism: witness Lawrence Venuti's three decades in bed with Friedrich Schleiermacher, the bourgeois nationalist theologian who as a German Romantic was occidentalistically conditioned to resist the capitalist "bring the author to the reader" regime of translation (see Robinson 2013b for discussion).

Nietzsche is perhaps the Western post-Romantic Occidentalist *par excellence*, and it is no accident that Heidegger and poststructuralist rereadings of Heideggerian "destruction" as "deconstruction" emerge out of Nietzsche. It is, however, something of a surprise that Harold

Bloom's "conservative" defense of the Western canon, precisely because it is steeped in Nietzsche and Romantic and post-Romantic poetry, is powerfully Occidentalist as well. This might even be the strand of his thought that unifies the apparent contradictions that I tracked in section 2.3: the Strong Poet whose "mastery" he admires is not the idealized Westerner, as he is for the patriotic NAS, but the dark enemy of the West, the outlaw, the terrorist, the Nietzschean superman, Milton's Satan (as read by William Blake). To the extent that Bloom's hero is a primitivist, he is not so much (a) rural or (b) religious or (c) ascetic or (f) organic or (g) nativist as he is an autochthone, a mythical figure born from the soil, rocks, and trees, a powerful animistic creature whose nature is difficult for us woman-born humans to comprehend. Thus while he may be (a) anti-urban, anti-decadence, and generally anti-modernist, he is also the quintessential Romantic; while he is (b) anti-secular, anti-rationalist, anti-theory, and generally anti-intellectual (like early Walter Benjamin, Bloom is strongly drawn to Gnosticism and the Kabbalah), he is also a brilliantly erratic theorist of (his own) literary greatness; while he is (c) no hedonist, his greatest pleasure is in negativity, pain, and brokenness. He is above all (e) a dark hero, and so oriented to honor and death; to the extent that he is anti-bureaucratic, the bureaucracies he seeks to undermine are academic, deans and department chairs and promotion and tenure committees that would bureaucratize genius (for which read "Harold Bloom").

Consider, for example, R. V. Young's (2005: 19–20) attack on him:

> It is a grimly ironic truth that Bloom's own Gnostic Freudian treatment of literature and, above all, of authors, opened the gates to the postmodern assassins of the Party of Resentment, who now conduct their scornful ritual over the "death of the author." Finally, it is precisely his hostility to Christianity and his effort to displace it, spiritually and intellectually, which has resulted in the most grievous damage to the literary tradition that Bloom claims to love. While he gazes unblinkingly at the devastation wrought upon the tradition by the postmodern assault, he is blind to the intimate and indispensable bond between the second "canon" and the Faith informing its

necessary model, the scriptural canon. Western civilization is the cultural embodiment of Christendom: when its cultural heart stops beating, all that is left is a corpse.

If the tonal parallels between Kirkland's attack on American "mystical" translations of the *Laozi* and Bloom's attack on American academia are striking in their Occidentalism, the tonal parallels between both of these Occidentalist Jeremiads and Young's orthodox Christian defense of the Bible and Western civilization against Bloom's attack is even more striking because it is so patently anti-Occidentalist. Young even chimes in with Bloom's castigation of the School of Resentment, which he renames the "Party of Resentment," and adds his own denunciations ("postmodern assassins" and many more); the only difference between Young and Bloom vis-à-vis that Party of Pariahs is that Young lays the blame for their rise at Bloom's feet. Bloom claims to love the Western Canon, but Young believes that one cannot love the Western Canon and hate Christianity, because the two are intimately intertwined. Bloom may be *religious*—oriented to ancient rituals and obedience to "higher powers," and so anti-secular, anti-rationalist, and generally anti-intellectual—but he has backed the wrong religion:

> The Christian begins the path toward salvation in the humble realization of his own culpable estrangement from his loving Creator to whom he must submit absolutely and on whose gracious mercy he depends utterly. The Gnostic finds the beginning of his path to salvation in the realization that the world is a great imposture, a prison of pain and frustration. His escape lies in recovering the intrinsic goodness within himself, the principle of illumination that he shares with other enlightened spirits. "If you are not to be hedged in by God's incomprehensible power," Bloom writes, "then you must dissent from the doctrine of Creation. You must learn to speculate about origins, and the aim of your speculation will have to be a vision of catastrophe, for only a divine catastrophe will allow for your own, your human freedom." *Your own, your human freedom*—not "the liberty of the glory of the children of God" (Romans 8.21). (Young 21)

Bloom is wrong to reject Christianity, not just because it is the one *true* (icotic) religion, but because it's the one *good* (ecotic) religion—and above all because it is the spiritual bone marrow of Western civilization. By undermining Christianity Bloom undermines not only the Western Canon but Western civilization—and has taught the next generation of humanities professors to do the same, with the result that "postmodern assassins" are set loose in our universities to destroy the West. And of course, as I'm sure Young knew, the original "assassins" or Fidai were what we would now call "Muslim terrorists" (an association made explicit by Lewis 1967), a radical sect of Nizari Ismaili mystics that used assassination for military ends. "Postmodern assassins" is an almost-explicit Orientalist slur.

From this angle, the clash looks like a religious war: the American translators of the *Laozi* think they are promoting a religion of surrender to large cosmic forces, but according to Kirkland they are promoting only Western individualism; Bloom thinks he is promoting a religion of transformative catastrophe, but according to Young he is promoting an anti-Christian and therefore anti-Western individualism. According to the American translators of the *Laozi* as attacked by Kirkland,

1. there is no God: [there is] only an impersonal reality called "Tao," and it doesn't have a will that I have to respect above my own personal desires;
2. there is no true moral authority outside of myself: anyone who says otherwise is trying to oppress me;
3. "Truth" is whatever I say it is.

According to Bloom as attacked by Young, what is important is "*Your own, your human freedom*—not 'the liberty of the glory of the children of God.'" The problem for both Kirkland and Young is individualism, the impulse to resist God, to treat God's Will as optional, to invest all decision-making power in the human individual rather than in omnipotent God, Who only wants the best for us. For Kirkland, that God is Daoist and therefore Chinese and Asian and therefore infinitely valuable; for Young that God is Christian and therefore Western and therefore infinitely valuable. For Kirkland, failure to surrender to that God is a Protestant/Romantic/Western rejection of the East; for Young failure to surrender to that God is an esoteric/Romantic/heretical rejection of the West. As Buruma and Margalit insist, Western Occidentalists tend to be zealous conservatives; but Kirkland is a conservative whose zeal is for religious Daoism, Young a conservative whose zeal is for Christianity, and Bloom a conservative whose zeal is for Jewish mysticism—and each would denounce the other two as horribly and perversely wrong.

## 3.5 Second Conclusion: Eurocentrism, Decentered

Where does all this leave us? At the very least, and perhaps also at most, caught in the middle. That middleness is the salutary burden of Sakai's notion of cofiguration. But note that that middle is radically decentered: not itself a center but a strandedness between putative centers. We recall Schleiermacher's (1813/2002: 87: 25–35) admonition against the phenomenological disorientations brought on by being stranded in this kind of middle, which he associated with cosmopolitanism:

> Denn so wahr das auch bleibt in mancher Hinsicht, daß erst durch das Verständniß mehrerer Sprachen der Mensch in gewissem Sinne gebildet wird, und ein Weltbürger: so müssen wir doch gestehen, so wie wir die Weltbürgerschaft nicht für die ächte halten, die in wichtigen Momenten die Vaterlandsliebe unterdrückt, so ist auch in Bezug auf die Sprachen eine solche allgemeine Liebe nicht die rechte und wahrhaft bildende, welche für den lebendigen und höheren Gebrauch irgend eine Sprache, gleichviel ob alte oder neue, der vaterländischen gleich stellen will. Wie Einem Lande, so auch Einer Sprache oder der andern, muß der Mensch sich entschließen anzugehören, oder er schwebt haltungslos in unerfreulicher Mitte.

> For true as it remains in many ways that one cannot be considered educated and cosmopolitan without a knowledge of several languages, we must also admit that cosmopolitanism does not seem authentic to

us if at critical moments it suppresses patriotism; and the same thing is true of languages. That highly generalized love of language that cares little what language (the native one or some other, old or new) is used for a variety is not the best kind of love for improving the mind or the culture. One Country, One Language—or else another: a person has to make up his mind to belong somewhere, or else hang disoriented in the unpleasant middle. (Robinson 1997/2002b: 235)

*Unerfreulich* "unpleasant" as that middle undoubtedly is for some, especially (g) nativist Occidentalists like Schleiermacher, it tends to be the intercultural and periperformative realm inhabited by translators and interpreters, and, writ large, in histories of intercivilizational engagement, by all those involved in cofigurative regimes of translation.

Do these reflections have any practical consequences for translators? Perhaps, but only if they are interested in understanding what they do, and why, and for whom—which is to say, only if they are interested in theory. What Sakai calls "*the* regime of translation," to the extent that it is involved in normalizing and naturalizing hegemonic (homolingual) assumptions about national languages and the bridges between them, would appear to be anti-theory, in the sense of discouraging the kind of self-reflexivity that might lead a translator to challenge (or even just consider) the purpose of a given translation job. "Don't think about the political or other agendas this translation is intended to serve; just strive for abstract semantic equivalence." Abstract semantic equivalence is safely universalist. It will offend no one. It is eagerly complicit in the mystification of all political and other agendas.

To be sure, this normative scenario for translation also yields a complex and delicate playground for the theoretically and politically sensitive translator who is inclined to tweak the norms just a little, to highlight the political implications of a given translation job ever so slightly, with the most subtly nuanced shadings of explicitation: subtle enough to be plausibly deniable, but explicit enough to generate a strategic level of unease in target readers.

The practical consequences for translation theorists are more pressing. That cofigurative strandedness in the middle, after all, tends to militate against facile accusations of Eurocentrism (or for that matter Sinocentrism), because the centers are not so much centers as they are nodes in a multibranching relationship. Not only is the cofigurative legacy of Orientalism not Eurocentric (it is at most Europhilic); it is also divided, inspiring and conditioning as it has done a cofigurative Occidentalist countertradition that is actively Europhobic. Whether this middleness would console that Chinese colleague of mine in Hong Kong, who came to me angry at being accused by a reviewer of Eurocentrism, I don't know; the model I've been developing here would still seem to suggest that you have to choose sides, and my guess is that he wouldn't be happy choosing either side. Nor is it likely to placate Andrew Chesterman, whose Popperian universalism seems implacable.

But it does serve to cast a rather negative light on the dogmatic narrowness and explanatory impotence of that universalism. The more practical and theoretical complexity that one must suppress in order to sustain the illusion that one's conceptual net is universal, the more obvious it becomes that one is engaged in mystifying a local interested agenda as a one-size-fits-all truth-and-method, and so seeking to whitewash the worst kind of circularity. To say that "All scientific endeavour is intrinsically universalist," after all, is to believe and imply that "All universalizations of Western science are intrinsically Western and intrinsically scientific, and therefore intrinsically universal(izing)." To my mind, whatever we can do to expose, demystify, and so ultimately undo that kind of circularity is to the good, and bids fair, to paraphrase Chesterman, to (1f) "advance" translation studies.

## 3.6 Third Conclusion: An Intercivilizational Turn?

We might want to say that what I'm calling an Intercivilizational Turn in TS is actually an offshoot—or perhaps even the main branch—of postcolonial translation theory. Throughout the 1990s postcolonial studies of translation were thought of as part of the Cultural Turn, but by the turn of the millennium they had moved past the study of specific colonial and postcolonial translation histories to the study of relations between larger civilizational entities, "Europe" and "Asia," or "the West" and "the East." One might even be inclined to describe the work of Sakai Naoki and others as a postcolonial theorizing of translation that has "outgrown" talk of postcoloniality: the power differentials in which the large intercivilizational (Sakai says "macro-spatial") encounters remain steeped increasingly seem *constitutive* of the specific histories of empire.

But of course in an important sense any study of colonial regimes of translation, or of any given decolonizing project when channeled through translation, always necessarily entails and enfolds broader intercivilizational perspectives. The colonial enterprise brings to the cross-cultural encounter not just two different languages and cultures but a proliferation of languages and cultures that tend to be not only hybridized[10] but also hierarchized, so that it matters whether a given linguistic or cultural impulse comes from the aggregate source of colonial power or the aggregate target of colonial power. The colonial powers might contend among themselves for hegemony in a given region, but without losing sight of the aggregate status difference between the contending colonizers and the "natives"; and the colonized might vie for status differentiation among colonized cultures, but without losing sight of the "inherent" "superiority" of the colonizer cultures. These "civilizational spells" continue to haunt us, even as we deconstruct them—even when, intellectually, we no longer believe in them.

And certainly the early postcolonial studies of translation exceeded the established disciplinary purview of TS. Not only were they not about textual equivalence; they weren't even about translation from a single source language into a single target language. Rafael (1988/93), for example, was a study not just of Spanish>Tagalog translation, but of the colonization of the Philippines (and all of its languages) for a European Christ who happened in this one instance to speak Castilian. Cheyfitz (1990) was a study not of translation from English into a single

Native American language (or back) but of the circulation of translational impulses and texts through the British and French colonial encounter in the New World. Niranjana (1992) took as her primary examples retranslations from Kannada to English, but her purview was the broad scene of post-independence Indian decolonization.

And arguably the first work of postcolonial translation theory, Asad (1986), was a signal intervention not only into British social anthropologists' work, but into the broad intercivilizational tensions and negotiations that inform(ed) the assumptions brought to that work in the field. Two key notions introduced by Asad that have proved resonant for what (I'm arguing) became the Intercivilizational Turn were the *power differentials* at work in translation, an orientation that was picked up among others by Jacquemond (1992), whose primary examples were taken from Egypt and France, strong representatives of Islamic/Middle-Eastern/North-African and Christian/European/Western civilizations; and the concept of *cultural translation*, the process "not of translating specific cultural texts but of consolidating a wide variety of cultural discourses into a target text that in some sense has no 'original', no source text" (Robinson 1997: 43).

While TS tends to continue to be focused on the accuracy of specific translations or translation histories from a single source language to a single target language—a focus that according to Sakai is *structured* by the "regime of translation"—it often seems as if translation scholars have to fight the temptation to expand their purview to larger intercivilizational encounters. A study of translations between Chinese and English, for example, could be thought of narrowly as a textual exchange between a single source culture and a single target culture; but so powerfully formative has Chinese been for Asia, and so representative these days is English for/of/in the West, that even a narrowly textual focus on that "language pair" would tend to adumbrate broad-based intercivilizational research. As my brief foray into the history of *Laozi* translations into English in section 3.3 suggests, an adequate exfoliation of that project would unavoidably have as its historical and cultural background translations of the *Laozi* into Latin, French, and German as well, and the various Christian missions into China beginning in the late sixteenth century, and the intellectual history of (borrowings from translations of Asian thought in) esotericism, Idealism, Romanticism, pragmatism, and phenomenology in the West (see Robinson 2015a: 77–82 and 2016a for discussion). Similarly, a study of translations from English into Chinese would push us inexorably toward intercivilizational research: a study of Shakespeare translations in China, say, would inevitably invoke as cultural background the various histories of Shakespeare translations and productions in other Asian countries and in other European countries as well, and the cultural tensions in both civilizational regions between conservatives/classicists/formalists and radicals/Romantics/experimentalists (whatever forms and names the two groups assume in the various culturally situated historical trajectories).

It is also striking that so much of this work—not just the research into postcolonial translation, and not just CTS—is going on outside the TS fold. Mary Louise Pratt (2002: 25), for example, promises to "illuminate the scene [of cultural translation in colonial Peru] through the work of two eminent thinkers about translation, Eliot Weinberger and Clifford Geertz"—leaving us dyed-in-the-wool TS scholars scratching our heads. Geertz is an anthropologist best known for his term "thick description" (1973); but for an application of that term to translation we turn to Appiah (1993), another voice from outside TS (a cultural theorist working in philosophy departments).[11] Geertz is undeniably an eminent thinker, and he has a single article (1983) with "translation" in the title; does that make him an "eminent thinker about translation"? Possibly; but who in the world is Eliot Weinberger? He turns out to be the English translator of Octavio Paz, apparently well known (and therefore "eminent") to Hispanists like Pratt; and he seems to have given a talk on translation at the Cultural Center, International Development Bank, in November, 2000. Does that make him an "eminent thinker about translation"? The offense we TS scholars take here—*we* are the eminent thinkers about translation!—reflects the dark side of the disciplinization of TS, precisely that which—because TS lacks a single unified methodology and theoretical framework—many have claimed is lamentably *lacking*.

And it is perhaps that very disciplinary myopia that causes us to flutter these days like nervous moths around the dangerous flames of "Eurocentrism" and "Orientalism," aware that these large (inter)civilizational trends have a significant impact on the thinking we do about translation, but feeling that we lack the theoretical and methodological tools (and perhaps the disciplinary authorities) to approach those flames with the requisite protection. I suggest that we do not currently know what we mean when we call a whole field like TS "Eurocentric"—certainly the surprisingly random guesses made by such a well-placed TS scholar as Andrew Chesterman as to the case his "relativist" opponents are trying to make would seem to confirm this. And while I am emphatically not suggesting that TS studies of translations from a single source language into a single target language are retrograde or in any way unnecessary, I do submit that there is this larger historical and cultural context that in many ways overshadows our current concerns, and that we would therefore do well to open our gates to those CTS scholars who are already brilliantly engaged in the study of such things.

# Notes

## Preface

1 I'm alluding here to Bakhtin (1929/2002: 117–18; Emerson 1984: 199), of course, who distinguishes among [1] "Прямое, непосредственно направленное на свой предмет слово, как выражение последней смысловой инстанции говорящего"/"direct, unmediated discourse directed exclusively toward its referential object, as an expression of the speaker's ultimate semantic authority" (199: the apparently single-voiced speech of a character), [2] "объектное слово"/"objectified discourse" (the speech of a character who is intended to sound like (1)), and [3] "двуголосое слово"/"double-voiced discourse," which Bakhtin analyzes into three subcategories ([a] "однонаправленное двуголосое слово"/"unidirectional [passive] double-voiced discourse," [b] "разнонаправленное двуголосое слово"/"varidirectional [passive] double-voiced discourse," and [c] "активный тип"/"the active type). See also Robinson (2003: 112–13) for a revised tabulation of these categories, flipping Bakhtin's on its head, so that the first type is *overt multiple voicing* (Bakhtin's [3c] "active" type), the second is *overt multiple voicing with a hierarchy imposed* (Bakhtin's [3ab] "passive" type), and the third is *covert multiple voicing with a hierarchy imposed*, in which "the speaker gives the impression of speaking with only a single voice, either his or her own or someone else's" (Bakhtin's [1] "direct unmediated" and [2] "objectified" types). I'm suggesting that Chesterman's reporting of his opponents' views falls into *covert multiple voicing with a hierarchy imposed*, with Chesterman attempting to "give[] the impression of speaking with only a single voice," namely someone else's, but actually double-voicing it along the lines of the "varidirectional passive" type, in which the objectified discourse is subtly shaded with the tonalities of disagreement.

## Chapter 1: Sakai Naoki on Translation

1   The TS scholars Liu (1995) cited were ten: Andrey Fyodorov (1953), Roman Jakobson (1959), Achilles Fang (1959), Georges Mounin (1963), J. C. Catford (1965), George Steiner (1975), Anton Popovič (1976), Antoine Berman (1984; Heyvaert 1992), Douglas Robinson (1991), Willis Barnstone (1993), and Eugene Eoyang (1993). In addition, she cited the pioneers of postcolonial translation theory, who do not typically consider themselves TS scholars: Talal Asad (1986—not in her "Selected Bibliography"), Vicente Rafael (1988), Eric Cheyfitz (1990), and Tejaswini Niranjana (1992)—an anthropologist, a historian, and two Americanists. And she cited work by four philosophers whose thinking about translation has proved extraordinarily influential for TS: Walter Benjamin (1923/72; Zohn 1968/82), Martin Heidegger (1950/86; Hofstadter 1971), Hans-Georg Gadamer (1960/2010; Weinsheimer and Marshall 1975/89), and Jacques Derrida (1985). Barbara Johnson (1985) was cited as well, from the same collection (Graham 1985) in which Derrida's "Des Tours de Babel" appeared; Johnson's ruminations on "Taking Fidelity Philosophically" don't generally inspire much comment from TS scholars.

## Chapter 2: The Casting of Civilizational Spells: Nietzsche as Precursor, Bloom as Ephebe

1   For a reading of this moment in Nietzsche in terms of colonizing counterregulation, see Robinson (2013a: §2.1).
2   Butler's reading of the paradoxes in Foucault's theory of discipline does not exercise me much—probably because, like the essentializing (side of) Foucault that Butler constructs, I am quite happy to assume "that the 'constructed' or 'inscribed' body [has] an ontological status apart from that inscription." I am too much a philosophical pragmatist to worry overmuch about the exact ontological definition of construction or inscription—to enter into the minute wrangling over the precise sense in which a body can be said to have any material form at all

apart from (or prior to) its cultural materialization, or what ontological status we should assign to the cultural force that *does* the materializing. My pragmatic answer to "what disciplines(/constructs/inscribes) us" involves the iterosomatic circulation of discipline in and out of bodies.

3   And of course more than one commentator has wanted to put Walt Disney in the Hitler camp, especially after Leni Riefenstahl reported that Disney was the only Hollywood producer willing to invite her to L.A. to promote her documentary *Olympia* (1938) one month after Kristallnacht.

4   I put scare quotes around "Saussurean" in order to distinguish the structuralist linguistics created by Saussure's Ph.D. students after his death from his actual notes (2002; Sanders et al. 2006), which actually, as I show in Robinson (2015a: Ch. 5), offer a theorization of language that is far more congruent with the model I develop here.

5   This somatic desomatization of the body, progressively iterated in Western culture at least since Descartes, has been the subject of increasingly intense philosophical scrutiny since the 1980s. See Barker (1984), Bordo (1987, 1993), Leder (1990), Ross (1998), Božovič (2000), Fiumara (2001), and the articles collected in Welton (1998). Much of this work rests on the philosophical rethinkings of Heidegger, Merleau-Ponty, Mauss, Freud, Todes, and other phenomenologists indebted to the idealized rethinking of the body in Husserl.

6   Here is Shklovsky's original: "Но самый обычный прием у Толстого, это когда он отказывается узнавать вещи и описывает их, как в первый раз виденния ..." (1923: 118).

## Chapter 3: East and West: Toward an Intercivilizational Turn

1   Emerson and Thoreau read Daoist classics in Guillaume Pauthier's French translations and Ruist classics in Joshua Marshman's 1809 translation *The Works of Confucius* and David Collie's 1828 translation in *The Chinese Classical Work Commonly Called the Four Books* (both of which Emerson had in his library and Thoreau found there upon first staying in the house in 1841). Inspired by these works, Emerson published a selection

(translated by Thoreau from Pauthier's French) of "Sayings of Confucius" in the 1843 *Dial*, and Thoreau quoted extensively from Mengzi in *Walden* (for this history see Christy (1963); Cheng [2000: 219n1]).

2   Kirkland tends to refer to adapters—poets or other writers who create "translations" of the 《老子》 *Laozi* with no knowledge of Chinese, by adapting other translations—as "pseudotranslators." Translation scholars reserve that term for producers of texts that have no source text, like James MacPherson's Ossian poems.

3   Kirkland tends to tar Confucianism with the same "Westernizing" and "secularizing" brush as what I've called the "omnibus Protestant/Enlightenment/Romantic nexus of easy secular individualism" that is the broad target of his attacks—but I'm told that there are voices increasingly being raised in China claiming that 儒道 *rudao* "Ruism" or "the Confucian Way" has always had a "higher power" as well, that Confucius thought of 天 *tian* "heaven" as a personalized spirit being, and that every Confucian thinker since has believed in exactly the same being as well. It may be too soon to identify these voices as a "movement"—they still sound too sporadic to constitute a significant groundswell—but it does seem as if several key claims in the scholarly consensus on Chinese religion-and-philosophy are under concerted assault.

4   Fourfold Biblical hermeneutics was developed as a strategy for dealing with the semantic complexity of the Bible as a text written over a 1,500-year period in dozens of different genres, for dozens of different audiences and different purposes. Theoretically any given passage in the Bible could be read on four different levels:

1. the historical (what actually happened)
2. the allegorical (the meaning of what happened in terms of systematic theology)
3. the moral (the implications of what happened for the ethical choices each individual must make in life)
4. the anagogic (the ways in which what happened, or how the story was told, alluded to "the mysteries of Jesus Christ," deep secret metaphysical and eschatological knowledge)

Thus the Song of Solomon might be read (1) at the historical level to refer to the writer/speaker's lust for a woman, (2) at the allegorical level as a symbolic account of Christ's love for the Church, (3) morally as encouragement to fidelity in marriage, and (4) anagogically as, well—who knows?

Obviously one of the great advantages of this sort of approach to a text for systematic theologians was (and continues to be, though less explicitly these days) that it was always possible to skip a level as not really "relevant" to the passage. In the Song of Solomon, for example, one could argue that (1) the sexy love poem had no significance at all, and could be ignored, suppressed—mainly, though one didn't need to spell this out, because the whole book is really too sexy to belong in a sacred text that tends to discourage this kind of sexual passion—and that (2) the story of Christ's love for his Church was the *true intended* meaning of the text.

For the Jesuit missionaries reading and translating ancient Chinese philosophical texts, this hermeneutic yielded a rather different advantage: even though it was a bit of a stretch to argue that the *authors* of those texts intended for them to be read on all these different levels as Christian theology, one could claim that *God* had inserted signs and signals into the texts to lead non-Chinese interpreters to their true Christian significance. It was, of course, usually easy enough to construct a (3) moral interpretation of a passage. And the Figurist approach applied by Bouvet and others, as studied by Collani (1981, 1985, 2012), applied the anagogic method to find traces of what Collani et al. (2008) call an *Uroffenbarung* or "Ur-Revelation."

5   See the Dedication to Alexander (1890):

> To those able and patriotic Statesmen, who are endeavouring to give new strength to the mighty Empire, founded and preserved by the wisdom of their forefathers, by infusing into it all that is most applicable belonging to the progress of the West; this attempt to draw more closely together two great peoples, who possess so many interests in common, is inscribed with every sentiment of sympathy and respect, by
> 
> THE AUTHOR

6   For example, he quotes the Lutheran Sinologist Victor von Strauß und Torney (1809–99) on his 1870 German translation of the 《老子》 *Laozi*:

> Wir meinen, jeder Unbefangenen, den man fragte, wie man in unserer Sprache das Wesen bezeichne, vom dem diess [*sic*] Alles ausgesagt werden könne, musste antworten: Gott, und nur Gott! Und wer die vorstehenden Aussagen zusammen fasst, dem kann gar kein Zweifel bleiben, dass L ein überraschend grosses und tiefes Gottbewusstseyn, einen erhabenen und sehr bestimmten Gottesbegriff gehabt habe, der sich fast durchgängig mit dem Gottesbegriff der Offenbarung deckt, sofern dieser nicht über ihn hinaus tiefer und reicher entwickelt ist was dem allerdings keiner Nachweisung bedarf. Aber ausserhalb Israels wird aus allen vorchristlichen Jahrhunderten nichts Aehnliches nachzuweisen seyn. (quoted in Alexander 1895: xv-n; the full text in German is available online at http://archive.org/stream/pts_latsstatek_3720-0690/pts_latsstatek_3720-0690_djvu.txt)

> We believe that any impartial person who might be asked, what word in our language would best apply to the Being of whom all this can be said, would be compelled to answer, 'by the word God, and by none other!' And how can anyone with a knowledge of the foregoing evidence have the slightest doubt of Lâo-tze having possessed, in a remarkable degree, a great and deep consciousness of God of so sublime and precise a nature, that it almost realizes the idea of God belonging to Revelation, though it is needless to remark that the latter greatly surpasses it in the profundity and fullness of its manifestations. But in all the centuries preceding the Christian era, no similar revelation was made beyond the one made to Israel. (Translated and quoted by Alexander 1895: xiv)

Alexander (xv–xvi) also notes that the Rev. John Chalmers (1825–99), though he too turns 道 *dao* into the loanword "Tâo," nevertheless adds: "I would translate it by 'the Word' in the sense of 'the Logos,' but this would be like settling the question which I wish to leave open, viz.:— what amount of resemblance there is between the Logos of the New Testament and this Tâo, which is its nearest representative in Chinese?

In our version of the New Testament in Chinese we have in the first chapter of St. John—'In the beginning was Tâo,' &c." Chalmers of course worked with his fellow Scottish Congregationalist James Legge (1815–99) on various translations from the Chinese classics, and like Legge was pastor of the Union Church in Hong Kong.

7   Originally written in French, *La Monadologie* was first published posthumously in German and Latin translation, and translated from Latin back into French by Diderot (1713–1784) for his *Encyclopedia* a half century later (1751–1772); it was not published in its original French form until 1840.

8   One prominent exception might be this radically literal (Hörderlinian) rendition by the prominent Russian-American Sinologist Peter A. Boodberg (1957) (Pyotr Alekseevich Budberg, 1903–72, who taught Chinese at UC Berkeley for four decades, beginning in 1932), prefaced by Boodberg's note:

> The following translation of the entire text has little literary merit. It reflects, however, to the best of my ability, every significant etymological and grammatical feature, including every double entendre, that I have been able to discover in the original in an endeavor to establish a solider philological foundation upon which a firmer interpretation of the _incipit_ of Taoist philosophy might be built.

> Lodehead lodehead-brooking : no forewonted lodehead;
> Namecall namecall-brooking : no forewonted namecall.
>    Having-naught namecalling : Heaven-Earth's fetation,
>    Having-aught namecalling : Myriad Mottlings' mother.
> Affirmably,
> Forewont
> Have-naught
> Desired—for to descry in view the minikin-subliminaria,
> Forewont
> Have-aught
> Desired—for to descry in view the circuit-luminaria;
>    These pairing ones at-one
>      Egressing,

> Diverse namecall :
> At-one—bespeak such : Darkling,
> Adarkling such, again adarkling
> The thronging subliminaria's gate.

What's interesting about this is that it is almost impossible to *read*—it must instead be *studied*, and preferably studied stereoscopically, tracking etymologies in both English and Chinese. This kind of virtual unreadability constitutes but a slight displacement of the mystical injunction "don't translate" (see Robinson 1996: 78–9).

9   This is a bit of an oversimplification: I mean that people adhere to *outdated* ideologies for mysterious reasons. When a group's ideological loyalties are in line with material conditions—especially ownership of the means of production—the causal sequence from base to superstructure is clear and unambiguous. But even in that ideal scenario Marxist ideology theorists are unable to explain how or why people adhere so tenaciously to an ideology—how it is possible, for example, for a person to adhere to a propositional belief fervently enough that destruction of that belief can be severely traumatizing.

10  That hybridization would include the borrowing of terms from, say, colonized India into other British colonies, like "amah" and "shroff," or into English usage in the U. K., like "kebab" and "pundit"; or borrowings from Hong Kong Cantonese into standard colloquial English, including humorous literal translations like "long time no see" (from 好久不見 *hou gau bat gin*) and "no can do" (from 不可以 *bat ho ji*), or calques like "chop chop!" (from 速速 *cuk cuk*) and "gung-ho" (from 工合 *gun hap*).

11  Note that several of these "extra-TS" texts have been assimilated into TS through anthologization—Asad (1986) and Pratt (2002) in Baker (2009: 2.223–47 and 2.3–14), Spivak (1993) and Appiah (1993) in Venuti (2000/12: 312–43)—but tend to remain outliers in the field, somehow mentally "marked" by TS scholars as speaking from outside the door. Eric Cheyfitz and Tejaswini Niranjana have told me that, though they haven't published on translation since the early 1990s, they still get invited to give guest lectures on translation—often, they say, because the inviter read about them in Robinson (1997b).

# References

Alexander, G. G. 1890. *Confucius: The Great Teacher*. London: Kegan Paul, Trench, Trübner.

Alexander, G. G., trans. 1895. *Lao Tsze: The Great Thinker With a Translation of His Thoughts on the Nature and Manifestation of God*. London: Kegan Paul, Trench, Trübner.

Ames, Roger T., and David L. Hall, eds. and trans. 2003. *Daodejing: "Making Life Significant"; A Philosophical Translation*. New York: Ballantine.

Appiah, Kwame Anthony. 1993. "Thick Translation." *Callaloo* 16.4: 808–19.

Asad, Talal. 1986. "The Concept of Cultural Translation in British Social Anthropology." In James Clifford and George E. Marcus, eds., *Writing Culture: The Poetics and Politics of Ethnography*, 141–64. Berkeley and Los Angeles: University of California Press.

Baker, Mona. 2006. *Translation and Conflict: A Narrative Account*. London and New York: Routledge.

Baker, Mona, ed. 2009. *Translation Studies*. 4 vols. London and New York: Routledge.

Bakhtin, Mikhail. 1934-5/75. *Slovo v romane* ("Word in the Novel"). In *Voprosy literatury i estetiki* ("Questions of Literature and Aesthetics"), 72–233. Moscow: Khudozhestvennaya Literatura.

Bakhtin, Mikhail Mikhaylovich. 1929/2002. *Problemy poetiki Dostoevskogo* ("Problems of Dostoevsky's Poetics"). Moscow: Yazyki Slavyanskoy kul'tury.

Barker, Francis. 1984. *The Tremulous Private Body: Essays on Subjection*. Ann Arbor: University of Michigan Press.

Barnstone, Willis. 1993. *The Poetics of Translation: History, Theory, Practice*. New Haven: Yale University Press.

Bassnett, Susan, and Harish Trivedi, eds. 1999. *Post-colonial Translation: Theory and Practice*. London and New York: Routledge.

Baumlin, James S. 2000. "Reading Bloom (Or: Lessons concerning the 'Reformation' of the Western Literary Canon)." *College Literature* 27.3 (Fall): 22–46.

Benjamin, Walter. 1923/72. "Die Aufgabe des Übersetzers." In Tillman

Rexroth, ed., *Kleine Prosa, Baudelaire-Übertragungen*, 9–21. Vol. 4, Part 1 of Walter Benjamin, *Gesammelte Schriften* ("Collected Writings"). Frankfurt am Main: Suhrkamp.

Bennington, Geoffrey, and Rachel Bowlby, trans. 1989. Jacques Derrida, *Of Spirit: Heidegger and the Question*. Chicago: University of Chicago Press.

Bergson, Henri. 1889. *Essai sur les données immédiates de la conscience* ("Essay on the Immediate Givens of Consciousness"). Paris: Alcan.

Berman, Antoine. 1984. *L'Épreuve de l'étranger: Culture et traduction dans l'Allemagne romantique* ("The Experience of the Foreigner: Culture and Translation in Romantic Germany"). Paris: Gallimard.

Bloom, Harold. 1973. *The Anxiety of Influence: A Theory of Poetry*. New York: Oxford University Press.

Bloom, Harold. 1975. *A Map of Misreading*. New York: Oxford University Press.

Bloom, Harold. 1994. *The Western Canon: The Books and School of the Ages*. New York: Harcourt Brace.

Boodberg, Peter A. 1957. "Philological Notes on Chapter One of The *Lao Tzu.*" *Harvard Journal of Asiatic Studies* 20.3/4: 598–618. Excerpted online at http://www.aiai.ed.ac.uk/~jeff/random-text/boodberg. Accessed January 20, 2015.

Bordo, Susan. 1987. *The Flight to Objectivity: Essays on Cartesianism and Culture*. Albany: SUNY Press.

Bordo, Susan. 1993. *Unbearable Weight: Feminism, Western Culture, and the Body*. Berkeley and Los Angeles: University of California Press.

Bouchard, Donald F., and Sherry Simon, trans. 1977. "Nietzsche, Genealogy, History." Translation of Foucault 1971. In Bouchard, ed., *Michel Foucault, Language, Counter-Memory, Practice: Selected Essays and Interviews*, 139–64. Ithaca: Cornell University Press.

Božovič, Miran. 2000. *An Utterly Dark Spot: Gaze and Body in Early Modern Philosophy*. Ann Arbor: University of Michigan Press.

Bradbury, Steve. 1992. "The American Conquest of Philosophical Taoism." In Cornelia N. Moore and Lucy Lower, eds., *Translation East and West: A Cross-Cultural Approach*, 29–41. Honolulu: University of Hawai'i College of Languages, Linguistics and Literature and the East-West Center.

Brent, Joseph. 1993. *Charles Sanders Peirce: A Life*. Bloomington: Indiana University Press.

Brower, Reuben A., ed. 1959. *On Translation*. New York: Oxford University Press.

Buruma, Ian, and Avishai Margalit. 2005. *Occidentalism: The West in the Eyes of its Enemies*. Harmondsworth: Penguin.

Butler, Judith. 1989. "Foucault and the Paradox of Bodily Inscriptions." *Journal of Philosophy* 86.11 (November): 601–7.
Butler, Judith. 1990/99. *Gender Trouble: Feminism and the Subversion of Identity*. Reprint. London and New York: Routledge.
Butler, Judith. 1991. "Imitation and Gender Insubordination." In Diana Fuss, ed., *Inside/Out: Lesbian Theories, Gay Theories*, 13–31. London and New York: Routledge.
Bynner, Witter. 1944. "The Tao Te Ching by Lao Tzu: The Witter Bynner version." Online at http://terebess.hu/english/tao/bynner.html. Accessed April 9, 2015.
Catford, J. C. 1965. *A Linguistic Theory of Translation: An Essay in Applied Linguistics*. London: Oxford University Press.
Cheng Aimin (程爱民). 2000. "Humanity as 'A Part and Parcel of Nature': A Comparative Study of Thoreau's and Taoist Concepts of Nature." In Richard J. Schneider and Lawrence Buell, eds., *Thoreau's Sense of Place: Essays in American Environmental Writing*, 207–20. Iowa City: University of Iowa Press.
Chesterman, Andrew. 2014. "Translation Studies Forum: Universalism in Translation Studies." *Translation Studies* 7.1: 82–90.
Cheyfitz, Eric. 1991. *The Poetics of Imperialism: Translation and Colonization from The Tempest to Tarzan*. New York: Oxford University Press.
Christiansen, Broder. 1909. *Die Philosophie der Kunst* ("The Philosophy of Art"). Hanau: Clauss und Fedderson.
Christy, Arthur. 1963. *The Orient in American Transcendentalism: A Study of Emerson, Thoreau, and Alcott*. London: Octagon.
Collani, Claudia von. 1981. *Die Figuristen in der Chinamission* ("The Figurists in the China Mission"). Frankfurt am Main, Bern: Peter Lang.
Collani, Claudia von. 1985. *P. Joachim Bouvet S.J. Sein Leben und sein Werk* ("P. Joachim Bouvet, S.J.: His Life and His Work"). Nettetal: Sankt Augustin.
Collani, Claudia von. 2012. *Von Jesuiten, Kaisern und Kanonen. China und Europa – eine wechselvolle Geschichte* ("Of Jesuits, Emperors, and Canons: China and Europe, an Eventful History"). Darmstadt: Wissenschaftliche Buchgesellschaft.
Collani, Claudia von, Harald Holz, Konrad Wegmann, eds. and trans. 2008. *Uroffenbarung und Daoismus. Jesuitische Missionshermeneutik des Daoismus* ("Ur-Revelation and Daoism: The Jesuit Mission Hermeneutics of Daoism"). Bochum: European University Press.

Collie, David, trans. 1828. Mencius, "The Shang Mung and the Hea Mung." In *The Chinese Classical Work Commonly Called the Four Books*, 171–352. Malacca, Malaysia: Mission Press.

Connor, Peter, trans. 1991. Jean-Luc Nancy, "The Inoperative Community." Translation of Nancy 1986/2004. In Peter Connor, ed., Nancy, *The Inoperative Community*, 1–42. Minneapolis and London: University of Minneapolis Press.

Crowley, Aleister. 1918. "The Tao Te Ching, by Lao Tzu." Online at http://terebess.hu/english/tao/crowley.html. Accessed September 16, 2014.

Damasio, Antonio R. 1994. *Descartes' Error: Emotion, Reason, and the Human Brain*. New York: Putnam.

Denzin, Norman K., and Yvonna S. Lincoln, eds. 2011. *The SAGE Handbook of Qualitative Research*. 4th edition. Thousand Oaks, CA: Sage.

Derrida, Jacques. 1985. "Des Tours de Babel." In Graham 1985: 165–207 (in English, translated by Graham) and 209–48 (in French).

Derrida, Jacques. 1987. *De l'esprit: Heidegger et la question* ("On the Spirit: Heidegger and the Question"). Paris: Galilée.

Diethe, Carol, trans. 1994/2006. Friedrich Nietzsche, *On the Genealogy of Morals: A Polemic*. Translation of Nietzsche 1887/92. In Keith Ansell Pearson and Duncan Large, eds., *The Nietzsche Reader*, 390–435. Oxford: Blackwell.

Emerson, Caryl, ed. and trans. 1984. Mikhail Bakhtin, *Problems of Dostoevsky's Poetics*. Translation of Bakhtin 1929/2002. Minneapolis: University of Minnesota Press.

Emerson, Caryl, and Michael Holquist, trans. 1981. Mikhail Bakhtin, *Discourse in the Novel*. Translation of Bakhtin 1934–35/75. In Michael Holquist, ed. *The Dialogic Imagination: Four Essays*, 259–422. Austin: University of Texas Press.

Eoyang, Eugene. 1993. *The Transparent Eye: Reflections on Translation, Chinese Literature, and Comparative Poetics*. Honolulu: University of Hawai'i Press.

Erlich, Victor, trans. 1975. "Parallels in Tolstoy." Translation of Shklovsky 1919/23. In Erlich, ed., *Twentieth-Century Russian Literary Criticism*, 81–5. New Haven and London: Yale University Press.

Fang, Achilles. 1959. "Some Reflection on the Difficulty of Translation." In Brower 1959: 111–33.

Felman, Shoshana. 1980. *Le Scandale du corps parlant: Don Juan avec Austin, ou, la séduction en deux langues* ("The Scandal of the Speaking Body: Don Juan with Austin, or, Seduction in Two Languages"). Paris: Seuil.

Felstiner, John. 1980. *Translating Neruda: The Way to Macchu Picchu*. Stanford: Stanford University Press.

Fiumara, Gemma Corradi. 2001. *The Mind's Affective Life: A Psychoanalytic and Philosophical Inquiry*. London and New York: Routledge.

Florida, Richard. 2002/14. *The Rise of the Creative Class—Revisited*. New York: Basic.

Florida, Richard. 2008. *Who's Your City? How the Creative Economy Is Making Where to Live the Most Important Decision of Your Life*. New York: Basic.

Foucault, Michel. 1971. "Nietzsche, la généalogie, l'histoire" ("Nietzsche, Genealogy, History"). In Suzanne Bachelard et al., *Hommage a Jean Hyppolite*, 145–72. Paris: Presses Universitaires de France.

Foucault, Michel. 1975. *Surveiller et punir. Naissance de la prison* ("To Surveil and to Punish: Birth of the Prison"). Paris: Gallimard, 1975.

Frye, Northrop. 1957/73. *Anatomy of Criticism: Four Essays*. Princeton: Princeton University Press.

Fuller, Steve. 2003. *Kuhn vs Popper: The Struggle for the Soul of Science*. Cambridge: Icon.

Fyodorov, Andrey. 1953. *Vvedenie v teoriyu perevoda* ("An Introduction to the Theory of Translation"). Moscow: Izdatelstvo Literatury na Inostrannykh Yazykakh.

Gadamer, Hans-Georg. 1960/2010. *Wahrheit und Methode*. Tübingen: Mohr Siebeck.

Geertz, Clifford. 1973. "Thick Description: Toward an Interpretive Theory of Culture." In Geertz, The Interpretation of Cultures: Selected Essays. New York: Basic.

Geertz, Clifford. 1983. "Found in Translation: On the Social History of the Moral Imagination." In Geertz, Local Knowledge: Further Essays in Interpretive Anthropology, 36–54. New York: Basic.

Giles, Herbert. 1886. *The Remains of Lao Tzu: Re-Translated*. Hong Kong: China Mail.

Goldin, Paul R. 2002. "Those Who Don't Know Speak: Translations of the *Daode Jing* by People Who Do Not Know Chinese." *Asian Philosophy* 12.3: 183–95.

Golffing, Francis, trans. 1956. Friedrich Nietzsche, *The Genealogy of Morals: An Attack*. Translation of Nietzsche 1887/92. In *The Birth of*

*Tragedy and The Genealogy of Morals*, 147–299. New York: Anchor/Doubleday.

Graham, Joseph F., ed., 1985. *Difference in Translation*. Ithaca: Cornell University Press.

Grayling, A. C. 2005. *Descartes: The Life and Times of a Genius*. New York: Walker.

Greenfield, Howard, trans. 1965/91. Albert Memmi, *The Colonizer and the Colonized*. Translation of Memmi 1957/66. Boston: Beacon.

Halpern, Richard. 1997. *Shakespeare Among the Moderns*. Ithaca, NY: Cornell University Press.

Harrington, Lewis, trans. 2006. Morinaka Takaaki, "Translation as Dissemination: Multilinguality and De-Cathexis." In Sakai and Solomon 2006b: 39–53.

Heidegger, Martin. 1950/86. *Unterwegs zur Sprache* ("Underway Toward Language"). Pfullingen: Neske.

Heyvaert, S. 1992. Antoine Berman, *The Experience of the Foreign: Culture and Translation in Romantic Germany*. Translation of Berman 1984. Albany: SUNY Press.

Hofstadter, Alfred, trans. 1971. Martin Heidegger, *Poetry, Language, Thought*. Translation of Heidegger 1950/86. New York: HarperCollins.

Hogan, Ron. 2002. "The Tao Te Ching: A Modern Interpretation of Lao Tzu." Online at http://www.beatrice.com/TAO.txt. Accessed September 20, 2014.

Hulme, T. E. 1911/24. "Romanticism and Classicism." In Herbert Read, ed., *Speculations: Essays on Humanism and the Philosophy of Art*, 113–22. London: Routledge and Kegan Paul.

Humphries, Jefferson. 1985. *Metamorphoses of the Raven: Literary Overdeterminedness in France and the South Since Poe*. Baton Rouge: Louisiana State University Press.

Jacquemond, Richard. 1992. "Translation and Cultural Hegemony: The Case of French-Arabic Translation." In Lawrence Venuti, ed., *Rethinking Translation*, 139–58. London and New York: Routledge.

Jakobson, Roman. 1959. "On Linguistic Aspects of Translation." In Brower 1959: 232–9.

Johnson, Barbara. 1985. "Taking Fidelity Philosophically." In Graham 1985: 142–8.

Kaufmann, Walter, trans. 1967/89. Friedrich Nietzsche, *On the Genealogy of*

*Morals: A Polemic*. Translation of Nietzsche 1887/92. In *Basic Writings of Nietzsche*, 14–163. New York: Random House/Vintage.

Kirkland, Russell. 1997. "The Taoism Of The Western Imagination And The Taoism Of China: De-Colonializing The Exotic Teachings Of The East." Presented at the University of Tennessee, October 20, 1997. Online at https://faculty.franklin.uga.edu/kirkland/sites/faculty.franklin.uga.edu.kirkland/files/TENN97.pdf. Accessed September 10, 2014.

Kirkland, Russell. 2004. *Taoism: An Enduring Legacy*. London and New York: Routledge.

Kobayashi Masayoshi (小林正美). 1992. "The Celestial Masters Under the Eastern Jin and Liu-Song Dynasties." *Taoist Resources* 3: 17–45.

Kobayashi Masayoshi (小林正美). 1995. "The Establishment of the Taoist Religion (Taochiao) and Its Structure." *Acta Asiatica* 68: 19–36.

Kuhn, Thomas S. 1962/70. *The Structure of Scientific Revolutions*. Chicago: University of Chicago Press.

Leary, Timothy. 1966. *Psychedelic Prayers, & Other Meditations*. Berkeley, CA: Ronin.

Leder, Drew. 1990. *The Absent Body*. Chicago: University of Chicago Press.

Legge, James, trans. 1861. *The Works of Mencius*. 1861. Reprint. New York: Dover, 1970.

Lemon, Lee T., and Marion J. Reis, eds. and trans. 1965. *Russian Formalist Criticism: Four Essays*. Lincoln: University of Nebraska Press.

Liu, Lydia H. 1995. *Translingual Practice: Literature, National Culture, and Translated Modernity: China, 1900–1937*. Stanford: Stanford University Press.

Liu, Lydia H. 1999a. "Introduction." In Liu 1999c: 1–12.

Liu, Lydia H. 1999b. "The Question of Meaning-Value in the Political Economy of the Sign." In Liu 1999c: 13–41.

Liu, Lydia H., ed. 1999c. *Tokens of Exchange: The Problem of Translation in Global Circulations*. Durham, NC: Duke University Press.

Liu, Lydia H. 2014. "The Eventfulness of Translation: Temporality, Difference, and Competing Universals." *translation* 4: 147–70.

Marshman, J[oshua], trans. 1809. *The Works of Confucius, Containing the Original Text, With a Translation, to Which is Prefixed a Dissertation on the Chinese Language and Character*. Serampore, Bengal, India: Mission Press.

Memmi, Albert. 1957. *Portrait du colonisé, précédé d'un Portrait du colonisateur*. Paris : Gallimard.

Miller, Alice. 1980/2002. *For Your Own Good: Cruelty in Child-Rearing and the Roots of Violence*. Translated by Hildegard and Hunter Hannum. New York: Farrar, Straus & Giroux.

Moga, Eduardo, trans. 2014. Walt Whitman, *Hojas de hierba. Edición completa y selección de prosas* ("Leaves of Grass: Complete Edition and Selection of Prose Works"). Barcelona: Galaxia Gutenberg/Circulo de Lectores.

Mounin, Georges. 1963. *Les problèmes théoriques de la traduction* ("The Theoretical Problems of Translation"). Paris: Gallimard.

Mungello, David. 1977. *Leibniz and Confucianism: The Search for Accord*. Honolulu: University of Hawai'i Press.

Mungello, David. 1982. "Die Quellen für das Chinabild Leibnizens" ("The Sources for Leibniz's Image of China"). *Studia Leibniziana* 14: 233–43.

Nancy, Jean-Luc. 1986/2004. "La Communauté désœuvrée." In Nancy, *La Communauté désœuvrée* ("The Inoperative Community"), 9–102. Paris: Detroits.

Neruda, Pablo. 1950. *Alturas de Machu Picchu*. Online at http://www.poemas-del-alma.com/alturas-de-macchu.htm. Accessed January 13, 2015.

Nietzsche, Friedrich. 1887/92. *Zur Genealogie der Moral: Eine Streitschrift* ("Towards a Genealogy of Morals: A Polemic"). Second edition. Leipzig: Naumann.

Niranjana, Tejaswini. 1992. *Siting Translation: History, Post-structuralism, and the Colonial Context*. Berkeley and Los Angeles: University of California Press.

Palmquist, Stephen R. 2000. *Kant's Critical Religion: Volume Two of Kant's System of Perspectives*. Aldershot: Ashgate.

Parkes, Graham, ed. 1991. *Nietzsche and Asian Thought*. Chicago: University of Chicago Press.

Peirce, Charles S. 1931–58. *Collected Papers of Charles Sanders Peirce*. 8 vols. Vols 1–6 edited by Charles Hartshorne and Paul Weiss; Vols. 7–8 edited by Arthur W. Burks. Cambridge, MA: Harvard University Press.

Peirce, Charles S. 1992/98. *The Essential Peirce: Selected Philosophical Writings*. 2 vols. Edited by the Peirce Edition Project. Bloomington: Indiana University Press.

Perkins, Franklin. 2004. *Leibniz and China: A Commerce of Light*. Cambridge: Cambridge University Press.

Pine, Red, trans. 1996/2009. *Lao Tzu's Taoteching: With Selected*

*Commentaries from the Past 2,000 Years.* Port Townsend, WA: Copper Canyon.

Pink Floyd. 1973. *The Dark Side of the Moon.* Los Angeles: Capitol Records.

Pogson, F. L., trans. 1910. Henri Bergson, *Time and Free Will: An Essay on the Immediate Data of Consciousness.* Translation of Bergson 1889. London: Allen and Unwin.

Popovič, Anton. 1976. *A Dictionary for the Analysis of Literary Translation.* Edmonton: Department of Comparative Literature, University of Alberta.

Porter, Catherine, trans. 1983/2003. Shoshana Felman, *The Scandal of the Speaking Body: Don Juan with J. L. Austin, or Seduction in Two Languages.* Translation of Felman 1980. Stanford: Stanford University Press.

Pratt, Mary Louise. 2002. "The Traffic in Meaning: Translation, Contagion, Infiltration." *Profession* 2002: 25–36.

Pym, Anthony. 1995. "Schleiermacher and the Problem of *Blendlinge.*" *Translation and Literature* 4.1: 5–30.

Quine, Willard V. O. 1960. *Word and Object.* Cambridge, MA: MIT Press.

Rafael, Vicente. 1988/93. *Contracting Colonialism: Translation and Christian Conversion in Tagalog Society under Early Spanish Rule.* Durham, NC: Duke University Press.

Ratner-Rosenhagen, Jennifer. 2011. *American Nietzsche: A History of an Icon and His Ideas.* Chicago: University of Chicago Press.

Redfield, Marc. 2003. "Literature, Incorporated: Harold Bloom, Theory, and the Canon." In Peter C. Herman, ed., *Historicizing Theory,* 209–33. Albany: SUNY Press.

Robinson, Douglas. 1985. *American Apocalypses: The Image of the End of the World in American Literature.* Baltimore: Johns Hopkins University Press.

Robinson, Douglas. 1988. "Dear Harold." *New Literary History* 20.1 (Autumn): 239–50.

Robinson, Douglas. 1991. *The Translator's Turn.* Baltimore: Johns Hopkins University Press.

Robinson, Douglas. 1996. *Translation and Taboo.* DeKalb: Northern Illinois University Press.

Robinson, Douglas. 1997. *Translation and Empire: Postcolonial Theories Explained.* Manchester: St. Jerome.

Robinson, Douglas, trans. 1997/2002a. August Wilhelm von Schlegel, "The Speaking Voice of the Civilized World." Translation of Schlegel 1803/1965: 34–6. In Robinson 1997/2002c: 220–1.

Robinson, Douglas, trans. 1997/2002b. Friedrich Schleiermacher, "On the Different Methods of Translating." Translation of Schleiermacher 1813/2002. In Robinson 1997/2002c: 225–38.

Robinson, Douglas, ed. 1997/2002c. *Western Translation Theory From Herodotus to Nietzsche*. Second edition. Manchester: St. Jerome.

Robinson, Douglas. 2001. *Who Translates? Translator Subjectivities Beyond Reason*. Albany: SUNY Press.

Robinson, Douglas. 2003. *Performative Linguistics: Speaking and Translating as Doing Things With Words*. London: Routledge.

Robinson, Douglas. 2008. *Estrangement and the Somatics of Literature: Tolstoy, Shklovsky, Brecht*. Baltimore: Johns Hopkins University Press.

Robinson, Douglas. 2011. *Translation and the Problem of Sway*. Amsterdam and Philadelphia: John Benjamins.

Robinson, Douglas. 2013a. *Displacement and the Somatics of Postcolonial Culture*. Columbus: Ohio State University Press.

Robinson, Douglas. 2013b. *Schleiermacher's Icoses: The Social Ecologies of the Different Methods of Translating*. Bucharest: Zeta.

Robinson, Douglas. 2015a. *The Dao of Translation: An East-West Dialogue*. London and Singapore: Routledge.

Robinson, Douglas. 2015b. "Towards an Intercivilizational Turn: Naoki Sakai's Cofigurative Regimes of Translation and the Problem of Eurocentrism." *Translation Studies* 8.3: 1–16.

Robinson, Douglas. 2016a. *The Deep Ecology of Rhetoric in Mencius and Aristotle: A Somatic Guide*. Albany, NY: SUNY Press.

Robinson, Douglas. 2016b. *Semiotranslating Peirce*. Tartu, Estonia: Tartu Library of Semiotics.

Robinson, Douglas. 2016c. "Benveniste and the Periperformative Structure of the Pragmeme." In Keith Allan, Alessandro Capone, Istvan Kecskes, and Jacob L. Mey, eds., *Pragmemes and Theories of Language Use*. Dordrecht: Springer.

Robinson, Douglas. 2016d. "Pushing-Hands and Periperformativity." In Douglas Robinson, ed., *The Pushing Hands of Translation and its Theory: In Memoriam Martha Cheung, 1953–2013*. Forthcoming. London and Singapore: Routledge.

Robinson, Douglas. 2017. *Critical Translation Studies*. London and Singapore: Routledge.

Ross, Stephen David. 1998. *The Gift of Touch: Embodying the Good*. Albany: SUNY Press.

Rutschky, Katharina. 1977. *Schwarze Pädagogik: Quellen zur Naturgeschichte der bürgerlichen Erziehung* ("Black Pedagogy: Sources for the Natural History of the Bourgeois Experience"). Munich: Ullstein.

Sakai Naoki. 1997. *Translation and Subjectivity: On "Japan" and Cultural Nationalism.* Minneapolis: University of Minnesota Press.

Sakai Naoki. 2010. "Theory and Asian Humanity: On the Question of Humanitas and Anthropos." *Postcolonial Studies* 13.4: 441-64.

Sakai Naoki, and Jon Solomon, eds. 2006. *Translation, Biopolitics, Colonial Difference. Traces* 4. Hong Kong: Hong Kong University Press.

Sakai Naoki, and Sando Mezzadra, eds. 2014. Special issue. *translation* 4 (Spring).

Sanders, Carol, Matthew Pires, and Peter Figueroa, trans. 2006. *Writings in General Linguistics.* Translation of Saussure 2002. Oxford and New York: Oxford University Press.

Saussure, Ferdinand de. 2002. *Écrits de linguistique générale* ("Writings in General Linguistics"). Edited by Simon Bouquet and Rudolf Engler. Paris: Gallimard.

Scarpitti, Michael A., trans. 2013. Friedrich Nietzsche, *On the Genealogy of Morals: A Polemic.* Harmondsworth: Penguin.

Schlegel, August Wilhelm von. 1803/1965. *Geschichte der klassischen Literatur* ("History of Classical Literature"). Vol. 3 of Schlegel, *Kritische Schriften und Briefe* ("Critical Writings and Letters"). Edited by Edgar Lohner. Stuttgart: Kohlhammer.

Schleiermacher, Friedrich. 1813/2002. "Ueber die verschiedenen Methoden des Übersetzens" ("On the Different Methods of Translating"). In Martin Rößler, with the assistance of Lars Emersleben, eds., *Akademievorträge* ("Academy Addresses"), 67-93. Part I of *Schriften und Entwürfe* ("Writings and Sketches"). Vol. 11 of *Kritische Gesamtausgabe* ("Critical Complete Works"). Berlin: BBAW.

Schmitt, Charles. 1966. "Perennial Philosophy: From Agostino Steuco to Leibniz." *Journal of the History of Ideas* 27: 505-32.

Schneidau, Herbert N. 1995. "Harold Bloom and the School of Resentment: Or, Canon to the Right of Them." *Arizona Quarterly: A Journal of American Literature, Culture, and Theory* 51.2: 127-41.

Schuchard, Marsha Keith. 2011. *Emanuel Swedenborg, Secret Agent on Earth and in Heaven: Jacobites, Jews and Freemasons in Early Modern Sweden.* Leiden and Boston: Brill.

Schultz, Susan M. 1996. " 'Returning to Bloom': John Ashbery's Critique of Harold Bloom." *Contemporary Literature* 37.1: 24–48.

Sedgwick, Eve Kosofsky. 2003. *Touching Feeling: Affect, Pedagogy, Performativity*. Durham, NC: Duke University Press.

Sheldon, Richard, trans. 2005. Viktor Shklovsky, *Knight's Move*. Translation of Shklovsky 1923. Normal IL and London: Dalkey Archive.

Sher, Benjamin, trans. 1990/98. Viktor Shklovsky, *Theory of Prose*. Translation of Shklovsky 1925/29. Normal IL and London: Dalkey Archive.

Sheridan, Alan, trans. 1977. *Discipline and Punish: The Birth of the Prison*. New York: Pantheon.

Shklovsky, Viktor. 1917/29. "Iskusstvo kak priyom" ("Art as Device"). In Shklovsky 1925/29: 7–20.

Shklovsky, Viktor. 1919/23. "Paralleli y Tolstogo" ("Parallels in Tolstoy"). In Shklovsky 1923: 115–25.

Shklovsky, Viktor. 1923. *Khod konya* ("Knight's Move"). Moscow and Berlin: Helikon.

Shklovsky, Viktor. 1925/29. *O teorii prozy* ("On the Theory of Prose"). Moscow: Federatsiya.

Smith, Douglas, trans. 1996. Friedrich Nietzsche, *On the Genealogy of Morals*. Translation of Nietzsche 1887/92. Oxford and New York: Oxford University Press.

Solomon, Jon. 2014. "The Postimperial Etiquette and the Affective Structure of Areas." *translation* 4 (Spring): 171–201.

Spivak, Gayatri Chakravorty. 1993. "The Politics of Translation." In Spivak, *Outside in the Teaching Machine*, 179–200. London and New York: Routledge.

Steiner, George. 1975. *After Babel: Aspects of Language and Translation*. London: Oxford University Press.

Venuti, Lawrence, ed. 2000/12. *The Translation Studies Reader*. Third edition. London and New York: Routledge.

Weinberger, Eliot. 2000. "Anonymous Sources: A Talk on Translators and Translation." *Encuentros* 39. Cultural Center, International Development Bank, November.

Weinsheimer, Joel, and Donald G. Marshall, trans. 1975/89. Hans-Georg Gadamer, *Truth and Method*. Translation of Gadamer 1960/2010. New York: Crossroad.

Weisman, Karen A. 1996. "Birthing an Ecstatic Anxiety: Harold Bloom's Western Canon and its Readers." *Salmagundi* 112 (Fall): 216–25.

Welton, Donn, ed. 1998. *Body and Flesh: A Philosophical Reader*. Oxford: Blackwell.

Whitehead, Alfred North. 1929. *Process and Reality: An Essay in Cosmology*. New York: Macmillan.

Young, R. V. 2005. "Harold Bloom: The Critic as Gnostic." *Modern Age* 47.1 (Winter): 19–29.

Zapf, Hubert. 1995. "Elective Affinities and American Differences: Nietzsche and Harold Bloom." In Manfred Putz, ed., *Nietzsche in American Literature and Thought*, 337–55. Columbia, SC: Camden House.

Zohn, Harry, trans. 1968/82. Walter Benjamin, "The Task of the Translator." Translation of Benjamin 1923/72. In Hannah Arendt, ed., Benjamin, *Illuminations*, 69–82. Glasgow: Fontana/Collins.

# Index

Abrams, M. H., 94
Alcott, Bronson, 127
Alexander, G. G., 121–4, 151–3
"Alturas de Macchu Picchu" (Neruda), 96
"American Conquest of Philosophical Taoism, The" (Bradbury), 110
Ames, Roger R., 131–5
*Anxiety of Influence, The* (Bloom), 56, 69, 97
Appiah, Anthony, 145, 154
Aristotle, 29
"Art as Device" (Shklovsky/Sher), 97–8
"Art as Technique" (Shklovsky/Lemon/Reis), 97–8
Asad, Talal, xxi, xxii, 144, 148, 154
Augustine, viii

Baker, Mona, 154
Bakhtin, Mikhail, 77, 82, 147
Barker, Francis, 149
Barnstone, Willis, 148
Batchelor, Kathryn, xiv
Baudelaire, Charles, 103
Baumlin, James S., 56, 62, 70
Beckett, Samuel, 26, 29, 92
*Befremdung* (Novalis), 97
Benjamin, Walter, 2, 148
Benveniste, Èmile, 20
"Benveniste and the Periperformative Structure of the Pragmeme" (Robinson), 76
Bergson, Henri, 72
Berman, Antoine, 148
Blake, William, 108, 137
Bloom, Harold, xxiii–xxv, 34–5, 37–8
  on the canon as pain-driven memory, 68–76
  and the disembodiment of translation, 92–103
  as Occidentalist, 136–40
  on the "School of Resentment," 56–67
  on slave morality, 60–7
Boodberg, Peter A., 153–4
Bordo, Susan, 149
boundaries, x–xi, xxii–xxiii, 16, 60, 104, 135
Bourdieu, Pierre, 77
Bouvet, Joachim, 107, 120–1, 125–6, 151
Božovič, Miran, 149
Bradbury, Steve, 110, 119–20, 128, 134
Brecht, Bertolt, 73, 97
Buddhism, 33
  Zen, 108
Burke, Kenneth, 108, 130–1
Buruma, Ian, and Avishai Margalit, 32–3, 116–18, 140
Butler, Judith, xiii, 50–5, 148–9
Bynner, Witter, 119, 128, 133

canons
  biblical, 57–8
  literary, 57–61, 74–5
Catford, J. C., 148
Chalmers, John, 152–3
Chan, Leo, xxi
Chang Namfung, xxi
Cheng Aimin, 130, 150
Chesterman, Andrew, xiv–xxiii, 59, 60, 82–5, 108, 142, 147
Cheung, Martha, xxi
Cheyfitz, Eric, 143–4, 148, 154

Christianity, in *Laozi* translations, 120–5
Christiansen, Broder, 72
Christy, Arthur, 130, 150
*Civilization and its Discontents* (Freud), 71
civilizational spells (Sakai), xii, xiv, xx–xxiii, 3, 13, 39–40, 135–6
  in Bloom, 56
  and canonization, 59–60
  as icosis, 78
  intergenerational, 65, 72
  master- and slave-spells, 65–7, 91
  priest-spells, 90
  proto-civilizational, 78
  and Schleiermacher, 25–30, 33
  universalizing denial of, 82–4
cofiguration, regimes of (Sakai), xii–xiii, xx, xxiv, xxv–xxvi, 22–5, 103–5, 107–46, 110, 117, 124, 125, 129, 133, 141
  as the enemy, 113
  as middles, 140
Collani, Claudia von, 120, 151
Collie, David, 121, 130–1, 149
Confucianism, 33, 107, 121
*Confucius* (Alexander), 151
continental philosophy, 129
Critical Translation Studies (CTS), 2–3, 67, 78, 114, 145–6
  tensions with TS, 119
*Critical Translation Studies* (Robinson), xxvi, 76
Crowley, Aleister, 128
cultural translation, 23
Cultural Turn in TS, 3, 142

Damasio, Antonio, 47–8
*dao* (道, Laozi), viii
  as "God" (Alexander), 122–4
  as the moon (Du), 114–15
  as process, 131–2, 134
  as "the Word" (Chalmers), 152–3

*Dao of Translation, The* (Robinson), viii, 76, 108, 145, 149
Daoism, 33, 37, 107–8, 111–35
"Dear Harold" (Robinson), 104
deconstruction, 136
*Deep Ecology of Rhetoric in Mencius and Aristotle, The* (Robinson), viii, 90, 145
defamiliarization (Shklovsky/Lemon/Reis), 97–8
Derrida, Jacques, 15, 28, 148
Descartes, René, 149
*Descartes' Error* (Damasio), 47
Dewey, John, 108
Diderot, Denis, 153
Diethe, Carol, 44–5, 50
*différance* (Derrida), 15
*Discipline and Punish* (Foucault), 52, 79
"Discourse and the Novel" (Bakhtin), 77, 109
Disney, Walt, 82, 84
  and Leni Riefenstahl, 149
displacement (Freud), 15
*Displacement and the Somatics of Postcolonial Culture* (Robinson), 148
domestication (Schleiermacher), 19
Du Weiming (杜維明), 112, 114, 129

ecosis, 67, 76, 78, 102, 139
Emerson, Ralph Waldo, 94, 107–8, 118, 120, 127, 130–1, 133, 149–50
*Encyclopedia* (Diderot), 153
Enlightenment, xxv
  and esotericism, 31, 59, 125
  and scientistic universalism, xiv–xv, 59, 136
  and Western individualism, 112–13, 119, 150
enstrangement (Shklovsky/Sher), 97–8
*Entfremdung* (Hegel/Marx), 97
Eoyang, Eugene, xxi, 148

## Index

Erlich, Victor, 99–101
esotericism, x, 31–2, 59, 108, 120, 125–9, 131, 133, 140, 145
   in *Laozi* translations, 125–9
estrangement, 79, 97
   device (Shklovsky), 72–3, 97–8
   as icotic counternormativity, 76
   in Tolstoy, 102
*Estrangement and the Somatics of Literature* (Robinson), 72–3, 97
ethnocentrism, ix, xii
Eurocentrism, viii, x, xviii, 24, 60, 142, 146
   panicked, xiii–xv, xxii–xxiii

Fang, Achilles, 148
Faulkner, William, 105
Feeling of the Foreign (Schleiermacher), 6, 11–12, 26
Felman, Shoshana, 41, 49
Felstiner, John, 94–7
Figl, Johann, 37
Figurists, 120–1, 151
Fiumara, Gemma Corradi, 149
Florida, Richard, 70
foreigners
   all of us to each other (Sakai), 15–16
   for Occidentalists, 116
foreignization (Schleiermacher), 19
   and deforeignization in Bloom, 104
Foucault, Michel, 20, 50–6, 69, 71, 74, 79, 148–9
"Foucault and the Paradox of Bodily Inscriptions" (Butler), 51–2
four-fold hermeneutic, 121, 150–1
Frederick the Great, 8–9
French Symbolisme, 104–5
Freud, Sigmund, 15, 42, 69, 71, 92, 136–7, 149
Frye, Northrop, 69
Fuller, Steve, 83
Fyodorov, Andrey, 148

Gadamer, Hans-Georg, 148
Geertz, Clifford, 145
*Gender Trouble* (Butler), 50–2
*Genealogy of Morals* see *On the Genealogy of Morals*
German Idealism see *Idealism*
German Romanticism see *Romanticism*
Giles, Herbert, 127
global English, as gold standard, 92–3
Gnosticism, 70
Goethe, J. W. von, 33
Goldin, Paul R., 110, 134
Golffing, Francis, 39, 40, 42–4, 47, 49–50, 80
Gramsci, Antonio, 74
Grotius, Hugo, 29

*habitus* (Bourdieu), 77
Hall, David L., 131–5
Halpern, Richard, 69
Harrington, Lewis E., 93
Hartshorne, Charles, 131
Hegel, G. W. F., 22, 129, 136
Heidegger, Martin, x, 16, 28, 33, 35, 108, 136, 148–9
"Heights of Macchu Picchu, The" (Neruda/Felstiner), 94–7
henolingualism (Robinson), 26, 30
Herder, J. G. von, x, 33
Hermes Trismegistus, 108
heterolingual address, attitude of (Sakai), x–xiii, xxiii, 10–21, 29
   somatic, 78
Hill, Michael, xxv
Hitler, Adolf, 84
Hogan, Ron, 134
*Hojas de Hierba* (Whitman/Moga), 96
Hölderlin, J. C. F., 153
homolingual address, regime of (Sakai), x–xiii, xxiv, 10–21, 27, 29, 104, 141
   and translation, 3–4

Hui, Isaac, xxi
Hulin, Michel, 37
Hulme, T. E., 129
Humphries, Jefferson, 104–5
Husserl, Edmund, 107, 149

Iamblicus, 108
icosis, xiii, 29–30, 67, 76, 79–80, 102, 109, 139
Idealism, 145
  German, 85, 108, 125
  and Romanticism, xv
ideology theory, 136
"In the Penal Colony" (Kafka), 52
individualism, 114–17, 130
*Inoperative Community, The* (Nancy), 16–17
intercivilizational
  cofigurations, xxiii, 107
  encounters, x, xii, 109, 141, 143–4
  projects (Orientalism/Occidentalism), xx
  research, 145
  Turn, vii, xxiii, 142, 144
interculturality, 141
intergenerational pain-based memory (Nietzsche), 41–2, 72
  and civilizational spells, 38, 40, 65, 67
  and the interpersonal-becoming-intergenerational body-becoming-mind, 77–8
internalization of mastery (Nietzsche), 52, 74
itericosis, 77, 80, 91

Jacquemond, Richard, 144
Jakobson, Roman, 2, 148
James, Alice, 127
James, Henry, 127
James, William, 108, 127, 130–1
Jeremiads, 138
Jiang Kanghu, 119
Johnson, Barbara, 148

Kafka, Franz, 50, 52
Kant, Immanuel, 85, 127
  and the Copernican Hypothesis, 129
Kauffman, Walter, 38, 43, 50, 86–7, 89–90
Kirkland, Russell, xxiv, 34–5, 37–8, 105, 107–40
  on Confucianism, 150
  on esotericism, 125–9
  on "pseudotranslations," 150
  on Romanticism, 129–35
  on three stages of *Laozi* translation, 119–35
*Knight's Move* (Shklovsky/Sheldon), 99
Kobayashi Masayoshi, 111
Kothari, Rita, xiv
Kuhn, Thomas, 83, 85
Kyoto School, x, 108

Lacan, Jacques, 15, 105
*Lao Tsze* (Alexander), 121–4, 152–3
Laozi (老子), viii–x, 110, 132–3, 152
*Laozi* (《老子》), 111–18
  translations of, xxiv–xxv, 105, 107, 112, 115, 119–35, 138–9, 144, 150, 152
Leary, Timothy, 128–9
Leder, Drew, 149
legalinguistic code (Nietzsche), 86–92
Legge, James, 153
Leibniz, G. W., 29, 107, 120, 125–6
Lewis, C. I., 130–1
literary canon, 57–61, 74–5
Liu, Lydia, 1–3, 81, 92, 117, 148
logic of feeling (Nietzsche), 91–2
Lung, Rachel, xxi
Lynch, David, 85

MacPherson, James, 150
Mallarmé, Stéphane, 103
*Map of Misreading, A* (Bloom), 56, 97

Marshman, Joshua, 130-1, 149
Marx, Karl, 72, 136
master-spells, 65-7, 77, 92 see also
    civilizational spells
McElduff, Siobhán, xiv
Melville, Herman, 127
Memmi, Albert, 66
Mengzi (孟子), viii-x, 130
Merleau-Ponty, Maurice, 149
*Metamorphoses of the Raven*
    (Humphries), 104-5
Milton, John, 137
mirror-stage (Lacan), 15
modernism, 136
*Monadologie, La* (Leibniz), 126, 153
Morinaka Takaaki, 93
Mounin, Georges, 148
*Mulholland Drive* (Lynch), 85
Mungello, David, 125

Nabokov, Vladimir, 26, 29
Nancy, Jean-Luc, ix, xi, 16-17
Napoleon, 30
*Neiye* (《內業》), 111
Neoplatonism, 108
Neruda, Pablo, 92, 94-7
Nietzsche, Friedrich, xxiii-xxv, 33-5, 59, 85, 92, 136
    and colonizing counterregulation, 148
    on guilt and debt, 80-2
    and icosis/ecosis, 79-80, 102
    on the internalization of mastery, 52, 74
    and *man* "one," 77-9
    on the mnemotechnics of pain, 42-56
    as Occidentalist, 136-7
    on pain-driven memory, 61, 68-72
    on slave morality, 38-41, 60-7
    on the somatics of law and economics, 69, 76-92
*Nietzsche and Asian Thought*
    (Parkes), 37

Niranjana, Tejaswini, xxi, 144, 148, 154

Occidentalism, xx, 9, 24, 30-5, 33, 110-36
    as conservatives vs. liberals in the West, 118
    as East-West cofigurative enterprise, 131-5
    on individualism, 114-17
    on ritualistic religion and foreigners, 116-17
*Occidentalism* (Buruma/Margalit), 32-3, 116-18, 140
*Olympia* (Riefenstahl), 149
"On the Different Methods of Translating" (Schleiermacher), 33
*On the Genealogy of Morals*
    (Nietzsche), xxiii-xxv, 34, 37-54, 56, 65-7, 79, 85
"one" (German *man*, Nietzsche), 77-9
Orientalism, viii, ix, xx, xxi, 24-6, 27-8, 30-1, 33, 110, 117-18, 121, 139, 142, 146
Ossian, 150

pain
    as discipline (Nietzsche/Foucault), 78-80
    -driven memory (Nietzsche), 61, 68-72
Palmquist, Stephen R., 127
"Parallels in Tolstoy" (Shklovsky/Erlich), 99
Parkes, Graham, 37
Pauthier, Guillaume, 130-1, 149-50
Paz, Octavio, 145
Peirce, Benjamin, 130-1, 134
Peirce, Charles Sanders, 108, 130-1, 134
periperformativity (Sedgwick), 76-7, 102, 141

of *man* "one," 77–9
Perkins, Franklin, 126
phenomenology, x, 145
*philosophia perennis*, 107, 121, 124, 126
Pink Floyd, 115
Plotinus, 108
Poe, Edgar Allen, 102–5
"Politics of Translation, The" (Spivak), xxi
Popovič, Anton, 148
Popper, Karl, xiv, xviii, xxiii, 83, 85, 142
Porphyry, 108
Porter, Bill, 115
*Post-colonial Translation* (Bassnett/Trivedi), xxi
postcolonial translation theory, 142–4
poststructuralism, 129, 136
pragmatism, x, 131, 145
Pratt, Mary Louise, 145, 154
*Problems of Dostoevsky's Poetics* (Bakhtin), 147
*Process and Reality* (Whitehead), 131, 134
Protestantism, 112–13, 116–17, 119–21, 124–6, 140, 150
pseudotranslation (Kirkland), 116, 150
"Pushing-Hands and Periperformativity" (Robinson), 76
Pym, Anthony, 6–7

Quine, Willard Van Orman, 2

Rafael, Vicente, xxi, 143, 148
Ratner-Rosenhagen, Jennifer, 56
Red Pine, 114–15, 123
Redfield, Marc, 56
regime of translation (Sakai), xii–xiii, 109, 141
religion, viii, 110, 112, 129, 138–9, 150

cofigurative, 125
for Occidentalists, xxiv, 33, 37, 46–7, 68, 70, 108, 112–13, 115–20, 139
and the *philosophia perennis*, 121
*Remains of Lao-Tzu* (Giles), 127
*Representative Men* (Emerson), 127
resentment, xxv, 60, 63–5, 73
and civilizational spells, 66–7
Party of (Young), 137–8
*ressentiment* (Nietzsche), xxv, 39–40, 61, 63–4, 66, 80, 86–8
School of (Bloom), xxv, 34, 61, 63–4, 138
and slave morality (Nietzsche), 60, 63
somatics of, 61, 90–2
*Rhetoric* (Aristotle), 29
Riefenstahl, Leni, 149
Robinson, Douglas, xiv, 2, 148
Romanticism, 131, 145
English, 97
German, x, 4, 9, 30, 35, 93, 97, 108, 113, 125, 136
in *Laozi* translations, 129–35
Ross, Stephen David, 149
Royce, Josiah, 108, 130–1

Sakai Naoki, vii–xiii, xx, 1–35, 65
on Asian theorists, vii–viii, 107
on civilizational spells, 13, 82, 84, 135–6
on cofiguration, xxv–xxvi, 103, 140–1
on the haunt, 67
on homolinguality and heterolinguality, xxiv, 10–21, 104
on regimes of translation, 109, 144
and Schleiermacher, 25–30, 33
Saussure, Ferdinand de, 149
Scarpitti, Michael, 44, 50
Schelling, F. W. J., 26, 108

# Index

Schema L (Lacan), 105
Schlegel, A. W. von, 33, 93
Schleiermacher, Friedrich, 4–9, 136
    on domestication/foreignization, 19
    on the unpleasant cosmopolitan middle, 140–1
    on witches going doubled, viii, xxiii, 12–14, 25–30, 33, 90
*Schleiermacher's Icoses* (Robinson), 13, 26, 29, 136
Schmitt, Charles, 126
Schneidau, Herbert N., 56
Schopenhauer, Arthur, 33
Schultz, Susan M., 56
scientism, xiv–xvi, xix, xxii, 37, 59, 115, 136
Sedgwick, Eve, 76
Shakespeare, William, 57, 92, 145
Shklovsky, Viktor, 72–3, 97–101, 149
Simon, Sherry, 51, 53–5
Sinocentrism, 142
slave morality (Nietzsche), 34, 37
    in Bloom, 59–67
    as a civilizational spell, 38–41, 65–7, 91
    and *ressentiment*, 39, 60–1
    *see also* civilizational spells
Smith, Douglas, 43–4, 50
social neuroscience, of somatic theory, 75–6
Solomon, Jon, 1
somatic markers (Damasio), 48
somatic theory, ix, 52, 56
    bureaucratized, 92
    on canonization, 74–5
    and desomatization, 149
    of estrangement, 72–3
    itero-, 149
    of language and translation, 78
    and libido (Freud), 69
    and social neuroscience, 75–6
    and somatic economics (Nietzsche), 69, 76–82

"Song of Myself" (Whitman), 94
Southern Gothic, 104–5
speech acts (Austin), 40–1, 49, 77, 86, 88
    desomatization of, 91–2
    translational, 16
Spivak, Gayatri Chakravorty, xxi, xxii, 154
Sprung, Mervyn, 37
Stalin, Joseph, 84
Steiner, George, 148
Steuco, Agostino, 126
Strauß, Victor von, 152
Strong Man (Nietzsche), xxv, 35, 37, 61, 63–4
Strong Poet (Bloom), xxv, 35, 63–4
subject-in-transit, translator as (Sakai), 18–21
Sun Yifeng, xxi
Susam-Saraeva, Şebnem, xiv
sway (Robinson), viii
Swedenborg, Emanuel, 108, 126–7

Taoism (Kirkland), 111–12
Tate, Allen, 105
"Theory and Asian Humanity" (Sakai), vii–viii, xx–xxiii, 3, 107
*Theory of Prose* (Shklovsky/Sher), 97
Thoreau, Henry David, 120, 127, 133, 149–50
"Those Who Don't Know Speak" (Goldin), 110
*tian* (天, Mengzi), viii–ix
*Tokens of Exchange* (Liu), 1–3, 81, 92–3
Tolstoy, Leo, 92, 97–103
"Tours de Babel, Des" (Derrida), 148
"Towards an Interdisciplinary Turn" (Robinson), xxvi
Translation
    all address is (Sakai), 16
    and homolingual address, 3–4

*translation* (special issue, Sakai/Mezzadra), 103
*Translation, Biopolitics, Colonial Difference* (Sakai/Solomon), 1–3
*Translation and Empire* (Robinson), 144, 154
*Translation and Subjectivity* (Sakai), 1–3, 109
*Translation and Taboo* (Robinson), viii, 13, 154
*Translation and the Problem of Sway* (Robinson), viii
Translation Studies (TS), xiii, 1, 13, 145
and the erasure of the translator, 18
and Eurocentrism, xiv–xxiii
and the Intercivilizational Turn, xxiii, 142, 144
and tensions with CTS, 119
*Translation Studies Reader, The* (Venuti), 154
translator
rhetorical suppression of, 103–5
as subject-in-transit and disimagined laborer, 18–21
*Translator's Turn, The* (Robinson), viii
*Translingual Practice* (Liu), 1–3, 148
Trivedi, Harish, xxi
Tu Weiming *see* Du Weiming
Tymoczko, Maria, xiv, xxv

universalism, xxi–xxii, 136, 141–2
and competing equivalencies (Liu), 81

and denial of civilizational spells, 82–4

Venuti, Lawrence, 19, 136, 154
*Verfremdung* (Brecht), 97

Wade, Thomas, 127
Wade-Giles romanization system, 127
Wakabayashi, Judy, xiv
*Walden* (Thoreau), 130
Weinberger, Eliot, 145
Weisman, Karen A., 56
Weiss, Paul, 131
Welton, Donn, 149
*Western Canon, The* (Bloom), xxiii–xxv, 34, 37–8, 56–76, 92
*Western Translation Theory from Herodotus to Nietzsche* (Robinson), 93, 141
Whitehead, Alfred North, 108, 130–5
Whitman, Walt, 94–7, 127
*Who Translates?* (Robinson), viii
witches going doubled (Schleiermacher), viii, 12–14
and civilizational spells, 25–30, 33
*Writing on General Linguistics* (Saussure), 149
*wuwei* (無為, Laozi), 115

"Yankee transcendentalism" (Bradbury), 119–20, 125
*Yijing* (易經, Book of Changes), 126
Young, R. V., 137–40

Zhu Chenshen, xxi
*Zhuangzi* (《莊子》), 111

www.ingramcontent.com/pod-product-compliance
Lightning Source LLC
Chambersburg PA
CBHW061831300426
44115CB00013B/2334